*To Steve &
Dorothy
Good luck
at BC!

Mark Jantzen*

The
Wrong
Side
of
the
Wall

An
American
in
East
Berlin
during
the
Peaceful
Revolution

Mark Jantzen

Map not to scale

For

Alice

Table of Contents

Preface

"So, you were in East Germany when the Wall came down?"
The polite, curious, intrigued question that I've heard so often.
"Yes", I replied, "I was, in East Berlin actually. In fact I lived about a ten minute walk from the Wall."
"That must have been something!"
Indeed it was. This book is a modest attempt to explain what life in East Germany was like, how the peaceful revolution came to pass, and what some of the ordinary people of that country thought before, during and after the momentous events that ended the division of Germany. I lived and studied in East Berlin from October 1988 to September 1991. I was there under the Mennonite Central Committee, the relief and development agency of the Mennonite and Brethren Churches of North America. Being personally committed to the Biblical teaching of peace, and supported by a church with the same commitment, made living in East Germany all the more interesting and challenging.

Having gotten married shortly after my return to the U.S. made me think about the similarity between the question I used to ask about 'how do you know you're in love?' and the one I was now to answer, 'what was life in East Germany like?'. No matter how much talking (or writing) one does, both questions are simply unanswerable.

The analogy doesn't quite hold for a number of reasons. Eventually most people fall in love, and through that experience, gain understanding. There are no more 'East Germany' experiences to be had, the way it was will never again be experienced. I have tried to present some of the background information necessary to understanding life in East Germany. I have also tried to convey some of the mood, the emotions that were an integral part of that life. One small part of that effort is the more or less consistent use of the initials of the official name of the country, GDR (German Democratic Republic). East Germans used the German initials, DDR (*Deutsche Demokratische Republik*) when talking about their country. It would just *feel* wrong to talk about 'East Germany'.

As part of the attempt to convey a little of the feel of the GDR, I have gathered and translated odds and ends of East German life; a song, a few stories, a few sermons and speeches. The East Germans knew their life better than I ever could. They can speak more powerfully about it. These tidbits are collected in a section at the end of the book called the Scrapbook.

Of course, if East Germans read this book, they might well be a bit disappointed to find so much general information about the GDR. There is no doubt that I have only been able to present bits and pieces of a very complex picture. Having to pick and choose, perhaps something of importance has been left out. All the same, I hope some of the magic, the zaniness, the hope and despair of those days in the GDR comes through in the following account.

There are many people to thank for their assistance. After hearing bits and pieces of this story, many people encouraged me to gather it together and write it down. The list of encouragers includes friends from the GDR and MCC administrators and colleagues. Without their many enthusiastic nudges, this book would have never been written. Marilee Diener and Fred and Angelika Fransen have read the entire manuscript, helpfully correcting numerous errors and making many valuable suggestions for improvement. Walter Sawatsky has been a source of encouragement and good counsel on matters of writing and scholarship. I want to thank my parents, Henry and Gretl Jantzen, for generously underwriting the major portion of the printing costs. And finally, the biggest thanks go to my wife, Alice, who not only provided me with the time to write, but also managed to balance giving practical advice and criticism with an abundance of loving encouragement.

Abbreviations and Terms Used

Berliner Zeitung: Party controlled daily newspaper in East Berlin

Buschfunk: Wilderness radio. A German expression for passing on news by word of mouth.

Bausoldaten: Construction soldiers. The GDR's provision for conscientious objectors to serve in a non-combatant role.

CDU: Christian Democratic Union. In West Germany, the right of center party. In the GDR, a partner party with the SED that gave Christians supportive of SED policies a minor role in politics.

CPC: Christian Peace Conference

CSSR: Czechoslovakian Socialist Republic.

DDR: *Deutsche Demokratische Republik*, (German Democratic Republic),

FDJ: *Freie Deutsche Jugend* (Free German Youth), the communist youth organization for high school and college age young people.

FDP: Free Democratic Party, the centrist party in West Germany.

FRG: Federal Republic of Germany, the official name for West Germany and now all of Germany.

GDR: German Democratic Republic, more commonly known as East Germany

Kinderkrippe: Day care center in the GDR for infants 18 months to 3 years of age.

IM: *Inoffizielle Mitarbeiter(in)*, Informal Co-worker, the designation for informants working for the Stasi.

Johanneum: The name of the red-brick dorm in downtown East Berlin where I lived the last couple of years. Occupancy is reserved strictly for theology students. It was built before the turn of the century by a philanthropist. The foundation he established for its upkeep went broke during the economic upheaval in Germany between the World Wars.

Junge Welt: Daily paper of the FDJ for high school and college students.

Leipziger Zeitung: Party controlled paper for the region around Leipzig.

MCC: Mennonite Central Committee, the relief and development agency of the Mennonite and Brethren Churches of North America.

Menno-Heim: The name of the large suburban house that served as a church and guest house for the West Berlin Mennonite Church and as a home of MCC'ers Tim and LaVerna Reimer.

ML: Marxist-Leninist; also short hand for ML courses required the first three years of study for all univeristy students.

Municipal Apartment Agency: *Kommunale Wohnungs Verwaltung* (KWV). The GDR government agency in charge of managing and renting out government owned apartments.

ND: *Neues Deutschland*, largest daily newspaper in the GDR. Its banner proclaimed it as the central organ of the Central Committee of the Socialist Unity Party. It gave the official party version of all events.

Neues Forum: (New Forum) One of the first and most popular grass-roots organizations to be formed outside of the party. At first illegal, it served to bring opponents of all stripes together in the waning months of 1989.

PDS: *Partei des Demokratischen Sozialismus* (Party of Democratic Socialism). The new name for the old SED.

SED: *Sozialistische Einheitspartei Deutschland* (Socialist Unity Party). The name came about due to a forced merger of the Communist Party and the Social Democrats in 1946, with the communists clearly retaining the upper hand.

SPD: Social Democratic Party, the left of center party in West Germany.

Stasi: Short for *Staatssicherheitdienst*, literally State Security Service, better known in English by the generic name, Secret Police.

Stempel: Official rubber stamp of any and all kinds; an important concept in the neat and orderly German society.

die tageszeitung: Left-wing daily newspaper in West Berlin.

Treuhand: Meaning 'Holding Company', this corporation was formed to take over GDR government owned companies in order to privatize them.

Verfassungsschutz: 'Constitution Protection Service', the West German agency responsible for keep tabs on any groups that may endanger the rule of law and the Constitution.

Volkskirche: People's church. Based on the historical practice of enrolling everyone born in the established church of the territory, thus all the people of a political area were members of the same church.

Chapter 1

Crossing the Wall

We pulled out of the Lehrter Stadtbahnhof station headed east, crossing the Spree river and then the Wall. I tried to get a good look at the guards in their tower. What a way to earn a living, I thought. Standing in that tower on the edge of the Spree, they could watch the West German flag waving in the breeze on the opposite bank of the river on top of the Reichstag, the old Imperial Parliament building. They also could watch the river itself, looking for any signs of swimmers trying to make it to the other side. Next to the Reichstag, one could just barely make out the row of white crosses wired onto the fence in front of the Wall, bearing testimony to a half-dozen swimmers, tunnelers or runners who didn't make it.

The S-bahn train slid past the gash the Wall made in the middle of Berlin, a gash that served as an 'air-lock' between two worlds. According to the government that had it built, the 'air-lock' of the Wall was to keep contamination from the West from seeping in. Unfortunately, it had been built with doors that generally opened only one way. The S-bahn slowed as it wove its way between the back walls of the pre-war tenements. S-bahn is the German word for above ground public transit. U-bahn means subway train, even in those places where the U-bahn goes above ground to cross the S-bahn, which on occasion darts underground. That kind of unexpected complication, like most complications in Germany, has something to do with history. The S-bahn I was riding on October 16, 1988, stayed above ground. It pulled into the Friedrichstrasse station, a dead-end.

Below us there was another S-bahn station, underground, for a north-south line, as well as a U-bahn station. Berlin was divided along city district lines after World War II. The middle district, called,

1

logically enough, Mitte, went with the eastern Soviet districts. It stuck out into West Berlin like a protruding wart. The districts to the north of Mitte became the French sector, those to the west the English sector. The American sector was in the south and southwest of Berlin. Forty some years later, it was thus possible to take West Berlin public transit into the former center of town, Mitte in East Berlin, just to change trains. That was, however, not my intent that morning. When I got off the S-bahn I headed for the 'air-locks' of the border crossing.

For Westerners going through the border was actually no big deal. It had long been possible to obtain a day-visa by simply showing your passport at the border, paying 5 DM ($3) for the visa and exchanging 25 DM ($15) for 25 M, East Marks. You had to return to West Berlin before midnight through the same border crossing where you came in (lest you turn into a pumpkin). With a day visa you were also required to remain within the city limits of East Berlin. Thousands of tourists did this every day. I, however, was not going for the day, but for three years, to study theology at Humboldt University in East Berlin and learn what I could about life in East Germany.

That was a bit more difficult to arrange. Professor Heinrich Fink, head of the Theology Department, had some problems getting my visa approved. As a stop-gap measure, he got me a two-week visa to attend a meeting of something called the Christian Peace Conference (CPC) in the town of Görlitz, in the southeast corner of East Germany. Since the conference only lasted a week, I'd have the second week to work out the details of my stay.

I walked past the stairs going down to the other platforms and thus back to West Berlin. I went straight to the 'air-lock' room. The 'air-locks' were all in row. They were actually booths consisting of a narrow passageway with a door on each end. In the middle of the passageway was a window. Behind the window was a border guard. Each booth had a sign to show which one kind of human being it would accept. There were three kinds; 1) East Germans, 2) West Germans and West Berliners, and 3) Others. The GDR had never recognized West Berlin as part of West Germany, although they insisted that East Berlin was part of East Germany - one of those historical complications. At any rate, that made West Berliners a species distinct from but related to West Germans. If you had any residual paranoia about Germans and their racial theories, you could wonder why they insisted on grouping people into Germans and Others. I tried to focus my disdain for the system on bureaucrats around the world, who divide people into groups just to be more efficient.

Some of the 'air-lock' doors were open on our side, that's where the lines formed. When it was my turn, I stepped into the narrow chamber to face a young border guard encased in glass, sitting behind a high counter. I pushed my passport and visa papers through the slot. He put them down behind the counter so I couldn't see what he was doing with them. I could see his shoulders rotating as he moved his arms back and forth, as if he were performing some magical incantations. That was followed by a number of solid thumps; the obligatory *Stempel*, rubber stamps of various types and colors. He glanced at the mirror up behind my head to get a view of my suitcase and tennis shoes. He pushed my passport back through the slot and hit a button. There was a short buzz, during which I could push open the door at the other end of the 'air-lock'. It rattled shut behind me.

One advantage of getting 'invited' to the GDR to attend a conference was that I could get out of paying the $15 a day required exchange. I just held up my passport with the business trip visa papers and walked past the line of Westerners waiting to exchange money. There was a final bottleneck to go through in front of custom officials, who on occasion waved people out of line for closer inspection. They just waved me on. I rounded one last corner and opened the door out into the east half of Friedrichstrasse station. I was through the border.

The S-bahn ran here too; it was also a dead-end station. In fact the East and West dead-end platforms were exactly parallel. There was a wall up to the roof in between the two halves of the station that gave both halves a paper bag, no-way-out-but-to-back-up feeling. My destination was within walking distance, so I didn't need to ride the S-bahn on the East side. I picked up my suitcase and headed out the door.

There were two lines outside. The one at the taxi stand reflected the shortage of taxis. The other was shorter and moved much quicker, it consisted of GDR pensioners going through the 'air-locks' in the wrong direction in order to spend the day in West Berlin. They were allowed out a set number of days per year. If they didn't come back, at least the GDR government could save itself the expense of paying their pensions. That row of 'air-locks' was in an extra building, marked alternately EXIT or emigration. One wall was all glass, but covered at ground level by a row of bushes so no one could look in. Middle-aged children were dropping off their mothers and waving good-bye. Grandma whooshed through the 'air-locks' and was gone for the day. Berliners have a long standing tradition, going back to the days before East and West, of giving government buildings biting, bitter-sweet nicknames. They called the exit 'air-lock' building the Palace of Tears. I walked between the ends of the two lines, turning up Friedrichstrasse, the street that gave the station its name.

The street crossed the river Spree right there. On the other side of the bridge on the right side of the street was an apartment building under construction. Then came the Friedrichstadtpalast, a building that looked like a theater of sorts. There were posters out front of women with long legs and short skirts. Behind it was a large empty lot. On the corner of the lot was the skeleton of a building, its back torn open, still in ruins 43 years after the end of the war. I turned the corner at the bombed out building onto Oranienburger Street. On one side was the huge empty lot and the ruined building, on the other a row of drab tenements, with shops on the ground floor and apartments four and five stories above. I climbed the stairs in one of these tenements, lugging my suitcase, and rang the door bell of the office of the Christian Peace Conference in the GDR.

Quick Introductions

That was the end of much time for reflection. There was a short flurry of introductions, a quick cup of coffee and I was assigned a car to ride in. Dr. Kraft, a professor of Ethics from the theology department, and I rode with a pastor to Görlitz. I started learning three important lessons about life in the GDR there.

I had no idea what the CPC was, but certainly got a crash course in that. It had been founded in 1961 at the initiative of a Czech theologian by the name of Hromadka. As I found out later, their conclusion that the Soviet-led invasion of Czechoslovakia in 1968 was also an act of peace cost them most of their credibility in the West. There were only about 500 members in the GDR, but some were in influential positions, like several of the professors of the Humboldt University. Beyond all the politics, it was an introduction to the ambiguity of trying to follow Christ in the GDR.

My official status at the conference was as a steward, a volunteer to help out where needed. There were a couple dozen East German young people serving in the same function as well as some older people. We had our own staff room to hang out in between assignments. There we could rub shoulders with some of the officials of the East German branch of the CPC. I listened in on a conversation between one of the officials and a young man. He had applied to attend university, but had been turned down. He felt that his being Christian had been the sole basis for the rejection. His grades in high school had been quite good and he had done his stint in the army as required. The older man he was talking to urged him to appeal his case, in effect to take the government to court, because discrimination on religious grounds was simply illegal in the GDR. The older man conceded that not all of the party members had figured that out, but it was Christians' responsibility to stand up for their rights. The young man seemed a bit hesitant to follow that advice, reminding me most of an unskilled, unemployed person in our society being told to just get off his duff and get a job. Good advice in both cases, no doubt, but not always easy to follow up on.

The CPC included only a tiny minority of the Christians in the GDR. It was considered to be at one extreme end of the spectrum in loyal support of the government. As in any society, or in any church, I later found a wide range of opinions in the GDR. The idea of a monolithic East German, a country full of fervent communists, was the first Cold War myth to be debunked during my stay in the GDR.

We were put up in student dorms. This had the disadvantage of cold showers, but the great advantage of allowing conference participants to talk to the students until the wee hours of the morning in the student cafe called 'In der Maus' (In the Mouse). With Görlitz being pretty much off the beaten track, not many Americans came to visit. I had purposely left my T-shirts and sweatshirts with English printing at home. I was white and had thinning hair; in short, at first glance I could pass for an East German. Once they found out I was American, they looked me over top to bottom, like a giraffe in the zoo. The Cold War and the lack of ability to travel had worked their poison. Few people believed intellectually that Americans were evil, or somehow deformed by capitalism, but this was a poison that affected the soul, a Cold War myth of their own. There seemed to be something enticingly repulsive about having a real American actually sitting in their cafe. I must admit to feeling the same way about sitting around with regular East Germans. Which ones were in the Party or working for the Stasi, the East German secret police? They had all served in the East German army and been trained to kill Americans (defend their country is how their army put it).

They had a lot of questions. Are American cars really that big? What was I doing here? What did I think of the GDR? Were there really homeless people in the U.S. like the newspapers claimed? What did people back home think of the GDR? They also talked about life in their dorm. It was three or four students in a small room, having to take shifts stoking the coal furnace in the basement, and hating cold showers as much as I did. In the evenings I spent with students there, I discovered people much like myself, yet shaped by very different experiences. That made real communication difficult.

My third important lesson came on the last evening of the conference. There was a formal reception given by Kurt Löffler, State Secretary for Church Questions, the ranking government official in charge of managing relations with churches. A beautiful cold buffet table had been set up. Right in the middle of it there were big bunches of bananas. People gathered in clusters, I joined the other stewards.

It started out very formal; a little chamber music, then a number of the kind of speeches that say nothing and are promptly forgotten. Some of the Latin American delegates went up to the far end of the table and started nibbling on the goodies. Instant mortification. "They shouldn't be doing that" some of the older people in our group whispered rather loudly. The younger ones just snickered and looked a bit jealous. Mercifully the speechifying ended soon. We all stormed the buffet table.

Two of the more petite young women made what was for them a dreadful discovery. The table was pretty big and those bananas were exactly in the middle, a long way off. They couldn't reach them. I happened to be standing right next to them.

"Hey, Mark, can you get us some bananas?"

"Well, uh, I guess so."

I grabbed two and passed them on.

"Don't you want any?"

Looks of shock and disbelief.

"No, thanks, I don't like bananas."

An almost audible gasp.

Obviously there was something special about bananas here that I was missing. Once they had finished eating the first round of bananas and before I helped them get seconds, I asked for an explanation.

"Well, it's just that you hardly ever see them."

Bananas don't grow in East Germany, or for that matter anywhere in the East Bloc, so they had to be imported. That meant paying hard currency, which the government claimed not to have much of, so bananas usually only showed up for Christmas. Like most things considered exotic or off-limits, this helped make bananas all the more exciting. Of course, their reaction to my dislike of bananas had more to do with youthful exuberance than anything else, but it did underline the intense curiosity about things Western that permeated East German society.

Taken in

There was one final important event at this conference. I met Imke. I had gone to Görlitz not knowing what I would do after the conference was over. Imke lived in Berlin and offered to let me stay with her and her husband for the final week of my two-week visa. I gratefully accepted. We caught a ride back to Berlin with a pastor friend of hers.

Micah, Imke's husband, hadn't, of course, known about her generous offer. Since they, like most East Germans, had no phone, she hadn't talked to him all week. He accepted Imke's dragging some strange guy along home with good grace. It wasn't until a few days later he told me that he had to report the fact that I was staying with them to his boss. He worked as a technician at a radio station, a position of some official responsibility. Anyone who fit into this nebulous category was required to report all contact with people from the West. If someone found out I had been staying at his place and he hadn't reported it, he would have been in trouble. He assured me that reporting on himself entailed no risk. Their inviting me into their home seemed all the more amazing.

They lived on Gleim Street, in a run down section of town with mostly pre-war tenements. It was a five minute walk from the nearest park, which also meant a five minute walk from the Wall. We went there on Sunday afternoon, a nice little park, with grandmas sitting on the benches and children playing on the grass and the playground equipment. There were little red and white iron barriers set up at the edge of the park, a couple of feet in front of the Wall. The activities in the park at least gave the guard in the tower something more interesting to look at than guards had in most places. The top floors of apartment buildings in the West could be seen on the far side of the death strip. I seemed to be the only one who took much notice of the Wall, it was part of the landscape for everyone else.

Not having phones made for interesting social interaction. We would go to visit people unannounced, I was always invited to come along, or they would just drop in on us. If it didn't suit, there was no problem in saying so, but generally it just suited. At one birthday party we went to, the conversation started out pretty general, similar to the discussions 'In der Maus'. It soon took a different turn, though, because this was a group of people that knew and trusted each other. The problems of the GDR got some very frank discussion. Several of the people there were looking for apartments, one of the biggest problems. The procedure was explained to me several times, but I never did quite figure it out.

It started at the local Municipal Apartment Agency (MAA), the bureaucracy in charge of all apartments. First you had to prove that you deserved an apartment. That wasn't hard, assuming you were old enough to move out on your own and not a student. Students were only allowed to live in dorms. If you deserved an apartment, you got a Deserves an Apartment Certificate. Next you applied for an apartment. Then you waited years, or got creative. Sometimes it was possible to find an apartment that had been abandoned, usually by people who had emigrated to the West. This was especially true in pre-war tenement districts. You could report it to the MAA and they might or might not let you move in. Or you could just break the door down, move in and start paying rent, then wait until the MAA caught up with you and made you pay a fine (and let you stay) or evicted you. Some companies provided an apartment as a way of attracting workers from a shrinking pool caused by a low birth rate and emigration to the West. Another possibility was to sublet a room from someone with a two-room apartment. When they moved out you might be allowed to keep the apartment. Like I said, I never did quite understand this system.

Signing up

I spent my time during that week trying to figure out what I'd need to get final permission to stay. Professor Fink's administrative assistant assured me that the State Secretariat of Church Questions had approved my stay. It would just be a matter of waiting for the paperwork to make the rounds of the University's bureaucrats.

Dr. Brigitte Kahl, a professor of Ecumenism, also had an administrative position that put her in charge of shepherding my paperwork through the channels. I had several meetings with her throughout the week. She also taught the Introduction to Old Testament class I was joining 6 weeks late. She encouraged me to read through the first five books of the Old Testament by next week in order to get caught up. Attending her class was the first time I ever had to read the Old Testament through start to finish, the first of many pleasant bonuses to studying theology in East Germany.

Another person I met during this week was Klaus Roeber. He had been a pastor for a number of years and was now back at the University working on his doctorate. He had been good friends with the previous MCC workers, who had been in West Berlin. He was assigned to me as a contact person for problems of any kind. He gave me a tour of the various University buildings where the department had lecture rooms. Thirteen years ago, the Theology Department had moved to a former construction workers' shack a block away from the intersection of Friedrichstrasse and Unter den Linden. They had been told that it was a temporary arrangement, while their old building was being renovated. They were still there. That made it necessary for the lectures to be held in other buildings.

Klaus took me to lunch at one of the restaurants on Unter den Linden, the 'Main Street' of East Berlin. Afterwards he gave me some advice on what to do if agents of the Stasi ever came to talk to me. They would try to intimidate me into agreeing to keep the conversation a secret. He said I should never agree to that. I should tell them that as a Christian I would need to talk about such a traumatic situation with fellow Christians and especially with my pastor. He also mentioned a few ground rules about what to talk about with people in general and what to avoid. The most basic rule was simply not to say things that you didn't believe in enough to back up no matter what. It just wasn't the type of society where you could say the first thing to pop into your head. This was probably all good advice, but it sure gave my paranoia a healthy boost.

The end of the week the bureaucratic process hit high gear. Dr. Kahl took me to the university's Office for Foreign Students, where I had to fill out two 'Immigration' applications. I also received my student ID and library cards, and without further ado, a little green booklet called Social Insurance Identification. As a student of the university, I was entitled to free health care at the university school of medicine, covering all office calls, prescriptions, in fact, absolutely all health needs.

I went to visit the dorm I had been assigned to, a long row of new, 11-story apartment buildings. They were located about an hour by bus from the university on Storkower Street. Frau Rönsch was the lady in charge, she said I could move in on Monday, October 31. She showed me the room. I would get one room of a three room apartment. I shared the bathroom with the other two guys in the apartment. A hot-plate on top of a small refrigerator in the hallway served as the kitchen. The apartment was up on the tenth floor. Foreigners were always put in apartments together, although some of the other apartments in the building had East Germans students in them. All the foreigners in this dorm were paying for their studies in hard currency, which is why we got single rooms. The East German students were packed in three or four to a room. On the other hand, we had to pay $75 a month rent. The East Germans paid 10 marks, about $6 at the official rate or 60¢ at black market rates at that time. The strangest part of the whole set up was the two different TV rooms. The Germans had broken down, hard-backed chairs and a black-and-white TV in theirs. We had a nice sofa and a couple of nice lounge chairs and a color TV in ours. Ours was locked and only foreign students were issued a key. Frau Rönsch didn't check very often, but if she caught a German in our lounge, they got a good chewing out. As a general rule, we just didn't mix much in the dorm.

On the 31st, I not only moved from Imke and Micah's into my new home, I also signed the final version of the contract with the University. MCC would pay them $5582 a year for what the theology department jokingly referred to as 'the exportation of theological education in a domestic setting'. That amount included the rent for my room and a stipend. University officials had also been 'touchingly concerned' about providing me with adequate pocket money. They suggested a monthly stipend of 500 East Marks, to be exchanged at the official rate of 1-to-1. That was a good deal for the government; the black market rate was about a tenth of that. East German students got paid a stipend of 200 Marks a month.

The only reason the government agreed to issue me a temporary residency permit was to get that $5582 a year. MCC and I were being drawn into the ambiguity of living in Eastern Europe. Every little bit of hard currency given to the government only helped them out. On the other hand, it was the only way to get into the country. None of the East Germans I talk to thought it was a bad compromise, but a compromise it was none the less.

There was another clause written into the contract I had to sign that gave cause for reflection. §6 stated: "Mr. Jantzen pledges himself to obey the regulations and laws of the GDR and not interfere in the internal affairs of the GDR as well as to respect the customs and traditions of the GDR". §10 - "The course of studies will be immediately ended if any laws or ordinances of public order of the GDR are broken." That made for a pretty clear veiled threat. If I didn't behave, the government had legal grounds on which to send me home.

Having filled out the 'Immigration' cards and been issued a residency permit, I found out that if I wanted to leave the GDR, I now had to apply for permission to 'emigrate' using the same procedure as GDR citizens. Of course, my applications were never turned down. Every time I wanted to leave the country, even to go to West Berlin for a day, I had to fill out two cards stating where I was going and why. The director of the Office for Foreign Students had to initial it, but he wasn't always around. Then I had to go across town to the police station responsible for the district where my dorm was located. They had a special department for foreigners that would stamp an exit and reentry visa into my passport for a 15 mark fee. The whole procedure took at least half a day and none of the offices were open on weekends, so I had to plan ahead a little if I wanted to go to West Berlin. Still, I was much better off than my fellow students.

East German universities were set up on a seminar group principle. A group of 20-30 students were together throughout their university stay. They had most of their classes together and thus got to know one another quite well. That type of rigid structure might well have made it easier for the Stasi to keep an eye on students, but it also made it easier for me to fit into student life in the theology department. I joined classes six weeks late because of my visa problems and was assigned to the freshmen class seminar group. There were about 25 freshmen and it was here that some of my deepest friendships developed.

Sometime during the first week of classes, the cafeteria offered bananas one day for dessert. I had learned my lesson in Görlitz; to not eat a banana would be to stick out. My dislike of them was rooted somewhere in the distant fog of childhood; it had actually been years since I tried one. So in the interest of fitting in to my new adoptive society, I dutifully took a banana and ate it. Not too bad! I wouldn't say I liked it, but I guess they're edible alright. It was at least one success of my coming to live in the GDR!

November 7 was the beginning of a series of lectures organized by the University to commemorate a night of terror 50 years before, November 9, 1938. On that night, at the instigation of the Nazis, a couple hundred Jewish synagogues were set on fire, thousands of Jewish business had their display windows smashed, thousands of Jews were arrested and some were even murdered[1]. Typical of the different approaches to this sad history taken in West Germany and the GDR were the different names used to denote this event. In the West it was called *Kristallnacht*, the night of crystal, referring to the broken windows of Jewish businesses. The East German name, *Pogromnacht*, the night of the pogrom, stood as a critique of that Western name, which highlighted broken windows instead of brutal murders and arrests. In the East, however, one was given the impression that it was Nazis, and not Germans, who were to blame, obscuring the painfully gray overlap between those two groups.

One of the special lectures for the memorial of that occasion was by a Jew who was living in Jerusalem. It was held in the French Cathedral, a church just off Unter den Linden, about a mile from the Brandenburg Gate and thus a mile from the Wall. The speaker had spent the war in hiding in Amsterdam, not too far from the house where Anne Frank had hidden. Unlike Anne, she was not discovered and survived the war. During question and answer time, someone asked about the current status of Jerusalem and the prospects of trading land for peace.

This woman was in favor of that trade with one major exception. She said Jerusalem could never be divided again. She said there used to be a wall between East and West Jerusalem, but once you tear a wall down in a city and the people are given the opportunity to learn to live with each other it's not possible to build a wall again.

Prophetic words. They got a nervous laugh from the audience, a number of quick glances over the shoulder. It defined the two central realities of East German life; a sad war followed by a sad division, symbolized by a sad wall. In those few short weeks, I found a lot of things that made no sense to me. I still figuratively looked over my shoulder in confusion and paranoia all the time. But in those few short weeks, I had found East Germans who laughed, who sang, who were shy or obnoxious, who were like people are everywhere, I guess.

And yet, unlike anywhere else, their lives revolved unconsciously, unseen, almost unknown, around a very sad war and a very sad wall.

Chapter 2

What Are You Doing Here?

I think the real reason I went to the GDR starts with the fact that Adolf Ott was a member of the Nazi party. He was also a devout member of the Protestant Church in Neureut, Germany. He was my grandfather.

People were always asking me why I would voluntarily move to the GDR, what I was doing there. I would usually pick a short, pat answer from my repertoire. I didn't like my old job, I wanted a change and this is where I ended up. There's a Cold War on and I wanted to come see the enemy for myself. I love Germany. It beats working for a living. My Bible has a verse in it about loving your enemies. Most people were satisfied with one of the short versions, so it wasn't very often that I had to think about the complex, longer version, the reason to make what turned out to be a life-changing decision.

That longer version started with my grandfather, Adolf Ott. I myself grew up on a dairy farm in the southeast corner of Nebraska. The economic realities of life might have been a bit harsh, but in general I had a sheltered and happy childhood. Small-town America, except for Mom's war stories.

During the war they lived in the town of Bretten, in the south of Germany, close to the Rhine Rver. Their house was on the outskirts of town, close to the train tracks and a train tunnel. As the war wound down, the German Army used the tunnel as a day-time bomb shelter for supply trains. The Allies, of course, knew this and made both ends of the tunnel a constant target, in the hope of burying the train.

They never succeeded but tried often enough. The pressure waves from the exploding bombs dislodged the tiles from the roof of Mom's house. Climbing up on the roof to straighten out the tiles after the Americans' bombing run became a daily task for a while.

Mom was fourteen, going on fifteen, the oldest of six children. She was terrified of being buried alive in the basement of the house.

14

She preferred to stand outside and watch the bombs fall, then run, pretending that bombs could be outrun. That drove Grandma crazy. Her sister, Irma, was the opposite. She spent all her time in the basement. One of their brothers, Friedbert, who would have only been five or six at the time, was playing outside in the yard one day. He misjudged the direction a plane low on the horizon was flying. He realized his mistake just in time, diving in the house as the American fighter plane strafed the courtyard and the house. One bullet shot the handle off the oven door, one of the 'souvenirs' of the war that remained in the family for years.

There hadn't been much school the last couple years of the war, because it was too dangerous to have the children all together. They would go on Mondays to pick up the assignments for the week and on Fridays to hand them in. Grandpa Ott had been drafted late in the war and ended up in a French prisoner of war camp. After the war, Grandma told Mom she'd either have to go to work or stay home with the youngest children. Mom decided she'd rather work. She started work at age fifteen, grinding off stove tops in a local factory.

Her part of Germany was in the American Occupation Zone, so she met her first Americans. The winter of 1945-1946 was very tough. The war had disrupted the harvest and the transportation network had been bombed out. The kids used to pick over the garbage dump out back of the Army's cafeteria. That's how Mom tasted her first donut. There were Army regulations against that kind of thing as being unsanitary. They started burning the garbage dump every day. Grandma was furious. "Someday the Americans will have to go hungry themselves for burning food like that when there are so many hungry people around!", she would say. There were also GI's who handed out food, especially to the kids.

Once a food rationing system was set up, one person from each family was required to watch a movie about the horrors of the concentration camps before getting their family's food coupons. Mom volunteered to go to the Americans' 'propaganda' movie on her family's behalf, since she could go with a girl friend of hers. They talked and giggled in the theater, not paying any attention to the movie until a man behind them scolded them to be quiet and pay attention. He seemed pretty upset about something. They didn't believe anything they saw anyway.

American War Stories

A German reading these stories would find them remarkable only in that my mother's immediate family suffered no deaths. Several uncles were killed, of course. Hearing these stories, told infrequently and with reluctance, was the start, and in many ways the most important part, of my orientation for a three-year stay in East Germany.

My father's war stories were much different, but painful in their own way. His family, as far as anyone knew, had been Mennonite since the time of the Reformation. For most of the local congregation and his family, that meant refusing to serve in the armed forces. He went to work for a neighbor who had enough 'points' in agricultural production to secure him a farm deferment.

Most people in our corner of Nebraska were Germans. From my own childhood I remember one old neighbor lady who had never learned English and had still managed to get along in our little village. There were, however, some sharp differences between the small group of Mennonites and the larger group of German Lutherans.

Up until World War II, my home congregation used German in their worship services. Now, with their refusal to go to war against the Germans, that looked very suspicious. I've heard some vague stories of uneasy relations between neighbors, maybe even an incident of yellow-paint splashing here and there, but mostly it's just never talked about. It is admittedly a difficult topic. It certainly isn't too realistic to expect to find great tolerance during as emotional a time as a war.

My parents talked German at home as their secret language, whenever there was something to talk about that they didn't want us kids to hear, like bedtimes or a discussion on the vegetable-eating policy. We picked up a little, but mostly that served as powerful incentive to learn German in high school.

We also took two trips as a family to visit Grandma. We met our German cousins. On the first trip in 1966, we were young enough to play together without needing a common language. By the second trip in 1974, they had learned a little English in school and my older siblings had learned a little German.

We were related to about half the village of Neureut. We visited in the homes of some of Mom's aunts. They were elderly women, plying us with *Spätzle* or *Dampfnudeln*, the culinary specialities of the area. They all lived in apartments attached to the houses of one of their children. I remember the apartments as being dark, and several had pictures of young men wearing German army uniforms hanging in prominent places. Wayward husbands who never came home. One got killed at Leningrad, another was missing in action at Stalingrad. We were told that we had to eat seven Dampfnudeln before we could even start keeping track. I think I only ever made it to five and almost burst. The pile was the same size when we left as when we came, it seemed to magically regenerate itself every time Mom's aunt took the platter into the kitchen.

My junior year in college, 1983-1984, was spent in Wuppertal, West Germany. I learned a lot about the Germany that had come to pass after my mother left and her memories of it ended. One day the students were gathered around TV sets all over the university. Must be some big soccer game, I thought. When I stopped long enough to look over someone's shoulder, I realized they were all watching the debate in the national parliament over allowing the stationing of Pershing II's, medium-range nuclear missiles. One source later reported that the Americans had deployed the first missiles while the debate was still being held, an affront to West German sovereignty. Not long after that, I was talking English with an American friend, heading into the cafeteria. Wham! The German in front of us had slammed the door in our faces as hard as he could. It bounced off the toe of my hiking boot, so no harm was done. Still, an interesting concept, someone hating you for being American. Certainly only a tiny minority of Germans felt that way. Many more were interested in becoming friends and I was warmly received in a number of German homes. Maybe I only remember that one act of hatred because it was so rare.

Joining MCC

After college, I got a job as a computer programmer in Lincoln, Nebraska. My salary was good, the people I worked with were great, but we did have to work quite a bit of overtime, including weekends. I had long been considering doing some kind of overseas voluntary work with the church, but part of the catalyst came from an unexpected source. After I had been at that job for about 6 months, I was asked to help train David, who had just been hired. The first thing David did on his first day of work was to lay a Bible out on his desk. There were few professing Christians in our company, so David's forthrightness sparked a few discussions and a fair amount of ridicule of Christianity, TV evangelists etc. For other, personal reasons, David wasn't with our company very long. After he left, our manager became aware of the type of discussions we had been having on company time. He knew I was a Christian, so he made a point of telling me that he appreciated that I didn't push my beliefs during office hours. He had nothing against it, our outside interests were our business. If we wanted to have religion as a hobby, fine, but it shouldn't interfere with work.

I had found a warm church home at First Mennonite Church in Lincoln. Our young adult bible study was very close. I was teaching the second grade Sunday School class. Having to work overtime on the weekends soon caused conflict. Once I had to find a substitute teacher on short notice, another time I had to leave for work right after Sunday School class. There are of course many people who have jobs that keep them from going to church on Sunday; medical professionals and people in service industries. It was the expectation that I treat my 'religion' as a hobby that was the last straw in my deciding to look for another job.

I decided I would apply for a position with Mennonite Central Committee (MCC). MCC is the relief and development agency of the Mennonite and Brethren in Christ Churches. I knew about their program in East Europe and asked to be considered for East Germany.

MCC was not an abstract church institution to our family. Dad had spent two years with MCC in Germany from 1949-1951. He drove truck, hauling refugees and supplies back and forth as needed. Mom was one of the first non-Mennonites to participate in a MCC visitor program that brought European youth to North American for a year. She was here from August 1953 to August 1954. She spent the first 6 months working in the Mennonite Hospital in Beatrice and roomed there with Dad's sister. They would go out to the farm on weekends. The rest, as they say, is history. MCC had become an integral part of the family history. My oldest brother spent 4 years with MCC in Bolivia working in agricultural development. When the option of going to East Germany came up, Mom was skeptical, ostensibly because communists couldn't be trusted, but I suspect it had more to do with the sheer distance involved. Dad just smiled. His mother had apparently had a similar reaction to his driving through East Germany to West Berlin a few days after the blockade was lifted in 1949.

Part of the family or not, MCC is also an institution. Making all the necessary arrangements took time and paperwork. There were apparently some reservations about sending single persons into settings with such extreme isolation from other North Americans as was typical of East Europe.

I had hoped to have things worked out by March, 1988. My sister and I had planned a trip to Europe for March and April. Although things with MCC were still very much up in the air, I went ahead and quit my job. During our trip, I made a quick detour to the MCC European office in Neuwied, West Germany. I hoped to ask if an exception could be made in my case so that I could be accepted to go to East Germany. George Epp, MCC Assistant Secretary for Europe, started the conversation by asking when I would be ready to go!

There were still many details to be worked out. George wrote to a few of his contacts in East Germany. Dr. Junghans answered from Leipzig, Dr. Fink from East Berlin. George sent me copies of their answers and asked where I wanted to go. In my ignorance, my only criteria to decide between the two was the fact that Axel, a friend of mine from Wuppertal, had moved to West Berlin. At least I'd know somebody there. George wrote back to Dr. Fink. Things seemed to be on track at last. I made plans to attend orientation at MCC headquarters in Akron, PA, the beginning of September. Immediately afterwards I would leave for Germany.

Exactly half way through orientation, word came from the MCC office in Neuwied that my visa application had been denied. I spent the next couple days muttering about immigration bureaucrats under my breath and wondering what on earth I would do now. After some consultations between George Epp in the Neuwied office, John Lapp and Anita Brendle in Akron and myself, it was decided that I would go to Germany. I was relieved that MCC was willing to risk a plane ticket on my being able to get a visa once I got to Berlin. I myself was not so confident.

I arrived in Frankfurt on September 21 and took the train to Neuwied. I had several days to get to know the staff in the office there. I was also able to spend some time reading through the files that the previous MCC'ers in West Berlin had left behind. John and Norma Thiessen had lived in the house that served as church building for the West Berlin Mennonite congregation, the Menno-Heim. They had worked at visiting Mennonites in East Germany and maintaining contact between the two congregations that had been split by construction of the Wall in 1961. As a student, I was expected to spend most of my time studying so as not to jeopardize my visa. However, it was clear that MCC expected that I contribute to the life of the Mennonite Church in East Germany.

Once I was over my jet lag, I took the train to West Berlin. Shortly after crossing the East German border, the border guards came through and handed out 'transit visas'. The official international agreements stated that the East German government granted West Germans, and by corollary other Westerners, the right to travel through East Germany. The bored expressions on the border guards faces and the faces of the West Germans in my compartment made it clear this was a well-worn routine. I hoped I managed to look bored too.

In West Berlin I moved into the Menno-Heim. I was finally close enough to East Berlin to figure out what was going on. I called Dr. Fink and arranged a meeting for September 28.

I went through the border crossing at Friedrichstrasse, shelling out the $18 for a day visa. I spent the morning walking up and down Unter den Linden. I tried to get a peek into the main university building, which is on that street. Right inside the front door was a little glass booth with a student sitting in it.

"ID!", she said to me as I looked at her uncertainly.

"I just want to look around."

"That's not allowed!"

Oh, well. I also got an offer to exchange money on the black market that I turned down. I was starting to wonder what I had gotten myself into here. I found the address that Dr. Fink had given me. It was a couple of blocks off of Unter den Linden, a church known as the French Cathedral. There was going to be a special assembly of the Theology Department and Dr. Fink wanted me to be there so he could introduce me to everyone.

There was a guy selling what passes in all of Germany for hamburgers and what passed in East Germany as cola, so I had a little lunch. That got rid of about a Mark and a half of the 25 East Marks I had to spend before going home. I went into the church and there was another student sitting in another glass booth. I thought.

"Can you tell me where the theology department is meeting?"

A long pause.

"This is a museum belonging to the Cultural Department of the City of Berlin. The other end of the church is still a church, you might check there."

Right, a church divided into a state part and a church part. The theology department was indeed meeting in the church half of the church. I was asked to stand up and was introduced as an American student having difficulties getting all the paperwork done on my visa, but I would soon be joining the department. Afterwards, a number of students came up and talked to me. Besides the standard 'What are you doing here', some of them also offered some very candid advice about the professors and the course of studies.

I went with Dr. Fink to his office in the construction shack that served as the theology department. It was getting late in the afternoon, so we couldn't talk very long. He told me about the temporary visa he would get for me to attend this meeting of the Christian Peace Conference. Mainly he reassured me that my visa problem would be worked out.

George and Agnes Epp had made arrangements to come to Berlin to help me finalize arrangements as well as introduce me to some of the Mennonites in West and East Berlin. We had another meeting together with Dr. Fink on October 5. He had just received word that my visa had been approved. We talked a while about the different courses I could take. One issue that had not been resolved was housing.

"What kind of apartment do you and your wife require?" Dr. Fink asked.

In the four years since I had last lived in Germany, I had become a little uncertain about my German. I must have heard something wrong.

"My wife?"

"Yes, in fact your visa request was turned down the first time because your wife is a West German citizen. That has been worked out now."

"But I'm not married!"

Pause. A little bit of paper shuffling. Wow, I thought, married! Maybe that's what they mean by a planned economy!

"Well, I don't know how that happened, but it doesn't matter. I'm sure we'll be able to find you a dorm room now with no problem."

He also gave me my visa to an international meeting of the Christian Peace Conference, which started in a week and a half.

Once we got out of Fink's office and had a good laugh, George explained how I had gotten my 'wife'. About 18 months earlier, he had written Dr. Fink about a couple that MCC wanted to sponsor to study at the Humboldt University. He was American and she was West German. Our applications must have gotten mixed up in the files.

Loving Enemies?

I remember the first time I watched the movie "Raiders of the Lost Ark". Of course, the Nazis, or the Germans, same difference apparently, were the villains. There is one scene where a couple of Germans in a jeep are forced off the road by the hero, Indiana Jones. The camera shows us a close up of the driver's face as he yells *Scheisse!* What I remember most about that scene is that I laughed, quite loudly, and no one else in the theater did. Embarrassment. I wondered if I was the only person in the audience who understood *Scheisse*, the most basic of all German swear words.

The episode seems symptomatic to me. One generation of Americans had learned to think of the Nazis, or Germans, as Evil personified. I thought of at least one of them as my grandfather. I was keenly aware of the evil that they had perpetrated, but couldn't bring myself to abhor my mother for having been in the *Bund Deutsche Mädel* the female equivalent of the Hitler Youth. It took me years to realize but the Germans in my world were more gray than black and white. It made me wonder if the same applied to my generation's Evil personified, the communists in East Germany.

I also grew up in a corner of the world where people were inclined to take their Bibles seriously. Dad would always tell incredulous German visitors that burglars would have easy pickings in our neighborhood on Sunday mornings because everyone went to church every Sunday. Of course, the various churches choose to accent different themes. Like the lowest bass note on our pipe organ, there was one theme in our church that was seldom heard but traditionally held to help undergird the whole structure.

"But I tell you who hear me: Love your enemies, do good to those who hate you, bless those who curse you, pray for those who ill-treat you." (Luke 6:27) Like a bad organist hitting that low note at the wrong time, this verse, when it was mentioned, brought discord to our congregation. We couldn't agree on what Jesus meant. In our congregation there is a conspicuous lack of saints, we all lash out in anger at times, are unloving or have other faults. Again it took me years to realize the contribution of our congregation to making peace. It tipped the scales in my decision to go to East Germany. It was the insistence that this message in the Bible, to love our enemies, presents us with a question that we have to ask ourselves again and again, even as a definitive answer eludes us.

When facing border guards, the frustration and loneliness of being so far from home among such strange people, or the endless question of what I was doing there, this question, and the God who inspired it, seemed very distant. It took time. I spent quiet evenings in snug apartments talking and laughing with my friends, the enemy. I shared communion with fellow questioners, who had found different answers than mine to some of life's questions. We played Frisbee together in the park under the shadow of the Wall. In all these activities I discovered the magic, the grace that was the real reason I was there.

Chapter 3

Getting Settled In

Part of my quest to get to know my new home was the mundane task of getting certain simple tasks done. One of the first jobs I had given myself was to find a way to keep in touch with developments back home by regularly reading *Newsweek* or *Time.* I wanted a solution that would not make me stick out too much in East German society. I hoped to blend into my new surroundings in order to really understand them. At the same time, I had to realize that my being so different, being able to travel to West Berlin and having hard currency, made really blending in impossible.

Now I knew it wouldn't be very practical to get a subscription to *Newsweek.* It would be intercepted in the mail. I didn't want to go to West Berlin every week to buy it. There would have been too much hassle to get the visa every time, plus it would have made me stick out as someone who could just go across the Wall. Somehow it didn't feel right to me to go to West Berlin for something as trivial as a copy of *Newsweek.* My fellow students couldn't go there unless their grandparents lived there and were celebrating a major birthday, like their 70th or 75th, or had died and were being buried. Those who had no immediate relatives in the West had no chance of going there at all.

I decided to start by looking in the library. The National Library, which had started as the library of the Prussian dukes and kings, was still on Unter den Linden, right next door to the main university building. I set out to find their periodical section.

"ID!" the doorman said to me as I entered the library.

I was told at the Office for Foreign Students that I would be required to carry my American passport as my official identification with me at all times. Both East and West Germans have government issued ID cards that they have to produce on demand of authorized authorities, most notably the police. I always assumed this was a holdover from Prussian bureaucracy. This doorman didn't look like much of a Prussian. I couldn't fathom why he would want to see my passport. I showed him my newly acquired student ID.

"Don't you have a library card?"

So that's what he was looking for. I had to admit I didn't.

"You can get one from the university", he told me.

I went back to the Office for Foreign Students and got a library card. I tried again when I had a little time to spare about a week later.

"ID!" the doorman said to me as I entered the library.

I showed him my library card.

"You need to sign in and get a *Stempel* (official rubber stamp)" he said, "the registration office is over there."

That was a relatively quick procedure. I showed the doorman the new *Stempel*.

"Coats and book bags are not allowed in the library" he said, "the coat check is over there."

That was a relatively quick procedure too. I showed him my *Stempel* again. This time he just nodded and I was in.

To my surprise I found both *Time* and *Newsweek* listed in their periodical department. There weren't any periodicals on display though. I asked the periodicals' clerk how I could find them. She showed me how to fill out a form.

"Put the date of the issue you want here" she indicated.

"I want the most recent one" I answered.

"OK, just write that then and lay the form on my desk when you're finished. I'll go get it for you as soon as I have a chance."

She brought me an issue of *Time* that was three weeks old. She said it was the most current issue there. I didn't see how it could take the mail to East Berlin three weeks longer than the mail to West Berlin. I also didn't see much point in arguing, so I read that issue and left. I had noted the date, so that I could specifically request the newest issue next time.

A week later I was back. The current *Time* wasn't available. The next day I tried requesting the latest *Newsweek*. The clerk brought me one that was only two weeks old. Progress, I thought. When I came back next week, she brought the same issue, now three weeks old. The next week she still brought me the same issue, now four weeks old. I was sure this was a communist plot of some sort. They probably kept track of people who showed too much interest in Western news magazines. I was a Westerner, though, and what possible reason could they have for not letting me read a *Newsweek*?

I went up to the periodicals desk and yelled at the clerk in a hushed whisper. All I wanted to do was read news from back home, I told her. Why can't the *Newsweek* be delivered on time. It seems a bit silly.

She looked a bit taken aback at the beginning of my tirade, then she shrugged her shoulders and said it wasn't her fault that the mail was slow. I left in disgust. There was another possibility for reading *Newsweek*.

A little farther up Unter den Linden, close to the Brandenburg Gate, the American Embassy was tucked away in a little side street. A number of students had told me about it. It had a small library with newspapers and magazines from States. It was open to the public. The Embassy also had East German police protection. Two or three policemen were on patrol out front. In fact, a little booth with reflecting glass windows had been built across the street from it. I had talked to several students who had gone into the Embassy just to see what it was like and to try out their English on the newspapers there. On their way home, in fact only a block or two away, their ID's had been 'randomly' checked by police. They assumed that their descriptions had been radioed from the booth to the police patrolling the area.

I didn't want to make a habit of being seen going in and out of the Embassy, but I did want to keep up with news from back home. A policeman was standing right in front of the door, but he didn't say anything when I went in. I poked around the library a little, then went back out. I kept waiting for a policeman to come up to me, but none ever did. That feeling of being watched certainly explained why not many people bothered to go in there.

Paranoia And Communist Plots

The members of the Mennonite Church in the GDR were mostly people who had lived in the area of Germany that was given to Poland after World War II. There had been a massive flight of civilians from that area in front of the Soviet Army in the waning days of the war. Out of the confusion of flight, exhaustion, hunger and death, individual Mennonites settled here and there, isolated and scattered. Over time some found contact with the congregation in Berlin. When the Wall went up in 1961, Walter Jantzen in East Berlin had taken the initiative to get the congregation registered and recognized in the GDR.

One result of having a congregation of 250 members scattered throughout the country is that they didn't get together very often. Church services were only held once a month in East Berlin, so it took some time until I got to know the people who came to worship services there. Renate Roeser was the first to invite me to her home. By coincidence, my dorm was around the corner from her apartment.

The middle of January I went there for supper. Her husband, Dieter, is a member of the local Protestant congregation. We spent most of the evening talking about Mennonite history, and as is typical for Mennonites, looking for mutual acquaintances. Dieter would occasionally tease us about being off in a different world, but put up with our choice of subject matter. In the course of the conversation it also came up that Renate worked in the National Library.

"What a coincidence!" I said, then added carefully, "I've been there several times to read the *Newsweek*, but it seems to get there rather late."

"Humm, that's strange, it gets to our department on time. You see, I work in the receiving department for Western magazines."

"You mean you get to see the *Newsweek* when it's delivered to the library?" I asked incredulously.

"Sure, no one in our department can read English very well, but we try to read *Newsweek* and *Time*. It gives us a little taste of the big, wide world" she said with a smile. "Not to mention the fact that our own newspapers are so worthless."

"Incredible" I said "so can you tell me why it takes weeks for it to get out to the reading room?"

Renate laughed.

"Well, I guess it lies around our department at least a week because so many people want to read it. It's probably the same in the periodicals department. If we all knew better English, it wouldn't take so long. Why don't you come up to my department if you want to read it? That way you'll get it fresh."

It was indeed a communist plot of sorts that had kept me from getting the latest issue of *Newsweek*, but not the kind I thought. Censorship of the GDR press made news from uncensored sources scarce items. That slowed down the circulation of Western news magazines in the National Library. I was too embarrassed to tell Renate what I thought the real reason was. So much for the omnipresence of the Stasi! They had their own vicious, efficient logic, but it didn't include watching absolutely everything. I had learned a valuable lesson. And for the rest of my stay, I went to visit Renate once a week at work and she made sure I got to read the newest issue of *Newsweek*.

Confusion At The Border

The Mennonite congregation in West Berlin held services twice a month. Since the Mennonites in the GDR met so seldom, on occasion I would go to the services in West Berlin. I also got together once in a while with my friend, Axel, who lives there.

Every time I wanted to go to West Berlin I had to fill out 'emigration' forms in quadruplicate in the Office for Foreign Students, get approval there and then go across town to the police station where I was registered. In spite of all my sympathy for my fellow students who couldn't travel, it sure didn't take long to get sick of this arrangement. I decided to apply for a multi-entry visa.

The secretary in the Office for Foreign Students didn't give me much of a chance of getting that approved. Regulations are not meant to be circumvented. Some of my friends suggested I apply on the basis of wanting to go to Mennonite church services in West Berlin. Since they were more frequent there than in East Berlin, they thought I had a good case. The government would theoretically be a little squeamish about restricting the religious freedom of foreigners. I handed in my petition. It was turned down flat.

The one concession they made was exempting me from paying the 15 Mark fee every time. My first 'free' visa was for a meeting of Mennonite lay pastors in Hamburg, West Germany. The lay pastors of the West Berlin congregation had agreed to give me a ride.

I 'emigrated' at the Friedrichstrasse station and met my ride in West Berlin. We drove to one of the *Autobahn* (Interstate) border crossings between the GDR and West Berlin. The border guard couldn't quite figure out what to do with my passport. It was obvious that I was living in the GDR. Equally obvious from the stamps in my passport was the fact that I had just 'emigrated' from the GDR to West Berlin. Now I intended to travel through the GDR with a West German. Should I be considered as reentering the GDR or in transit through it? He finally had to call his supervisor to sort it out. We had to wait an extra 10 minutes. They decided I would travel 'in transit'. That meant that like the West Germans I could not under any circumstance exit from the *Autobahn*. In addition, as a foreigner, I had to pay a $3 transit fee. I would travel the GDR as an alien, although I had a residency permit. Historical complications.

Life Beyond The University

Most days were not that exciting. I'd get up, go to class, eat lunch in the cafeteria, do homework. Student life was basically not that much different than here. There were about 25 students in the freshman class. Class schedules didn't allow for many electives the first two years, so we had most of our classes together. In time I got to know the students. I still didn't know what to expect from these people who had such different experiences than mine. It seemed about half the students were preacher's kids or children of church employees of one kind or the other. Some fathers were even important church officials. Another large group of students came from working class families that had kept a strong commitment to the church. A few students came as first-generation Christians.

Petra's parents were both party members. She had the normal childhood, had managed to get into university. After she decided to join the Catholic church, her troubles began. She started getting bad grades in some of her classes. One day she was called into some administrative office and told she would no longer be able to study. She was quite sure it was because of her commitment to be a Christian. Her parents couldn't understand how she could throw her life away like that. Their already strained relationship became nonexistent. Petra got into nurses training and worked as a nurse for several years before deciding to study theology. The Humboldt University's theology department had a new tradition of admitting one Catholic student each year, so she joined our class. The prospects of finding employment as a woman in the Catholic church were admittedly slight. She wouldn't even think about joining the Protestant church.

Iris Wujanz comes from a farm family in the southeast of the GDR, in the village of Nechern. She was a Sorb. The Sorbs are a Slavic tribe, the only non-ethic Germans who have survived in Germany through the last thousand years. Their language is still spoken in some of the rural villages. She invited me to spend a weekend at her parent's place.

They still had their farmyard and even a few pigs. The house and barn were connected, the garage and workshop were in a separate building. They hadn't gotten around to putting in an indoor toilet yet. Their 'outhouse' was actually in a corner of the pig barn.

Officially they even still held title to their 40 acres of farmland. It's just that they had to rent it to the collective farm. The GDR government had started voluntary collectivization in the 1950's. When they surprisingly couldn't get every farmer to volunteer, in 1960 they finished the process by force. The collective farms were called LPG's, from *Landwirtschaftliche Produktions Genossenshaft*, which means agricultural production cooperative. Officials from the LPG came around and got all the livestock out of the barns. They were driven together to a central location and taken care of there. On the face of it, this was a more efficient way to handle livestock. In Nechern one farmer had been so distraught about losing his cows that he hung himself. Iris's father thought that most East German villages had a story like that. Many left for West Germany. The Wall was build in 1961.

Mr. Wujanz worked pumping gas in the collective farm's gas station. The state run gasoline company, Minol, had never gotten around to building a gas station in Nechern, so his station ended up being used by all the locals too. Not that it mattered much to him, his salary came from the LPG regardless of how much gas he pumped. Mrs. Wujanz worked as a milker in the LPG's dairy barn, 600 cows. Iris' brother, Daniel, was a tractor driver, which meant he didn't have to work too hard in winter. He took me on a tour of the whole LPG.

"Just in case any one asks, you're my second cousin, OK? It's not actually allowed to show our farm to Westerners."

The East Germans had their own tractor company, called Progress. The tractors didn't look too bad. Daniel said the LPG was better off than people trying to buy a car. They only had to wait a couple years between ordering a tractor and delivery, with cars it was more like 16 years.

The Sunday I was there was one of the more important religious holidays in Germany, *Totensonntag*, literally 'Sunday of the Dead'. Its a time to remember those who had gone before. It meant the church was uncharacteristically full. After a sumptuous noon meal, we went for a walk. As we passed the village cemetery, the conversation turned to funerals.

"The communists forgot to plan for death", Iris's sister Edith remarked. "When your average Joe gets buried, they make the mayor give a little speech. It's very pathetic. The poor guy never knows what to say."

Living Illegally

There were two big disadvantages to the dorm that I was living in. The first was that none of the students I saw every day in class lived anywhere close. The second was that it was about an hour bus ride from the University. The buses were often crowded, so much of that time was spent standing. Even worse, it meant I had to get up an hour earlier then if I lived somewhere close by. Since the Theology Department only had one small lecture room in its construction shack, most of the classes I had were held somewhere else. One place they were held was in the Johanneum.

This was an red brick building that had been built in the late 1800's as a dorm for theology students. There was room for about 35 students. It was five stories high, with an open central stairway. There was one large meeting room on the first floor that the Theology Department used as a classroom. The building was located close to the Friedrichstrasse station. In fact, a West Berlin S-bahn line went right under the basement. The passing trains made the whole building vibrate. So even if the students couldn't go visit West Berlin, they knew if the public transit there was running on time!

Most of the students living there were freshmen and sophomores. The general pattern seemed to be to use the Johanneum as a convenient place to live while trying to figure out how to 'acquire' an apartment by bending the rules. Once I found out that there was a room available, I decided to try my luck at bending the rules myself. A student doing post-graduate work was in charge of the Johanneum. He agreed to rent me a room and sign me in the building's registry. Theoretically, someone from the police came by once a year to check it. Since the University, and thus the government, were making $75 a month off my rent in the other dorm, it was obvious I couldn't officially move in here. Renting two rooms was, however, actually illegal, since space is rented based on need. As a single person, I didn't 'need' two rooms. We decided it would be OK to just go ahead and do it. If someone took exception to it, we would both plead ignorance.

Since I couldn't officially move in, I only brought along the books I needed for class and a few clothes. I soon discovered a flaw in my plan to only live in the Johanneum part time. The building was heated by large yellow tile ovens, one in each room. (This is another way of saying the hallways and bathrooms weren't heated.) There was a big pile of coal in the basement. Everyone had a coal bucket and an ashes bucket. You had to carry the coal up and get it started burning, a little like starting a fire in a barbecue grill. Katharina and Angelika were freshmen, roommates and living in the dorm. I asked one of them to show me how this was done. They both came and along the way to my room, Christian, another freshman joined us. They thought it humorous that I was so helpless in figuring out how to perform such a fundamental and simple task of daily life. I thought about the life and times of Charles Dickens.

Well, once the fire was going, you had to leave the bottom oven door open for about an hour to provide a draft. For best results, it was to be closed when the coal bricks had burned all the way through, but were still red hot. If the door was closed too soon, there was a slight possibility of gas building up and the oven exploding. If it was closed too late, all the heat would draft up the chimney. If it was done right, the heat would transfer to the tile and then radiate into the room. Three to six hours later, depending on the outside temperature, your room was warm. This whole procedure was not conducive to just popping in and out.

One day as Katharina, Angelika and I were walking back to the Johanneum after class, Katharina asked me what its really like in West Berlin. We were only a ten minute walk from the Wall. Since neither Katharina nor Angelika had immediate relatives there, they would have to wait another 40 years, until they were 60 years old, to visit there themselves. I thought for a second how crazy it was that I had come 10,000 miles to tell these two people what the other half of their city ten blocks away was like! Of course, there was no way to really tell them. On a lark I made up a wild story.

"Well, you know, there's actually nothing there. The apartment buildings and tree tops that you see over the top of the Wall are made out of cardboard. The whole thing is financed by the West German government and the CIA to fool East Germans."

For a second, Katharina had that wild look in her eyes that people get when they have a profound insight. Then she realized I was pulling her leg. I relented and tried to explain what West Berlin was really like. I'll never forget that look though. She simply had no way of knowing what was over there and had to be willing to believe anything for a second or two.

I only had my room in the Johanneum about six weeks when I got a visitor out at my other dorm. Sylke was the woman who had moved out of the room in the Johanneum that I had moved into. She had found an apartment of her own to 'occupy'. Since then, however, her boyfriend had proposed to her and they were planning to get married. The catch was that her boyfriend was a West German. He wasn't planning on moving to her country, so she was going to move to his. That meant getting permission to marry and then emigrate from the GDR government. In the last couple of years this had gotten to be fairly routine, but of course, their request could always be turned down. Such decisions were pretty arbitrary. In order to not give the government any excuse to harass her, she wanted to move back into her room in the Johanneum, which was her 'legal' place of residence. She had come to ask me to move out.

Who am I to stand in the way of love? Besides, she hoped to be married by summer, so that I could move back in then and not have to worry about lugging coal up, ashes down and shivering for hours until my room warmed up.

English And Russian

One of the best ways to get to know students outside of class was through informal English teaching. Russian class was mandatory in the GDR starting in the fifth grade, English was taught starting in the seventh grade. There was little doubt which one was preferred. East Germans had ample opportunity to travel to other East European countries (except Poland, of course, since the authorities were afraid they might come home with the 'Polish virus' of Solidarity). Russian was also the first foreign language taught in schools in Hungary, Romania or Czechoslovakia. When young East Germans went on vacation to those countries, general disdain of Russian was so great that the common language of understanding among young people was English. Since they couldn't travel to England, Canada or the USA, their English was never very good. But many students were determined to improve it.

I had only been there a month when Uta, a senior, invited me to come to her apartment to join a small group of students. They met once a week to practice English. They felt a bit frustrated since none of them knew English well enough to definitively settle arguments that arose about the best way to say something. Everyone brought something along for supper. We would spend about an hour talking English. By then everyone but me had a headache, so we would switch to German. It was a wonderful setting for getting my questions about life in the GDR answered.

The winter semester of the Humboldt University runs from October to January. The month of February was free. February 1989 was time for one of the theology departments trips to the Soviet Union. There was room in the group for me, so I was the only freshman allowed to go along, another advantage I had over my fellow students. This one, however, was based solely on the graciousness of the professors leading the tour group towards a foreign student. Before we left, we had a couple of organizational meetings. At one of them, a church official responsible for contacts with churches in Eastern Europe gave us Bibles and religious literature in German and Russian to take along. We were supposed to help our less fortunate brothers and sisters! Since part of the trip's cost was covered by the university, one could even say that the GDR government was financing the delivery of Bibles to the Soviet

Union! I was the only one who found this amazing, for the East Germans this was simply the way things were.

Our group was to visit Riga, the capital of Latvia, Tallinn, the capital of Estonia and Leningrad, now St. Petersburg. We made a pretty good team. I was not legally allowed to take East German money out of the country, but could carry all the hard currency I wanted. The East Germans could take out a limited amount of their own currency, but no hard currency (real money, as they called it). We divided the money up according to legality right before the border. I got a lot of the group's hard currency and someone carried my East German money for me. There wasn't much of a customs check anyway, and then the money was returned to its respective owners.

Although the trip had been arranged through the official Soviet tourist office, our professors had pretty much been allowed to set their own agenda. We met with church officials of all kinds. The literature in German was collected from students' suitcases and handed over to Bishop Kalnins of the German Evangelical Lutheran Church in the Soviet Union. The Russian materials were handed over at the various seminaries we visited. One of those seminaries was Catholic. When the students there asked why women were allowed to study theology at our seminary and what we thought of abortion, one of our professors had to take over the job of translating. The official translator provided by the travel agency wasn't up on all those theological terms.

The most amazing part of the journey for the East Germans was the freedoms they saw in the Soviet Union. In Riga, senior citizens with posters demanding independence from the Soviet Union lined the steps of the government building across from our hotel. They did the protesting during the day, since they had time. Students and workers came to take their place in the evenings. We were in Tallinn on the day that the Estonian flag was hoisted on the old city walls for the first time since Estonia was annexed by the Soviet Union in 1940. The Estonian government had declared a national holiday so every one could celebrate. The streets were jammed with people. Soldiers mingled easily with the crowd, police were hardly to be seen. The Lutheran bishop and the head of the Supreme Soviet of Estonia gave speeches one after the other, both were carried on local TV.

When we got to Leningrad, we visited a Museum of Atheism. This used to be anti-Christian propaganda on display in a former church. The East Germans had looked forward to visiting here, so they could poke a little fun at the heavy-handed tactics of the Soviet government. To their great disappointment, the displays had been changed to a fairly even-handed evaluation of the good and the bad associated with Christianity in Russia. One of our professors almost literally fell over when she heard the museum director talk about the introduction of Christianity to Russia as having been a positive development, all in all.

That kind of freedom to demonstrate and that kind of willingness to give Christianity a new and more objective look were still unthinkable in the GDR. And all their lives, those East German students had been drilled with the slogan 'To learn from the Soviet Union is to learn how to win'!

Shortly after we returned from the Soviet Union, some new MCC'ers arrived in West Berlin to start a three year term there. Tim and LaVerna Reimer, and their three children, Diedre, Tobin and Karl, were from Winnipeg, Manitoba. They would live in the West Berlin Mennonite congregation's house, the Menno-Heim. Their assignment was to help maintain contact between the Mennonites on both sides of the Wall. More importantly for me, they became friends with whom I could ponder the strangeness of life in Germany and God's way of working there.

Thus after five months in the GDR, many pieces were falling into place. I was past the stage of figuratively looking over my shoulder. My fellow students and my own experience had taught me the invisible lines that framed acceptable and unacceptable behavior in that country. The government could be criticized in private, but not publicly. I was into a routine of study and visiting, stoking coal ovens and learning. My nerves calmed down enough that I could start to reflect on what, indeed, I had gotten myself into.

Mothers being what they are in close-knit families, mine and Joel's, who lives in Montana, figured out that we were second-cousins and living in different halves of the same city. Although we had never met before, they suggested we get together. Joel was one of 12,000 American servicemen stationed in West Berlin. I figured it would make for an interesting visit, so I called him up.

He invited me over for supper right off the bat. It was towards the end of his tour of duty, so we didn't get together very often before he and his family went back home to the States. We did get together often enough to make me wonder. I asked him once what the point was of putting an army in a place where it's surrounded by Soviet forces to start with. He replied that if the Russians wanted to try and take West Berlin, they would be in for a heck of a fight. If they could tie down some of those forces, it would make things easier for the main forces further west. He didn't expect it would ever come to that. He was just doing his part to keep the peace.

If there were 12,001 Americans working for peace in the city of Berlin, how did I know that this one was right and those 12,000 were wrong? Were we both working for the same thing with different methods? What would have happened if there had been funds available and enough people interested to put 12,000 students in East Berlin? And what if those 12,000 people had resolved to ask themselves the question of what Jesus meant when he said "Love your enemies"?

As Joel showed me around the neat and orderly American army base, in the neat and orderly city of West Berlin, I thought about the pollution and drabness of East Berlin. I thought about the offensiveness of having to learn how to live your life within invisible lines for fear of getting stomped on by the government. I thought about faith and hope and how much energy it takes to keep them going and where that energy comes from. I think I had more questions than answers.

Chapter 4

Half Truths and Half Lives

Having settled into life in the GDR, I realized there was still one huge gap in my knowledge of the society there. After living there six months, I had not yet spoken to a single member of the Communist Party! One could certainly pick them out in a crowd. As part of the membership initiation they were given the party's emblem as a lapel pin. However, church membership and party membership were mutually exclusive. Since I had only gotten acquainted with people at the theology department and the Mennonite church, that ruled out learning to know party members. Actually, roughly 35% of the total population was at least nominally Christian and only about 17% of the adult population were members of the party[2].

I thought about attending Marxist-Leninist class at the University as a way of finally meeting a communist. Since I wouldn't be getting a degree from the Humboldt University, I was not required to attend such classes. Before deciding to go, I asked some of the students what went on in there. ML classes, as they are known, were required the first three years for all theology students. The three years were divided into philosophy, economics and something called "Scientific Communism". None of that sounded very attractive. However, there was also another dynamic at work.

Theology students were not screened for admission strictly by the usual method, which was to check for correct thinking as well as academic ability. Thus, they were known as an unruly bunch when it came time to settle down for ML class. The teacher of the freshmen ML philosophy class, Frau Maihorn, had volunteered to take the troublemakers on, out of a sense of challenge. This made the whole process sound more interesting. I decided to sit in on a least a few sessions, just to watch the action. If I learned a little something about philosophy along the way, which wasn't very likely, I guessed that wouldn't hurt anything either.

It took me a couple of weeks to get some basic vocabulary down. There were elections coming up and Frau Maihorn and the students obviously had two different definitions of democracy in mind. In the course of the discussion I found out both types even had names. Not surprisingly for communist thought, the names had something to do with classes, or rich and poor. The kind of democracy I had grown up with was called bourgeois, or upper middle class, democracy. Since you needed money to win elections, that system guaranteed that only rich people would win elections and write laws. The official name for that kind of system was a dictatorship of the bourgeois[3].

The kind of democracy they had in the GDR, and hence the big D for Democratic, was called socialist democracy or the dictatorship of the proletariat. It guaranteed that the party of the working class, in the GDR the Socialist Unity Party or SED, always won. Since the working class is the majority of the people in any industrial nation, making sure their party always won was real democracy.

The other term I had to learn a new definition for was 'communist country'. To my great surprise, I found out the GDR wasn't a communist country! It was socialist. The difference has something to do with how history develops. The official line was that Karl Marx had discovered scientific principles that show how history unfolds and thus what the future will bring. Capitalism will mess things up so badly that there will be a revolution, like the one there was in Russia in 1917. Then comes a phase of socialism, where the party runs the government in order to get things ready for communism, at which time government will disappear. I decided that if I was going to be able to talk to these people, I'd better learn their language, as it were. In fact, outside of ML class, everyone assumed the Communists' definition of socialism when they used that word, so I learned to call the GDR a socialist country. On the other hand, most people assumed the Western definition of democracy, so I never called the GDR democratic.

The real fireworks in ML class got started when we talked about that great philosophical question of materialism versus idealism. I just concentrated on observing the dynamics between the students and Frau Maihorn. The discussion had to do with how human beings got to be the way they are. The principle we were supposed to learn was that when the first person learned to use a tool, i.e. learned to work, that shaped how he or she thought and lived. From there it was a straight line to the importance of work, the working class, and the rule of the SED. Unfortunately for that principle, the students were being very obstinate.

"How do we know that the first person to learn to work didn't *think* of a tool first and *then* use it?" This could mean that thinking, or the power of ideas, was more important than the things that are created. A few students even pointed out that making creativity and ideas so important might leave room in a human being for a soul.

Well, they managed to string this discussion out over the span of several classes. Frau Maihorn kept urging us to try to understand what the texts we were reading actually said. We needed to peel back the layers of interpretation and deal with what Marx really wrote. (Our New Testament professor later made the same argument, albeit with a different set of texts.) As far as the students were concerned, it boiled down to the teacher's opinion versus theirs. As far as Frau Maihorn was concerned, the students were having trouble grasping some very basic *facts*. After the umpteenth round of her trying to get us to understand those facts, one of the students came unglued.

"I'm too old to believe all those stupid stories!" she yelled. "What's the point of learning all this old crap about classes? That has nothing to do with how we live today! We're all people, not classes!"

The room was dead silent.

Frau Maihorn took getting yelled at quite gracefully. Class was almost over anyway, so she talked a little about this and a little about that. Then she dismissed us. The next week we moved on to a different topic.

There was actually a very important lesson to be gleaned from that whole episode. When Marxism started out, it owed a great debt to and was in dialog with the philosophy of its day. In the course of time, however, it had changed from a theory that might be true to a dogma as solid as anything handed down by revelation. Once the Communist Party came to power and opinions clashed, there was the silence that follows utter disagreement between an iron-fisted ruler and the subdued ruled. The party filled that silence with propaganda, long speeches, orchestrated demonstrations, censorship and jail sentences. During strikes in East Berlin in June 1953 that silence was filled with the rumble of Soviet tanks, in August 1961 with the sounds of concrete slabs grating together to build the Wall. Those sounds still echoed in the silence between those who used communism as a dogma to prop up their rule and those they ruled.

Frau Maihorn was one of the true believers in communism. She knew that it should work by persuasion, not coercion. The student who made that outburst certainly never got in any kind of trouble for it, not even a bad grade in ML class. But with a different communist it might have turned out differently.

Methods of Control

The very first article of the constitution spelled it out. "The GDR is a socialist state... It is the political organization of all working people, urban and rural, under the leadership of the working class and its Marxist-Leninist party"[4]. The leadership of the SED had taken Marxist theory and written it up as law. Marxist-Leninist theory explained everything and promised everything would always get better and better. It all depended on material circumstances and how they were organized. Specifically this meant having the people own all the factories, mines and farms, called the means of productions. Once that was accomplished, most problems that had plagued society for thousands of years would cease.

Since this was a fact, proven by Marxist theory, the leaders would not tolerate any criticism, indeed such was regarded as a criminal act. At the same time, by wanting to be in control of everything, they laid themselves open to being blamed for everything that went wrong. Any number of institutions, rites and rituals were set up to build and manifest that control of the party over all areas of life. Mostly the party worked to cajole, lull or intimidate people into agreement.

One tactic to assert control was to only allow organizations that recognized the party's "leading role" as outlined in that first article of the constitution. The Free German Youth (FDJ) was founded as such an organization and gradually all other youth organizations were forced to become part of it or close down. Only one labor union was allowed on the same principle. Of course, it represented the party's interests, not the workers. The Society of German - Soviet Friendship promoted positive relations between the GDR and the Soviet Union. It had very inexpensive dues, required no effort, but was considered to look good on a resume. All you had to do was sign up and thus give at least implicit support to the government's rapport with the country that had helped defeat the Nazis. At the same time it was implicit support for that country which had imposed another type of dictatorship. There were even four other political parties, but they all existed on the basis of recognizing the primacy of the SED.

The party also thought it important to project their idea of "everything is always fine" through the media. The most important newspaper in the GDR was the *Neues Deutschland* (New Germany), called the *ND* for short. It was the official mouthpiece of the Central Committee of the SED. Some people spent a lot of time trying to read between its lines to see what changes were on the horizon. Anything one read in the *ND* could be quoted with impunity in public. This gave incentive to everyone to read it, looking for even a whiff of criticism.

The problem with the paper was that everything in it concerning the GDR was so obviously slanted. What one read in the paper did not reflect the surrounding reality. Many of the articles about other countries came considerably closer to the truth, but because of the lack of credibility, they were never believed either. For example, the *ND* loved to point out problems in capitalist countries like West Germany and the USA. My friends would ask me incredulously if there were really 3 million homeless people in the States. They would have been willing to dismiss it as a completely fabricated lie.

Television was a different story. The East German news broadcasts were, of course, similar to the newspapers. TV signals didn't require a visa, though, and with West Berlin in the middle of the GDR, West German TV stations could be received quite well in most parts of the GDR. East Germans were always up on West German politics, and Western TV shows like Dallas and Alf. Getting a good reception of West German broadcasts was a high priority. The tenements fairly bristled with antennas pointed west.

The southeast corner of the country was simply too far away to get good reception. It had won the nickname "Valley of the Clueless" for this reason. Unlike East German TV, which only showed the problems of West Germany, the West Germans showed some of the problems of their own country on the news. Of course, they also showed some of the problems in the GDR as well. Those East Germans who could watch both views of the world considered themselves the best informed people in the world.

It was rumored that for that very reason, the number of people applying to emigrate from the GDR to the West was highest in the area where they couldn't watch West TV. Those people were more likely to dismiss the news of unemployment, drugs and homelessness in West Germany as so much propaganda. The Wujanz family lived in such an area. Through church connections they had gotten to know enough people from West Germany to know the problems there were real. When I visited there, the village was all excited about the possibility of getting cable TV that would include West TV. The government had issued a permit to a group of private individuals to start a cable company. They had managed to get a satellite dish somehow. That was so incredible and unexpected that it lent some credibility to the rumor about the 'Clueless' being a real problem for the government.

The same procedure of control was applied to theater and movies. Thus the most interesting part of any performance or movie was to see what the actors and producers had managed to do with the limited freedom they had. For example, the play 'One Flew Over the Cuckoo's Nest' is set in an American asylum. In one production of it that I saw in East Berlin, there was no noticeable editing of the script to sneak in a protest. The set was generically institutional. The only noticeable oddity was the cleaning cart. They had simply taken a shopping cart from the local grocery store. There was no decoration, no attempt to hide what it was. There were a few cleaning supplies in it, a mop was tied to its side. I spent the whole play trying to figure out what that was suppose to symbolize. Shopping in grocery stores where you can't find everything you want drives you crazy? The grocery store as an asylum for the mentally disturbed? GDR society, symbolized by a shopping cart, as an asylum? Maybe it didn't mean anything at all, maybe it was just to make one wonder.

About the same time a movie came out called 'Treffen in Trevers' (Meeting in Trevers). It was about a love triangle during the French Revolution. The word of mouth advertisement that I heard, urging everyone to see it, made as much of a tiny little subplot as of the love story. One of the men in the triangle was a German revolutionary who fled to France. He was pursued by Prussian secret agents, who were very subtly supposed to be a reflection of the latter day Stasi secret agents. Anyone not interested in a love story was at least supposed to go to the movie to see those agents.

There were a number of theories students would offer to explain how it was possible for actors and directors to sneak such scenes past the censors. The most popular one was that those censors were a bit stupid. They just didn't get the joke. Another possibility was that the directors put in so much objectionable stuff that the censors only took out the worst and then felt they had done their job. The theory that made the most sense to me, though, was the most chilling. It went like this: theater would more typically be attended by intellectuals. The censors deliberately allowed a little criticism. Intellectuals were to be enticed to think that things couldn't be that bad if one could use a shopping cart to depict the whole GDR as an asylum. And if things aren't that bad, there's no need to risk one's neck to try and change them; the theater as an intellectual pressure valve.

Rites and Rituals

The system was built on the attempt to bend reality to match a theory. A number of rites and rituals were established to underline this. To participate in the rites was in some sense an admission that you were willing to deny reality and embrace the party's theory. To not participate brought one into conflict with society and might have meant that one suffered disadvantages of various kinds.

A few of the rites had been borrowed from the Nazis. The Nazis had used organized torch-lit processions to celebrate their ascendancy to power. The SED organized torch-lit parades. The Nazis had a Hitler Youth for boys and a *Bund Deutscher Mädchen* for girls, complete with distinctive uniforms. In the GDR there was a co-ed organization that started with younger children. They were called Young Pioneers. Their uniforms looked similar to those of the Nazis youth organizations, except with different colors.

Some rites had been borrowed from the Soviet Union. October 7, 1949 was the day the GDR was founded. It was a national holiday and celebrated by a military parade every year, the same way the anniversary of the Revolution was celebrated in the Soviet Union. A big viewing stand was set up to one side of Frankfurter Allee, one of the main streets in East Berlin. It used to be called Stalin Allee. All the dignitaries would gather there and people would line the street for quite a distance in either direction. Most of the apartment buildings along that street were ten to twelve stories high. Like on any national holiday, people were expected to fly the flag. The balconies along Frankfurter Allee were hung with alternating flags. One set of balconies would have the GDR flag from top to bottom, the next set would have a plain red flag, in honor of the international socialist movement. The Party organized visits to everyone living in those apartments to make sure they hung the right flag out on the right day. They bought the flags for the people and handed out small rewards, like flowers or chocolates. There were flags out all over the rest of town as well, but nowhere was it as systematic as here.

Another big parade was held every May 1, the traditional European Labor Day. For this ritual the emphasis was on the workers. The biggest parade was in Berlin, but there were festivities all over the country. The stage was set exactly the same as on October 7, with flags and a viewing stand. A number of weeks in advance, all the newspapers published the only acceptable slogans for the demonstration on the front page. Party members in every factory and office made sure that someone there made a nice banner with one of the official slogans. Instead of military columns, the parade consisted of workers of all sorts. All the different businesses had prearranged meeting points well up the parade route. There they congregated, unfurled their banners and sauntered down the street in front of the viewing stand. As they past, they were to turn towards the reviewing stand, smiling and waving at their leaders.

I had a chance to participate in the May 1 parade of 1989. Humboldt students were also expected to go as a group. One of the reasons for having people congregate in groups according to where they worked was to take attendance. Not showing up would be noticed. One never knew what disadvantages might follow at work or at school for one's children. You just didn't know for sure.

Most of the theology students didn't go. As a rule they would end up working for the church. The church was the only employer that wasn't expected to send its employees to the parade. Church employees and theology students were thus sheltered from pressure at work, one of the main avenues of control for the party. The gathering place for the University was quite a ways up the parade route, and I didn't want to walk that far, so I tried to join in a little closer to the viewing stand. That's when I noticed the whole route was roped off. All along it there were volunteer security guards; some party members perhaps, some from the FDJ. I couldn't talk my way past any of them. What looked like a joyful celebration was undergirded by heavy security. I later found out that agents of the Stasi would join the parade right before the viewing stand, walk past it with the people to make sure no one made a dramatic gesture of opposition right in front of the leaders, then circle back and join in again.[5]

I went down to the end of the parade, just past the viewing stand. As the parade disbanded, most people headed straight for the subway instead of going to the midway that had been set up with food booths and rides. They were merely putting in their time, sacrificing half of their holiday based on the vague threat that something bad might happen if they skipped out. The official tally was 750,000 marchers. East Berlin has a population of 1.1 million, so even if the count was somewhat exaggerated, it was an amazing amount of people to turn out to smile and wave at leaders they would throw out of office in six months.

Another key ritual that forced people to show support for the government was the election process. Municipal elections were held nationwide on May 7, 1989. In one of the strange twist of German politics, I as a foreigner was allowed to vote. Elections had been held a few months before in West Berlin, which has a significant percentage of foreigners. One of the issues of that campaign was if all those foreigners should be allowed to vote in municipal elections. In order to show the GDR's superiority to West Berlin and West Germany, a law was quickly passed allowing foreigners to vote in all GDR elections.

As already mentioned, their elections were based on a different concept of democracy. The goal was to get as high a percentage of people as possible to support the slate of candidates. There was no way to choose between them.

The whole election ritual was much more intricate than the parades. It started several weeks ahead of time. In order to vote, you had to present an Election Authorization Certificate. These were hand delivered by election officials to all eligible voters at their place of residence. You had to sign for their receipt. As a foreign student, I received my certificate from the Theology Department. The only suspense to the whole procedure was how high voter participation would be. Historically the official results were that more than 99% of the people had approved the candidates suggested by the SED and the other parties.

Before going to vote, I asked around to find out what the expected procedure was. The ballot consisted of a list of names, given without party affiliation or the office the candidates were running for. After handing in the certificate and showing your ID to make sure no one voted twice(!), you were expected to take your ballot, fold it, and drop it in the urn. That's why the students talked about 'folding', instead of voting.

I heard contradictory stories about the possibility of a 'no' vote. A few people said that if you crossed the names out, that counted as giving those candidates a 'no' vote. Most people seemed to think that it was only counted as a no vote if all the candidates names were individually crossed out. Apparently booths were provided for voting no. I was told to take along my own pen, since the booths only had pencils in them. Everyone I talked to agreed that going into a voting booth or failure to vote at all was marked down by the election officials and added to one's file.

Elections were always held on Sundays. Since officials didn't want anyone to use being away for the weekend as an excuse not to vote, the polling places were open at various times before the election for people to vote ahead of time. Since I was going to be out of town on election weekend, I went in early to vote. I thought it would be too much of an adventure to pass up. The polling place for students was in the university itself. I went up to the young woman, obviously a student, who was serving as an election official. I showed her my Election Authorization Certificate and she asked to see my ID. I plunked my US passport down on the table. Her eyes widened a little. She gave me a ballot, crossed my name off her list, and pointed me to the election booth. I had a hard time keeping a straight face, because I knew she would point any East German voter straight to the urn.

I went to the booth. Sure enough, there were several pencils there, but no pens. I pulled one out of my coat pocket. Since I wasn't sure what constituted a 'no' vote, I decided to make a pretty pattern on the ballot. I crossed out the first name, then left the next one. Then I crossed out two names and left one. Then I crossed out three and left one. I made it up to five lines before I ran out of names. It looked quite nice. I folded my ballot and put it in the urn.

Beyond all the silliness, there was a purpose to the rituals, theories, and organizations in the GDR. The people who had to live under that system were forced over and over to publicly show support of the government, regardless of what they really thought. They didn't have a magic passport like I did that would allow a way out. They were constantly confronted with decisions. For many people, it was the price you paid to get by and be left alone. For such people the decisions were not particularly difficult. A few people, however, saw the decisions for what they were, an attempt to suck you into the system. It was difficult to go smile and wave at the leaders, to vote for them and then make any protest against them seem credible. For those people the decisions became moments of soul-searching.

The lines of acceptable behavior were fleshed out by the fear of the Stasi. I quickly found out that criticism and political jokes told in a small circle of friends wouldn't get you in much trouble. If you did something at work, or even worse, publicly, you attracted the attention of the Stasi and things got more serious.

A final component in this system of control was the fact that some of the propaganda was simply true. Few people in a Western democracy would deny the importance of money in winning elections there. The net worth of people in Congress probably doesn't very closely match the national average. Homelessness, crime and drugs are really problems in our society, in part *because* of the way our society is set up. Western capitalist society certainly gave the SED plenty of ammunition. They would take that truth and wrap it in the theory they claimed was true. It wasn't easy for people caught in the system, and unable to travel to see for themselves, to sort through the maze of half-truths.

The end result of this whole system is that people divided their lives in half. In their public life they said what was expected and a lie. In private they would say what they really thought, the truth. They learned to watch out for themselves and not worry about any problems there might be in society. The East Germans called it the niche society. Everyone lived in a niche. From there they would sally forth into the make-believe world of GDR society.

Thus when East Germans went out on the streets to demonstrate six months later, they were not only making a statement about their government, they were calling on all the courage they could muster to put the halves of their lives back together. The action also carried with it the hope of freeing the truth from its half-prison.

Chapter 5

Creating Communist Personalities

One beautiful day in the summer of 1989 several friends and I were walking down Gleim street towards the Wall. To our left there was a park, to the right, tenements. Directly ahead were three huge concrete planters plunked down on alternating sides of the street and reaching out well past the middle of the street. They forced any traffic to slow to a crawl in order to weave through them. That was not a bad idea on a street right next to a park where lots of kids play, but that's not what the planters were there for. Just beyond them a red and white metal railing ran across the street, resting on posts sunk right into the asphalt. Twenty yards beyond it the Wall ran across the street.

All of a sudden three boys, nine or ten years old, came tearing around the corner behind us on their bikes and went flying down the street. They wove through the concrete planters, turned their bikes sideways, slammed on the brakes and slid to a stop well short of the metal barrier. They had obviously finished their favorite bike race obstacle course. Instead of turning around to go back to the start line, this time there was a bonus attraction at the end of the race. A door had opened in the Wall and a group of soldiers came out. It might have just been a change of shift or maybe they were doing some repair work on the Wall. At any rate, they mostly stood around and talked with each other. The boys watched them intently for a while. Once it was clear the soldiers weren't going to provide any excitement, they finally turned their bikes around and headed back up the street.

The whole time they had never quite gotten up to the metal barrier, much less made any hint of going beyond it for fun or on a quick dare. Some things were not thinkable in the GDR, even to young boys.

If the party was concerned about getting adults to at least behave in public, in children it saw a golden opportunity to clear up the whole problem of unruly subjects right from the start. The education system was carefully thought out and planned to create "communist

47

personalities". The kids laughed at the thought, but it was an attempt to be reckoned with.

Day Care

Since almost 90% of the women worked outside the home in the GDR, child care was important. As with many other things in the GDR, it was a question of availability, not affordability. The day care system was heavily subsidized. It was divided into two types of day care, *Kinderkrippe* for children up to three years old and Kindergartens for children three to six years old.

According to law, first-time mothers were given a year's maternity leave without pay, each subsequent child born entitled them to a year off with partial pay[6]. At the end of the year, they could place their child in a *Kinderkrippe* and return to their old job. If no *Kinderkrippe* spot could be found, they continued to receive partial pay and official leave until one became available. At age three, the children moved into the Kindergartens, much like day care centers in the U.S. Of course, mothers could always choose to quit their jobs and stay home, but few did. Even fewer fathers took advantage of the legal possibility of taking paternity leave in lieu of the mother's maternity leave.

Both types of day care centers were staffed by trained personnel. They promoted the learning of motor and social skills and provided excellent health screening. Along with these positive aspects were some ambiguous ones. The issue of how childhood development is affected by spending so little time with parents was often debated. And there were some downright negative aspects. Once paramilitary training was required in the high schools starting in 1978, toy soldiers and tanks were distributed to all day care centers. This was part of a campaign organized at all levels of the school system to encourage children to have a positive view of the military. This fit in with the general plan to influence children to think differently than their parents, if their parents were hostile or indifferent to the government.

Grade School

Children started school at age six. One important aspect of starting school was joining the *Jungpionier* (Young Pioneers), the communist children's organization. Some teachers were specially trained to be leaders. They organized field trips, recycling campaigns for old newspapers and other special activities. The initiation ceremony was suppose to be one of the highlights of starting school (see the Scrapbook page 172).

Grade schools usually started the day with the *Pioneer Gruss*, the official salute of the Pioneers. The class stood as the teacher said "For peace and socialism: be prepared!". The children were taught to raise their right hands above their head, all five fingers pressed together to make a flat surface, and answer "Always prepared!". Depending on the teachers and principal's attitude, those few children whose parents chose to keep them out of the Pioneers either had no trouble at all or were sometimes made fun of.

The textbooks were well coordinated between classes, so that when songs like "Best of Friends" (Scrapbook page 174) were sung in fourth grade music class, the lyrics were analyzed and explained in German class. The basic skills of reading, writing and arithmetic were taught quite well. The one-sided textbooks always contained at least some truth. Children were not able to figure out on their own what was missing. Of course, hearing all this makes the system sound more effective than it actually was. Talking to children from these grade schools reminded me that children have their own way of dealing with deception on the part of adults.

As part of my required social work internship, I spent five weeks in the spring of 1989 in a church affiliated home for abused and neglected children. Within a few days of arrival, the two sixth-grade girls taught me the following 'poem' that was making the rounds in their school. They giggled the whole time they were teaching it to me. Laughing at some of the grimest aspects of life was typical of East German humor, here at a sixth-grade level. The poem was a remake of Goethe's "King of the Elves". His original involved a midnight ride of a father to bring his ailing son home only to have the boy die in his arms on arrival.

Wer reitet so spät durch Kraut und Rüben?
    Es ist der Mark, der will nach drüben.
Erreicht die Grenze in Mühe und Not.
    tritt auf ein' Mine, bums, ist er tot!

Who's riding so late through cabbage and cress?
    If it isn't Mark, he's heading West.
He reaches the border with strain and in fear,
    steps on a mine, boom, he's dead, oh dear!

Christianity was taught in history class as having started out as a movement among the poor and enslaved (Scrapbook page 176). It was shown to have very quickly become something that had been misused to help keep in power rulers who exploited their subjects. Since both statements had some truth to them, what were students to think? In general the atmosphere was created that the church was something dangerous that one had best keep away from.

This was demonstrated by visitors we had at one of the Mennonite church services in the summer of 1989. When the door bell rang at the renovated apartment that served us as our church, I was closest to the door so I answered the bell. There were two boys who appeared to be 9 or 10 years old. I invited them in. They looked up, down and all around to see what this strange 'church' was like. They asked what we were going to do. I told them we would have a church service with some singing and a sermon from our pastor. After that there would be some cake and coffee for everyone, and they would be very welcome to stay for that. I asked them if they would like to come sit with me. To my surprise they agreed. We went into the largest room of the apartment, which was set up as a sanctuary. There were chairs for about forty people.

We had barely sat down when the one who appeared to be the spokesman for the two whispered to me that they had "to go get somebody". Then they were off in a flash. I laughed to myself and figured that was the end of their visit. In a very short time, however, they had returned with two girls about the same age in tow. All four of them sat down in the row of chairs in front of me. They were very well-behaved through the whole service. Afterwards we cleared out the chairs and set up tables in a big circle so we could sit down to enjoy cake and coffee. The children quickly agreed to stay for that.

I made sure to sit next to them in order to find out more about them. An added incentive to sit by them was that they had strategically placed themselves in front of one of the cake platters. In between bites I managed to find out that they lived close by. They had seen our sign out front and had come out of pure curiosity to see what a church was like! Once the cake platter was cleaned off, and it didn't take them long, they scooted on out the door. We later realized we had failed to ask their last names or exact addresses. They never came back. It seemed typical of the atmosphere of mystery and distrust about Christianity that the school system tried to create that young children would come sit through an otherwise somewhat boring church service out of curiosity! (Another possibility that an East German friend pointed out is that one of their parents worked for the Stasi and had sent them to check us out. Who knows?)

High School

The Youth Dedication ceremony, called *Jugendweihe*, was the official initiation rite for young people into the ranks of adults. Organized by the party for the first time in 1955, it was firmly grounded in the educational system of the GDR. The teachers were active in organizing the ceremony and in holding the special sessions of instructions that proceeded it. The heart of the ceremony was a solemn pledge given by the young people. It included defending the constitution of the GDR and the principles of socialism from the attacks of the imperialist countries. All the students participating were also given a book, not available in any bookstore, that was a one volume statement of communist philosophy and practices.

For the young people involved, the real attraction of the *Jugendweihe* was the presents. It was customary to receive a substantial present of some kind from one's parents, like a moped or a stereo. Grandparents and other relatives chipped in with lesser presents.

The fact that this occured at the age of 14 and at a time of transition from the 8th to 9th grade was by no means a coincidence. It was deliberately planned to compete with the churches' rite of confirmation. The pressure put on by the party in the 1950's was more than most people cared to withstand. The *Jugendweihe* was considered one of the extracurricular activities necessary to get ahead. By 1960, almost 90% of all 8th graders were taking part in the Youth Dedication ceremony.

The churches initially declared the dedication incompatible with receiving confirmation. It was felt that the whole ceremony and pledge were so firmly based on atheist principles that it didn't make any sense to confirm the same young people a couple weeks before or after they had pledged their loyalty to the socialist state. Unfortunately that usually meant that those young people were just lost to the church. By 1960, the Protestant Church had by and large given up trying to prevent their young people from taking part in the *Jugendweihe*. Instead they postponed their confirmation by a year. By forcing such an important decision at such a young age, the state established the precedent of people giving in just to get along. Any attempts of protest in high school brought implicit or explicit charges of going back on that solemn pledge (and those great presents).[7]

The FDJ was not formally linked to the Youth Dedication services. However, since 14 was also the age of transition from the Pioneers to the FDJ, the two were linked in the minds of most young people. The

FDJ had an official shirt, dark blue with the emblem of a rising sun. It was to be worn on special days in high school. The FDJ was the official sponsor of the youth clubs that organized dances and other social events for young people. There was literally nothing for young people to do, short of going to church, that was not connected in some way to the FDJ.

One prominent example of the FDJ's influence on the wider society was the annual Pentecost Meeting. Again the religious significance had been usurped by the party to its own ends. Those FDJ'ers deemed most worthy, i.e. loyal, were rewarded with a trip to the Pentecost Meeting in Berlin. This was a week-end long festival with lots of displays, concerts, eating and drinking, all free or at low prices. The residents of Berlin usually made a point of being out of town on that weekend. Those who remained had to put up with a huge horde of young people in blue shirts. The only happy side-effect was the reappearance in the grocery stores of certain rarity items. In the local grocery store where I usually shopped, I was amazed to find that strawberry yogurt, ketchup and tomato juice had all arrived on the Thursday before Pentecost.

The statutes of the FDJ made it very clear that the organization's main function was to support the politics of the SED. The FDJ called itself the 'fighting reserve' of the SED. In addition to support for the party, "the Free German Youth encourages the youth of the GDR in their irreconcilable hatred of Imperialism and its reactionary politics."[8] Imperialism was the code word for capitalist countries, particularly West Germany and the USA.

Another avenue of teaching the hatred of enemies was the military education that was part of the high school curricula. This included learning to shoot and throw 'clubs', suspiciously shaped liked hand grenades, at targets in sport classes. There was also a special two week class in which boys were taught to march in military formation and encouraged to get into better physical shape. During the same time, girls spent two weeks in civil defense camps learning to respond to natural disasters, for which marching in military formations was also apparently essential.

These activities were clearly framed by talk of needing to protect oneself from imperialist aggression. There was rarely any official talk of Americans as enemies. The capitalist system was the enemy, similar in a way to most Americans not considering Soviet or East German individuals as enemies. It was, however, too difficult a distinction to keep up in more informal settings. Then it quickly became a matter of talking about the 'Americans' invading Panama or the 'Americans' having attacked Vietnam, not the American government, where the blame officially was placed. It was the exact mirror image of the thinking I had so often heard expressed back home.

Of course, high school kids as a group do not easily lend themselves to herd management techniques. In the early '80's, a time when medium-range nuclear missiles were being placed in both West Germany and the GDR, a peace movement was started among high schoolers. The Soviet Union had donated a large sculpture of a man beating a sword into a plowshare to the United Nations, which put the statue on display at its headquarters in New York. A picture of it was included in the *Jugendweihe* book of the time. The Protestant Church adopted it as the symbol for its annual 'Ten Days of Peace' festival. Stickers and patches with a likeness of the statue surrounded by the words "Swords to Plowshares" were handed out and started to appear in high schools all over the GDR. The government like peace movements only if they served its purpose, so it moved to squash this one. Police ripped patches off the clothes they were sown to or confiscated jackets entirely. Students were threatened with expulsion. Protests that the very same thing was pictured in the *Jugendweihe* book were to no avail, the next edition of the book was minus that picture.

Many of the problems of becoming an adult were the same in the U.S. and the GDR. Like adolescents everywhere, the youth of the GDR knew how to make adults especially upset and seemed to enjoy doing it. Every school child knew that Erich Honecker, the leader of the party and the GDR, had spent 10 years in Nazi concentration camps. They likewise knew that Nazis and Communists considered themselves deadly enemies. Thus the easiest way to make the authorities mad was to draw Nazi graffiti or shout out some of the old Nazi slogans.

April 20, 1989 would have been Adolf Hitler's 100th birthday. On the short walk from my dorm to the bus stop early that morning, I saw several swastikas and a "Happy Birthday" painted on the sidewalk and on the buildings. While certainly an inexcusably stupid thing to do, it was not so much a resurgence of Nazism as a statement of thumbing one's nose at authority.

A similar incident was related to me by my sixth-grade poet friends. In their small village, which was close to a Soviet military base, someone had painted anti-Soviet slogans on a wall near their house. The next day, officials came to their school and told all of the students that their school had been selected for a scientific experiment concerning handwriting analysis. They were to take dictation, which would then be analyzed to test some fancy new theory. The students could hardly believe their ears when the officials started their dictation. They were to write down anti-Soviet slogans, the very same ones as on the wall! Obviously, the officials were from the Stasi, the secret police, and they were hoping to find some incriminating evidence on one of the students. A few of them wrote their slogans with great abandon, many were just very confused. The perpetrator eventually came forward and confessed. He had to finish his education at a school for juvenile delinquents.

University

By the time students made it to the university, they were starting to come to grips with some of the lies they had been told. Many of the male students told me that the time they spent in the army had really opened their eyes to the contradictions of their society, for example, in the words freedom or democracy. As peons subjected to constant verbal abuse in the National People's Army, they didn't feel very free. Most theology students had served in non-combatant civil engineering units, called *Bausoldaten*, the East German equivalent of conscientious objectors. The extra abuse they received heightened the tension with the state. Many of the female students had gone through the same process. For some it was their relationships to boy friends going through a difficult army time, for others it was entering the work force.

Leaving the sheltered and slanted world of the GDR educational system for a brief stint in the 'real world' lent urgency to the questions students would ask me about the truth of newspaper reports of problems in the West. The actual confrontation with what they knew all along, namely that the official representation they were given did not match the reality of life, was an impetus to critical thinking. That does not, however, mean that the process of rethinking what they had learned was simple or straight forward.

Thomas was at once typical and atypical in this regard. Typical was the fact that he rejected the communist ideology. He had been a member of the FDJ. He even volunteered for a longer tour of duty with the army. By serving three years instead of the required eighteen months, he guaranteed himself the right to study forestry, his real interest at the time. He was assigned to the Friedrich Engels Guard Regiment, a unit that did the ceremonial duty for foreign dignitaries. The unit also provided the guards for the Memorial for Victims of Fascism and Militarism. This was a small building on Unter den Linden street right next to the main building of the Humboldt University. There was an eternal flame burning in the middle of the building in honor of those victims. The goose-step changing of the guard ceremony had become a tourist attraction for those Westerners who came to East Berlin on a day visa. Thomas's duties sometimes included commanding that ceremony.

His army time was also, typically, a time of questioning. The nature of his questioning was quite atypical. Although nominally Protestant, he investigated all kinds of churches and religions during this time. Most of these groups were very small and difficult to even find, but Thomas really made the rounds. He visited at length with Seventh-Day Adventists and adherents of Far Eastern religion. The Mennonite church was also on his list of churches to check out. Once his army duty was finished, he started forestry studies near Dresden. He also met regularly with a couple there that had loose ties to the Mennonite church and who had a small library of Mennonite literature.

His studies were not working out as planned, but his interest in Mennonite teaching had grown. Renate helped get him a job at the National Library. Jochen Jantzen, a Mennonite church board member and owner of the building where the church had its apartment, let him move into a couple of rooms connected to the church office. Knuth Hansen, the pastor, helped with some of the paperwork necessary to facilitate a move to East Berlin. It wasn't long until Thomas joined the church.

Most of my theology student friends found that their time in the army led them to ask questions different from those basic to Thomas's quest. They were not looking for a different church to provide answers. They were asking questions, though, about relating to the government.

Some of our late night bull sessions were devoted to this topic. On the one hand, the government provided a semblance of full employment and housing for everyone. On the other hand, it was equally dedicated to lying, spying and persecution of all those who were outspokenly different. The students were all clearly against the latter, but were not at all sure which one of the two was more important. There was no doubt that the two were connected. The state provided physical security for all its citizens at the price of personal freedoms. Many of the older generation saw this more clearly than we did as students. They had also become more resigned to the status quo.

There was a budding realization among the students that a fraud had been perpetrated on them. The security offered was only a bribe to cooperate. The unwillingness to give in to the despair of ever changing that arrangement caused the percentage of young people who favored change, while still a minority, to be larger than the percentage calling for change in other generation groups.

Chapter 6

The Church in Socialism

The wheat fields had been turned into apartments; mile after mile of ten, twelve or sixteen story apartment buildings. The debates in Marxist-Leninist class about the nonexistence of a soul in human beings were reflected in the ugly functionality of socialist suburbs. The village of Marzahn, which gave this new suburb of East Berlin its name, seemed quite lost in the middle of this field of concrete.

The apartment buildings were built like huge erector sets. Preformed concrete slabs were set together quickly and efficiently. The same pattern was used over and over. If you visited the different types of apartments in one apartment building, you knew the floor plans of the housing for millions of East Germans. The same type of planning went into deciding how many schools, grocery stores, barber shops and post offices to put where. There were originally no plans to put churches anywhere.

A lot of young families moved to Marzahn because there wasn't anywhere else where they could start out on their own. The central heating at least meant they didn't have to worry about lugging coal up the stairs. The average age of the population in the northern district of Marzahn was 27. Of the 100,000 people who moved to this former wheat field in the 1980's, 3,000 joined the newly organized Protestant church congregation. Maybe ten percent of them were active in congregational life. They had managed to make arrangements to build their own church building.[9] There was also a small Catholic congregation and a tiny Methodist one. Thus, there were perhaps 500 active Christians among 100,000 people.

The pastors of Marzahn-North also helped out on occasion in the village congregations just outside city limits. As a guest of one of these pastors, Bruno Schottstädt, I sat in on a regular church service in one of those little villages. Four members had come for the service. We went through the liturgy, Bruno gave his sermon standing right in front of the first two pews, which easily held the congregation that morning.

A fellow student, Fidus, shed light on a different aspect of Christianity in the GDR. Her father is the General Superintendent in Wittenberg. General Superintendents are the first level in the Protestant church hierarchy below bishops. This position in Wittenberg meant that he served concurrently as pastor in the Castle Church in Wittenberg. It was here on October 31, 1517 that Martin Luther nailed his 95 theses to the church door, symbolizing the start of the Reformation.

It also meant that Fidus' father and his family got to live in the former monastery attached to the church. Luther had been a monk there. After leaving his order and getting married, he established what is often called the first Protestant parsonage in his old monastery. It was here that Fidus grew up. When American tourists weren't gawking at the table that might well have been pounded by Luther during his 'Table Talks', she could use it to play house.

Christians in the GDR were both a tiny herd of forlorn sheep and a group firmly embedded in some of the greatest traditions of Christendom. As such, they were involved in both questionable compromises and in standing firm.

How Did The Church Get Here From There?

The Thirty Year's War, 1618-1648, was fought mostly on German territory, causing great destruction and loss of life. Upon its conclusion, the religious aspect of the war was solved with the agreement that the religion of the ruler of a territory would dictate the religious affiliation of the ruled. Since the Lutherans didn't have a Pope, they looked to the ruler of the territory to provide leadership for their church. Those territories remained the basis for Protestant church organization in the GDR, eight of them in all.

On October 31, 1817, the three hundredth anniversary of Luther's thesis nailing, Friedrich Wilhelm III, King of Prussia, celebrated communion with his wife. What was remarkable about that event is that Friedrich was Reformed and his wife was Lutheran. He was also tired of the rigmarole of having both types of Protestant Churches in his kingdom. He hoped their forced union would provide him with a better grip on the ship of state.

At any rate, it made the nomenclature for churches in Germany a little more complicated. Those parts of the GDR in the north and south that never officially became part of the Kingdom of Prussia remained strictly Lutheran. The church in the former Prussia, the middle of the GDR, was called Unified. Strictly Reformed territories existed only in a few small areas of West Germany.

After the first world war, the King of Prussia, and the other nobility that headed these churches, no longer had a role to play in German politics. This also meant that the Lutheran and Unified churches no longer had an official head. Among the solutions was the founding of a confederation of *Evangelisch* churches for all of Germany. This was a nice way of including the Lutheran, Reformed and Unified strains without hurting anyone's feelings. *Evangelisch* is a bit awkward to translate into English, however. Evangelical in the North American sense of the word these churches are not. Thus they are often simply called Protestant in English.

As long as these Protestant churches were under the auspices of the various rulers, most subjects born in the region were duly baptized and considered members. This arrangement created something called a *Volkskirche* (People's church), since basically all the people belonged to the church. It insured that almost every village had its own church. In addition, under this arrangement the church always supported the policies of the ruler, who was after all the head of the church.

Since the GDR contained the heartland of the Protestant Reformation, about eighty percent of the population was Protestant at the end of the second world war. After the Soviet Occupation Zone became the German Democratic Republic in 1949, the party started serious work on reducing the influence of the church. Only non-Christians were allowed to hold upper-level posts in government, industry and other important positions. The introduction of the Youth Dedication Service was the real test of power. The church was not able to rally the population to make a stand. This was one weakness of the old *Volkskirche* concept. Most people had simply been born into the church. They were told that church, state and society should form a seamless whole. When the new state forced society to literally take a left turn, those nominal church members could see no reason to listen to the church's plea to hold the course. The result was a drastic decline of church membership. By 1964, slightly less than 60% of the population was Protestant.[10] By 1991, although no accurate figures were available, it's likely only around 30% of the population considered themselves members of the Protestant church.

Although Germany had been divided into two countries, the organization of the Protestant Churches in Germany continued as one. When both Germanies rearmed and integrated their armies into NATO and the Warsaw Pact in the 1950's, things got a bit tricky. The Protestant Churches in Germany signed a contract with the West German government to provide chaplains for the West German army. Of course, the government of the GDR had no interest in a similar arrangement. They were, however, quite indignant at the thought of the Protestant Church providing what amounted to aid and comfort to their enemy. From that point on, government officials refused to talk to officials of the Protestant church who lived in West Germany.

After the Wall was built in 1961, it became almost impossible for the leadership of the Protestant Church to meet together, since Westerners were denied entry visas and Easterners were routinely denied exit visas to attend conferences. In 1968, the government wrote a new constitution for the GDR. The paragraph on religious freedom was to be interpreted to mean that church boundaries must end at the nation's boundaries. In order to avoid breaking the new law, and a renewed direct confrontation with the state, a Federation of Protestant Churches in the GDR was created in 1969. There was now a separate Protestant Church for the area of the GDR.

By the early 70's the state was forced to realize that the church would not just disappear once the fear of hunger and poverty was banished. This hope had been based on Marxist-Leninist theory and the pragmatic politics of wanting to get rid of serious opposition. The church was forced to realize that the state, which it considered to be a crazy socialist experiment, would also not disappear in the near future. They worked out a compromise. By creating a separate GDR institution, the church backed off from its role of underlining the unity of Germany. The state hoped this would help lend the GDR respectability in the world.

This compromise started the church rethinking some traditional assumptions. The question was how this new church federation should relate to socialist society. It did not want to be against or beside society, but somehow "in" it. This formula was quickly reduced to the church being the "Church in Socialism". The significance of this was a shift from the church taking a stance against socialism to looking for areas where they might be able to cooperate. It mirrored the shift from saying either confirmation or socialist youth dedication to allowing both.

On the other hand, it was certainly not the case that the church gave the state everything it wanted. With the church accepting a role "in" society, the conflict shifted to what that role should be. The state wanted that role limited to regular worship services. Some church help with the care of the mentally and physically handicapped would also be welcomed. Ideally, the church should also support the building up of communist society. On the first count, the church was very reluctant to let the state define what a religious worship service should be like. For example, the occasional jazz worship services attracted considerable numbers of young people. The state considered them "irregular" and tried to shut them down. At a different level, the church's protest of this policy was based in part on its history of encompassing all of the people in its territory and in part on the belief that Christian faith must speak to all aspects of society. Thus, the church expressed concern about a wide variety of topics, much to the displeasure of the government.

The education of young people was one such topic. Privately, church leaders repeatedly asked for talks with the officials of the Ministry of Education to correct some of the inaccuracy in the textbooks. More public were attempts to organize training for peace. This specifically meant teaching children not to believe that they should hate their enemies. The church refused to accept the state's demand to not meddle in society on this issue.

For a church with such a long history of agreement with the state, this process of separation opened up a whole new field of discussion. The separation from and then opposition to the state was followed by a sort of compromise. This had its own logic to the church leaders, but not all of the members could follow it. Especially younger members had their problems. Part of it was probably the generation gap. All the same, by this time young people who were loyal to the church had made a real commitment to it. In some cases this meant giving up vocational dreams to maintain that commitment. After the Wall went up in 1961, the draft was introduced. With the separation of church and state, some in the church had started to question the assumption that Christians should always defend the state if required by law to do so. For some it was only clear that Christians should by no means defend an atheist state. For others, the Bible and/or their own logic taught that warfare was wrong.

Those young men who were drafted but wished to be considered conscientious objectors were offered the opportunity to serve as *Bausoldaten* or 'building soldiers'. They worked mostly on civil engineering types of projects. They were under army jurisdiction and plainly helped the cause of national defense. However, they did not have to take part in the regular basic training. They were not required to carry firearms.

This was a new phenomenon for the church. There had been only one Protestant conscientious objector in World War II. The young men who faced the pressure of the government and the army to achieve even this limited right of conscientious objection formed the visible backbone of the new peace movement. They didn't always agree among themselves on all points. A few served prison sentences instead of agreeing to serve under the army's jurisdiction. After almost thirty years of this arrangement, the government became quite used to especially pastor's sons serving in this capacity. One of my fellow students, whose father was a pastor, told me that when he told the army recruiter that he wanted to serve as a *Bausoldat*, the recruiter merely shrugged his shoulders, approved his request and that was it.

The church also took some time to adjust. The *Bausoldaten* and others started peace seminars and gave lectures in their home churches upon return from the army. The church leadership and the older generation were forced to rethink their own positions. In time, the leadership embraced at least some of the new thinking. Some of the young people pushed their position so far as to get into trouble with the state. The leadership usually felt that was pushing it too far and tried to keep the lid on things by getting the young people to back off a little.[11]

Part of the general confusion that arose here was due to the nature of the Protestant Church as an institution. As such it was the only institution in all of the GDR to exist independently of the party. Its mere existence, not the number of members or quality of its theology, gave it importance. Since it had been a *Volkskirche*, it had buildings and employees in all towns and many villages of the GDR. However, a church must also be more than just an institution. Many of the theology students thought the leadership was too concerned with keeping the institution intact. Whenever the issues dear to young people's hearts caused conflict with the state, they felt let down by the leadership's counsel of patience, reconciliation and accommodation.[12]

I was surprised to find such a tangled mass of relationships and history in such a state of flux. From North America, the GDR appeared to be a great, gray monolith, never changing. From the inside there was more change than one could keep up with, although it came in small increments. Christians in the GDR had to make difficult decisions of how to apply their faith to daily life. There was no such thing as avoiding compromises of some kind in such an all-encompassing state. Unlike back home, one was more often conscious of making decisions as a Christian.

Daily Lives

The first decision to make was if one would relate to the church at all. The statistics show most people decided not to. Thus for most people, the church and religion played no role in the daily lives of most East Germans. Bishop Hempel of Dresden put it well when he said that the only Bible most East Germans read are the actions of simple Christians' living out their daily lives.

The state had managed to link material advancement, getting good jobs, promotions and being left alone, with avoiding the church. The desire to have a comfortable life with a car, a nice apartment and as few hassles as possible from the government became the primary goal for most people in the GDR. That desire in itself was not bad when compared, say, to the desire to conquer foreign lands. So many people making their own personal material well-being the most important thing in life became a more difficult obstacle for the church to overcome than communist ideology.

Of course, life, and the decisions to be made, were more complicated than any simple decisions between God and materialism. One example was when we decided to start a Bible study group in the Mennonite church.

There was only one Mennonite church in the GDR. This one congregation of 250 members covered the whole country. A congregation in Berlin had been the only Mennonite congregation before World War II in the area that became the GDR. With the shift in borders following the war, parts of what were once Germany became part of Poland. Many Germans had already fled those areas in front of the advance of the Soviet army, others were forced to leave later. The area around the city of Danzig, now called Gdansk, had been home for many Mennonites. Many of those who had fled had only made it as far as the Soviet Occupation Zone. They settled down there and tried to start a new life.

Thus the Mennonite Church in the GDR, with about 250 members, was a collection of many different stories of flight and uprootedness. As life slowly returned to normal, those scattered Mennonites reported their whereabouts to the congregation in Berlin. When the Wall went up in 1961, the congregation was divided. The traditional meeting place of the Mennonites, the Menno-Heim, was in West Berlin. Walter Jantzen, a lay leader living in East Berlin, took over leadership in the GDR. He regularly visited the scattered members and held church services in different towns around the country.

Being that scattered out made congregational life on a daily or even weekly basis impossible. Many members had married Protestants or Baptists and raised their children in those churches. Other members had not raised their children as Christians at all, for fear that the children would not be able to get along in society if they were Christian. The membership was largely senior citizens. When Thomas joined, he became only the third member younger than 30.

Thomas was interested in trying to revive some kind of youth work in the Mennonite church. We talked about having a weekend retreat. We hoped some of the members could get their grandchildren to come. We also talked about starting a weekly Bible study. One of the other 'under-30' Mennonites also lived in Berlin, Axel Roeser, Renate's son. His job involved working some evening shifts, but he agreed to come as often as he could. Tim would come over from West Berlin, so we would be at least four people. We agreed to do both, start a weekly Bible study and hold a youth retreat.

We got the Bible study going first. We each invited a person to come along. Thomas invited a person from work, Stefan. Axel brought along Torsten, a friend of his from his chess club. I asked Angelika, a fellow student. Soon Ulrike, a high schooler of Mennonite background who lived on the outskirts of Berlin, joined our group as well. Although she had a round trip commute of three hours, she became a faithful attender. We also made a poster to hang in the window of the church apartment where we met. It was on the ground floor and right on the sidewalk, so any passersby would be sure to see it.

Our poster brought in a couple of curious young people. Typical of the atmosphere at the time was the question at the back of our minds. Were these people genuine seekers or sent here by the Stasi? It seemed very unlikely that the Stasi would bother with such a small group. Of course, if the Stasi managed to make us paranoid, they had already gained something. The point was, you never knew. And we didn't.

A more serious problem we had to work through was with the church board. Advertising for religious meetings like our Bible study from the window of an apartment was definitely in the gray area of the law. If any heat came from the government, it would go to the church board and not to us. It's one thing to say one's commitment to Christ must always come first. It was quite another to contemplate having an agent of the Stasi come visit you at home and rake you over the coals for such a small matter. We worked out a compromise. We would only put up the poster on the actual day of the meeting. As is the nature of compromises, none of us were really happy with it. These were the types of decisions that Christians had to make in the GDR. The soul-searching that went on at this level probably won't make it into history books that only look at the church in the GDR as an institution.

Freedom of Worship

There was an Events Ordinance that covered the legality of religious events. It had been passed into law early in 1971. It required all public events to be announced to (and approved by) the police. Specifically religious activities, such as worship services, communions and baptisms, were exempted. In general, if the event was led by someone working full-time for the church and was held in church buildings, it was not regulated by the government.[13] There were some early struggles over the interpretation of these measures. An understanding of sorts was reached by trail and error on the part of the church, since the court system of the GDR was not designed to give precise, binding judgments.

The main reason church attendance was so low thus had little to do with police measures or church attendance being outlawed. As mundane as it might sound, the reason was simply that people didn't want to go to church. Unlike some of the other East Block countries, attending church was not the main problem. It was how Christianity affected one's relationship to the state that the state was most interested in.

Starting already in the '70's, a few people began to address some of the needs they saw in GDR society that they felt the government wasn't taking care of. Human rights obviously topped the list. Environmental and peace concerns were not far behind. In fact, these three areas were seen as being interrelated. They were also areas where the government would not tolerate much public discussion.[14]

Some of the people in these groups were Christians, others weren't. Since there was no where else for them to meet, they would ask if they could meet in church rooms. The church could hardly turn them away, especially if some of the group members were also church members. Sometimes these groups wanted to hold bigger meetings. The state, of course, was opposed to this. It might break their monopoly on providing all the answers to questions. The debate about what was or wasn't a 'worship service' flared up again.

Was it a worship service if they sang a hymn once in a while during the meeting? Some of the non-Christians couldn't see why they should have to sing or pray at their group meetings. Some Christians couldn't see what business it was of non-Christians to tell the churches what to do. Many times the individual decisions were made by the local pastor and local church board. They were the ones who would feel the heat. If it was a really big event, then, of course, the church leadership at a higher level got involved as well.

The role of the church in the revolution that was brewing in the GDR is hard to pin down. It was thrust on the church by non-Christians who brought their dissatisfaction with society into the church. It was claimed by those in the church who insisted the church must be more than just an institution or a place to worship. The church insisted on non-violence because the liberation from supporting the state gave it the freedom to see the teaching of the Bible in a non-violent perspective. The church taught non-violence because the state had an absolute monopoly on the instruments of violence. No other tactic had any chance for success.

It was the soul-searching of individual Christians that gave the church so much diversity. The answers they found in their search are not answers that we can simply apply to our settings. What I learned from my friends in the GDR, my Christian brothers and sisters, was the courage to ask the questions.

Chapter 7

Starting To Fit In

I felt there had to be more to teaching English than just having people learn English. When we met at Uta's for supper and English conversation, I also tried to bring in a little something about life in America. That's how we ended up looking at Far Side cartoons.

You would think cartoons would be an easy way to explain American culture. You don't need many words. Some of the cartoons didn't even have captions. On the evening we talked about the Far Side, we went to the park right next to the Wall, in order to get in the proper mood to contemplate the wackiness of life. Sitting in the shadow of the Wall was the perfect setting, you would think, for studying the Far Side.

It didn't work at all. For one thing, German newspapers don't have regular cartoons, so the East Germans were not in the practice of trying to decipher those things. Mostly though, those cartoons were probably just too weird. Oh, well, win some, lose some. We had been meeting together long enough that the success of the evening depended more on how much fun we had than on how much we learned.

Numerous students had asked me to help them learn English. Most of them had had several years of English in high school, but had not really used it since. Not being allowed to travel, they had never gotten to be fluent. We could never have fit all those interested into Uta's small apartment, so I looked for a different solution. The theology department finally moved to a new building, still just off of Unter den Linden street, in February, 1989. Now there were plenty of classrooms available. I made reservations for one of them on a weekly basis and put up a sign announcing informal English class. About 20 people showed up the first day. That number quickly dwindled over the next weeks to a half dozen, but they were then faithful attenders. We talked about newspaper clippings and articles from church periodicals. If I learned about their culture and churches, but they knew nothing about mine, it didn't seem like we could really communicate. Starting to communicate on a two-way street helped me feel better about calling the GDR home.

A number of other things had fallen into place by now that also made me feel like I was getting settled in. For some mysterious reason, the regulations regarding multiple entry visas had been changed. I was able to get one for three months. Now I could leave the country whenever I wanted.

Friends from West Germany came to visit me in East Berlin in early summer. As West Germans, they could use more border crossing points than I could. I felt more like a real East Berliner when I walked with them to the border crossing on Bundes Street. They said good-bye and were gone. I couldn't have followed them even if I wanted to.

Sylke's marriage license had been approved, so she moved to West Germany. I moved back into the Johanneum. I felt a little guilty about having single rooms in two different dorms while so many other people were doubled up, so I volunteered to move into one of the Johanneum's double rooms. Since there hadn't been any problems the first time I moved in, this time I brought more of my stuff and settled in. Now I was only a ten minute walk from the university. And it was summer, so there was no need to worry about firing up the oven.

Another touch of home that one often saw downtown were American soldiers. According to the international agreements that governed Berlin, they could not be searched at the border. They were required to wear their uniforms. They could buy East German money very cheaply in West Berlin. Taking that money into East Berlin was against East German law, but they couldn't be searched, so that didn't matter. Whole buses of them would come over to go shopping. Of course, there wasn't much to buy. Children's clothes, shoes and toys were big favorites. There were a few books in English in the bookstores too. All of these items were subsidized by the government, and using the black market exchange rate, a real bargain. A day of inexpensive shopping could be wrapped up by taking the whole family out for steaks for the equivalent of a couple of dollars.

The British and French soldiers stationed in West Berlin had the same arrangement. Soviet and East German soldiers had to wear their uniforms whenever they went out in public. It was not uncommon to see groups of soldiers from some of these five different countries all shopping in the same big department store at Alexanderplatz in East Berlin. The American soldiers liked to get their pictures taken with the goose-stepping guards at the Memorial to the Victims of Fascism and Militarism.

It was a very strange feeling for me to hear American English spoken on the streets of East Berlin. The East Germans had varying reactions. Some were upset that the soldiers could come and buy subsidized goods. Their tax dollars were going to help out U.S. soldiers! Even worse, some of the goods they were buying up were hard to come by. It didn't seem fair that rich foreigners should be allowed to buy them up just because they happened to be in town when the goods became available. *Neues Deutschland*, the main party newspaper, carried an Associated Press article about it in June, 1989. The commander of the U.S. forces in West Berlin was reported as thinking about putting limits on the amount and types of purchases, in order not to strain relations with the East German government.

A different type of response was typified by a man named Gerhard Schöne. He was a Christian folk singer. He played mostly in churches, having been denied access to public stages. He had, however, been allowed to cut a few albums. They sold out very quickly. He had one ballad on his *Live* album called "Dear Enemy in the Distance". He introduced it like this:

"Have you ever noticed that the American soldier at the cash register in the book store is buying a picture book for children age five and up, a book with colorful monkeys and rhinoceroses? That he smiles at you and fumbles with a button on his uniform when you smile back and that this moment, just a second or two, was very strange? So desperate. Utopian. Ridiculous. Hopeful. Timeless. Short. Disarming."

Falling Apart

I was feeling settled in. My German had improved to the point where I didn't have to think about it. I understood enough of how the system worked to have lost some of my paranoia. I wasn't looking over my shoulder all the time anymore. I had found new friends.

Just when I thought I had East German society figured out, it started falling apart. It had been rotting for a long time, in fact, much of the rottenness went back to its foundation as a system imposed by a victorious Soviet government. The signs of the rot, usually well hidden, became publicly apparent in the summer of 1989.

Since the Soviet Union had created the GDR, it's not surprising that the changes in the Soviet Union were behind its collapse. This does not mean the GDR was simply a puppet of the Soviet Union. There were many differences. The standard of living was higher in the GDR. Government policies towards the churches were more lenient.

There was a special and complicated relationship to West Germany. All the same, the GDR was not completely sovereign. The Soviet Union had a history of intervening in East European countries to protects its own interests. Soviet tanks had crushed protests and revolts in East Berlin in 1953, in Hungary in 1956 and in Czechoslovakia in 1968. There had been riots and unrest in Poland multiple times; 1956, 1968, 1970, 1976, 1980/81 and 1988.

With the advent of *glasnost* and *perestroika*, it was clear that some kind of change was afoot in the Soviet Union. This gave people in the GDR hope. Up until then, the GDR had sooner or later followed most of the innovations coming from the Soviet Union. It became apparent that this time it would be later. There had been a changing of the guard among the leadership in the USSR. The GDR still had Erich Honecker and associates. They showed no interest in making any fundamental changes. In fact, in November, 1988, they took the extraordinary step of banning *Sputnik*.

Sputnik was a literary magazine published in the Soviet Union. It was translated into several languages, including German, and distributed in the GDR. It was not very widely read. It was, however, in the forefront of official publications in the Soviet Union that were probing some of the dark secrets of Soviet history. One of the topics it hit upon was the relationship of the Soviet Union to the Communist Party in Germany in the 1930's. Some of the conclusions drawn were not very flattering to the German Communists. Since the SED saw itself as the heir of the Communist Party, it took a dim view of airing out the skeletons in the family closet. *Sputnik* was banned. The very idea of banning a publication from the Soviet Union, the helpful big brother, was a signal that something rotten in the system was working its way to the surface.

East Germans watched the democracy movement in China with great interest. It seemed the students got even bolder while Gorbachev was there. Shock and sadness were the reactions to the news of the massacre in Tianammen Square on Sunday morning, June 4th. West German TV showed what footage there was of the gruesome brutality. It was a cold slap in the face to read the Monday morning *Neues Deutschland* headline: "People's Liberation Army of China Puts Down Counterrevolutionary Revolt". The newspaper article talked about the brutality and violence of the demonstrators. Its last sentence concluded that the actions of the army "met with the approval of the masses and the students."

Two days later, during our Introduction to the New Testament class, a petition was passed around. It protested the massacre in

Beijing. It was to be handed over to the embassy of China located in East Berlin. The rumor was that the embassy was completely sealed off by East German police. There was apparently no way to get into the embassy to leave off the signatures. Almost everyone in the class signed it anyway.

Other events that day overshadowed the massacre, at least for students in our department. One was the news of Polish election results. Those elections had been held on June 4th, the same day as the Beijing massacre. They were not completely free, with stipulations designed to keep the Communists in power. In spite of the obstacles, Solidarity had defeated the Communists, and other opposition groups, hands down. Perhaps more importantly, the Polish Communist Party admitted its defeat must mean the eventual loss of its power. And the Soviets had no objection. The Poles were the first in Eastern Europe to prove beyond doubt that Soviet hegemony could be thrown off. That fact slowly seeped into East German consciousness. It would no longer be a matter of facing Soviet tanks, but rather East German security forces.

The event that got our immediate attention that day happened during the class Church History of the Middle Ages. A typewritten sheet was passed through the rows. Since there was no access to photocopiers, information was often passed around this way. This sheet announced a demonstration starting from the administrative offices of the Berlin-Brandenburg Protestant Church. It was the one month anniversary of the May 7 elections.

Election Fraud

Of course, there had long been suspicions about election fraud in GDR elections. The opposition groups, however, were better organized and more numerous during those elections than at any other time. They had sent people to watch the counting of the ballots in some of the polling places. This event was officially open to the public. Usually only election officials and party members had attended. The opposition people went this time as well, pulling out paper and pen to tally the votes as they were read out. In most cases the minute they started doing that, someone, probably from the Stasi, came up to chew them out, trying to intimidate them. Those who stood their ground were generally allowed to stay.

All of these unofficial results were brought together. In those areas where opposition members had attended a significant number of the polling places, it was easy to show that something didn't add up. In most cases, even one polling place had read off more 'no' votes than were later officially listed for an entire city district. This unofficial tally indicated that up to 20% of the people had either not voted or voted 'no'. Considering that either one of those actions would lead to getting a black mark in your file, that was an amazing percentage.

One of the groups that had decided to protest this election fraud was called "Rejection of the Practice and Principle of Separation". The name referred to the government policy of calling for East German citizens to 'separate' themselves from West Germans. This policy formed the basis for the need for East Germans in certain jobs to report all contact with Westerners. Westerners were to be regarded as some kind of disease to be avoided if at all possible. Members of the opposition group "Rejection" were Christians, some of them pastors, who thought that kind of attitude towards other human beings was simply unacceptable for Christians, indeed for anybody.

Since they were in the business of encouraging people to treat other people with respect and dignity, this group was the one that had called for this particular demonstration. They wanted to hand in a *Eingabe*, an official petition, asking the government to check into the evidence of election fraud they would also submit. According to East German laws, every citizen had the right to hand in such petition to the government, which was then required to give an answer. Of course, everyone knew that the government wouldn't take the petition seriously. That was the point of a demonstration to accompany the petition to where it would be handed in. Such public actions of protest always got the government's attention.

Some of the students knew members in this group. In the discussion after class, they said that the church leadership had distanced itself from the demonstration. That meant that the demonstrators shouldn't count on church leadership going to bat for them to lighten potential prison sentences or fines. There were reports of the efforts the Stasi was making to keep people from going. Some of the students were very determined to go, others seemed noncommittal.

We had moved our English class for that day to the student lounge because the chairs there were more comfortable. Tim Reimer, the MCC'er living in West Berlin, had come as a special guest. We walked into a bit of a hornet's nest in the lounge. Professor Fink, the head of our department, was having a heated discussion with his son, Daniel, who was in my class. Daniel was one of the students determined to go to the demonstration. What's more, since he was taking care of his baby son for the afternoon, he was planning to take him along.

Professor Fink was very upset at the idea of taking a baby to something a potentially dangerous as a demonstration.

More of the students came into the room for English class. Many others were milling around in the hallway. Daniel left, but Professor Fink invited all of the students into the lounge for a discussion about the demonstration. He said the president of the university had called. He wanted Fink to make sure his students knew that demonstrating was illegal. The students immediately interpreted this as a threat of expulsion, which Fink denied. The students were pretty emotional. They were fed up with reasoning and talking. They wanted something to happen, something to change. Fink argued that nothing would be accomplished. The demonstration would be even less than an empty gesture, since he was sure the government would break it up before it even got started.

West German TV teams had already reportedly set up their cameras for the place where the demonstration was to start. This meant that the government would be even more determined to stop it, to prevent bad publicity. It also meant that people only interested in getting permission to emigrate to the West would come to the demonstration. They would try to get on to West German TV and then get arrested. Once in prison on charges of illegally demonstrating, chances were they would be bought free by the West German government, which paid the GDR government for the release of political prisoners into West German custody. To take such an extreme route showed their dedication to getting out of the country. Their actions, however, tended to discredit those who wanted to stay in the GDR and affect change.

The discussion broke up when the students decided it was time to go to the demonstration. That pretty well took care of English class for that day. Tim, his family and I had already made plans to eat supper together, so we did that instead of going to the demonstration.

The West German radio news reported on the demonstration in the evening, saying 120 people had been arrested. I got a full report the next day from some of the students who had been there. Most had been stopped at the subway exits by police and prevented from getting to the gathering point. In an attempt to get the demonstration out of public view and lessen the likelihood of arrests or violence, church leadership had suggested that the demonstrators meet in the Sophien Church instead. Here the demonstrators and the Stasi had played a game of cat and mouse. Any attempt to leave the church grounds with banners of protest led to arrests. At the same time, the Stasi didn't enter the church courtyard to make arrests. It had been a very harrowing experience for the students I talked to.[15]

A couple hundred people had been involved in that demonstration, a pretty small group for a city of over a million inhabitants. They hadn't managed to change anything. The wider population seemed to see such demonstrators as just a bunch of fruitcakes. The protests continued every seventh of the month after that, but with even fewer participants. The arrests continued as well every month. Carrying banners was sure to get you arrested, so more creative tactics were tried. One month the leaflet called for people to gather at Alexanderplatz to all laugh out loud, to laugh at the election results. Another month, everyone was asked to bring a whistle along, to 'whistle' at the results. (Shrill whistling is the same thing as booing in German culture.) None of these actions really got off the ground, but the leaflets being circulated among students was a sign that not everyone had given up.

Wall Day

In late summer, I visited relatives in West Germany with my parents, who had come for a short visit. I also spent two weeks at a international church work camp in the GDR. Since the university was not in session and many people were on vacation, the political activities in the country calmed down a little. Or maybe I had lost touch by being out of town.

One thing that was hard to miss, if you read the newspapers anyway, was the anniversary day of the building of the Wall, August 13. *Neues Deutschland (ND)* devoted several pages to this momentous event. There were two reasons given for building it. The first was that not being able to closely regulate who entered and left the country made it too inviting for political opponents to destabilize the GDR. This took the form of economic plundering. Black market trade boomed. West German firms were accused of hiring away skilled workers who had received their educations at GDR government expense. Western intelligence agencies were accused of acts of arson and sabotage. This reason was half true insofar as the Wall was in fact necessary to insure the continued existence of the GDR.

The second reason was even more far-fetched. 1961 was a time of great tension between the USA and the USSR. The *ND* printed a nice little map of NATO maneuvers prior to the building of the Wall. They were drawn as arrows coming at the GDR from all directions. Putting up the Wall had supposedly squashed NATO's invasion plans. To show the danger associated with defending the Wall against the enemy, a full page of photos of soldiers shot at the Wall was also printed. It was not clear, however, which of them had been shot from the west side of the Wall and which had been shot by fellow East Germans trying to escape.

A definite consequence of the Wall, called a benefit in the *ND*, was that a measure of peace and quiet returned to the GDR. People had been leaving the GDR at the rate of about 2,000 people a day. Keeping qualified workers at home and the realization that the GDR wouldn't go away led people to take making a life for themselves more seriously. There was eventually a rise in the standard of living.

Erich Honecker had recently been quoted in the *ND* as saying that the Wall would remain standing another 50 or 100 years if necessary. It would be there as long as the conditions that led to its existence continued. He portrayed those conditions as the desire of Western countries to do away with the GDR. The real reason the Wall had been built was to keep the GDR going. Only three months after 'Wall day' 1989, the party was maneuvered into a position of having to tear down the Wall in an effort to keep the GDR going.

One thing about the Wall was always clear. To tear it down would mean the end of the GDR. Thus it didn't top the list of demands that the opposition groups had. There was little point in asking the government to commit suicide. One of the demands therefore was to just make it easier to travel. Pensioners could already do so with impunity. People with immediate family in the West could as well on certain occasions, like birthdays and anniversaries. Less than 1% of the people who went stayed in the West. To do so would have meant leaving family behind, since families were rarely allowed to travel together.

The issue of the Wall was always there. Once flight had been ruled out, however, the focus had become more how does one live in the GDR. In time, for a few people, that became the question of how to affect change in the GDR. The events of August and September, 1989, swung the emphasis back over to leaving the GDR for the first time since 1961.

Chapter 8

Run Away! Run Away!

Susanne lived in the south of the GDR. Through a mutual acquaintance, she found out about American Mennonites and that one of them was even living in East Berlin. She wrote me to ask some questions. I invited her to come to Berlin for a weekend and visit the congregation there as the best way to answer her questions. Instead she sent me the following postcard, postmarked Siegen, West Germany.

Dear Mark,
Now unfortunately I won't be able to come to Berlin to visit the Mennonite congregation. That's too bad, but I have gone to West Germany illegally and won't be able to go back to the East anymore. Here in the West one can live in freedom, I hope, more so than in the East. The opportunity to leave via Hungary was a one time deal for us. So now even if we haven't learn to know each other, I want to thank you anyway for your invitation and wish you all the best!
Susanne

While some people were making difficult decisions about how to try to change things in the GDR, other people made equally difficult decisions about getting out of the country. The Wall did not just run through the middle of Berlin. As part of the 'Iron Curtain', it ran from the Baltic Sea coast in the north, along the borders of various Eastern European countries, down to the Black Sea coast. On May 2, 1989, Hungary became the first country to put a crack in it. They started to remove the barriers and barbed wire along their border to Austria.

In Hungary, changes came about through the Communist Party itself[16]. Reformers inside the party felt the only chance they had of staying in power long term was to make some changes. One of these was to have better relations with the West and their immediate neighbor, Austria. And if relations were improving, why bother with extensive barriers on the border? They started taking down the barbed wire along the border to Austria. There was no great danger of Hungarians skipping the country. It wasn't easy for them to get permission to settle in Western European countries. Besides, there was no where else in the world where they could speak Hungarian.

A crack in the 'Iron Curtain', however, made the question of leaving very immediate again for East Germans. There was a country that would grant them full citizenship rights, West Germany. They wouldn't have to learn a new language or culture.

The West German government had never fully recognized the legitimacy of the GDR. From the very beginning of both countries, the West German government claimed to be the only legitimate successor to the Imperial Germany. The basis for this claim was the fact that the GDR government had never been endorsed by real, secret ballot, democratic elections. The West German constitution, in fact, was written only as an interim document, pending German unification. Since the West German government felt those Germans living in the GDR had no legitimate government, it acted as if it were responsible for them.

That meant GDR citizens could get West German citizenship, no questions asked. They qualified immediately for all government programs; unemployment, student loans, job training or whatever. For East Germans who were given permission to visit in the West, the West German government even handed out 100 DM ($65) of 'greeting money'[17]. Since their own East German currency was worthless in the West, that little bit of pocket money helped them to feel that they were not totally destitute on their visits.

These kinds of regulations to make East Germans feel officially welcomed included all kinds of obscure provisions. West Germany has a 14% sales tax. Foreigners who bought large items in West Germany to take back home with them could get exemptions from that tax. That's what I wanted to do when I decided to buy a computer in West Berlin and take it back to East Berlin with me. It took me a whole day to track down the right office to get a tax exemption form. When I explained my plan to a clerk there, he told me I couldn't qualify. As far as the West German sales tax exemption law was concerned, the GDR was not a foreign country!

That whole line of reasoning, of course, made the GDR government furious. They saw the tactics of making GDR citizens seem welcome in West Germany as part of a plot to lure people over there. Sure they got $65 when they came, but if they got laid off two years later, would the West German government help them find a job then? Like all of the communist propaganda, that accusation had a little truth to it. Not enough of it, however, to convince many East Germans. Thousands still went to great lengths to get to West Germany. According to rumors, between 500,000 and one million people East Germans had applied for permission to emigrate to the West. Permission to do so had been granted at the rate of 20,000 - 40,000 a year during the 80's.[18]

Official West German government policies were, of course, not supported by everyone in that country. Some people were upset that East Germans could get $65 for nothing. Others felt unemployment was high enough, and the country crowded enough, without welcoming more people. Many West Germans had little idea of what daily life in the GDR was like. East German visitors to West Germany got a more ambiguous greeting from the general population.

The division of Germany also meant that many families were divided. The hundreds of thousands who left the GDR before the Wall went up added to those divisions. Most people in the GDR had relatives of some degree or the other living in West Germany. Of course, not everyone had close enough relatives to qualify for permission to travel to the West. For those who did, all these levels of relations between governments and people made for interesting family visits.

The Crack becomes a Gap

August is traditionally the biggest month for vacations in Germany. GDR citizens liked to travel to the other East Bloc countries. That was at least a little more exciting than staying in their own small country. Those other countries also had West German embassies. At the end of July and beginning of August reports on West German TV indicated that scores of East Germans were camping out in those embassies in Prague, Budapest and the West German consulate in East Berlin. They refused to leave until they were allowed to go to West Germany[19].

This was not the only time tactics like that were used by people desperate to leave the GDR. This time, though, it was a quite a number of people all at the same time in a number of different places. It was the leading story in West German news media. That in turn meant the East Germans heard all about it. The GDR government issued a statement about the people holed up in embassies on August 7.

"According to reports of Western media, politicians and officials of the FRG (West Germany), a few GDR citizens are visiting embassies of the FRG in other countries in order to present personal concerns. According to international law, representatives of the FRG have no rights or responsibilities concerning citizens of the GDR. Their concerns are the sole responsibility of the GDR, in whose laws all citizens are equal. Legal exceptions for individuals cannot be gained by visiting the embassies of other countries."[20]

The whole issue of people wanting to leave the GDR was addressed by the "assistant speaker of the GDR Foreign Ministry, Dr. Denis Ruth: 'For several days now, West German media have been leading a vocal campaign on behalf of a few GDR citizens, who have illegally been granted permission to stay in the FRG embassy in Budapest for the expressed purpose of illegally entering the FRG. ... The Foreign Ministry of the FRG, which has joined this campaign, should know that according to international law the embassies of the FRG have no right to become active on behalf of GDR citizens, for example, in the area of travel and visa concerns.' ... The speaker pointed out that from Jan. 1 to July 31,1989, 3,5 million GDR citizens had traveled to non-socialist countries, including 3.233 million to the FRG and West Berlin. 'It is also not unknown in Bonn how humanely the GDR, according to her laws, handles questions of allowing families to move together.'"[21]

Of course, this was the typical government explanation; it was all West Germany's fault. The stupidity of that explanation was not remarkable. The fact that the GDR government acknowledged the problem publicly was. And the problem only got worse.

On August 9, the GDR TV news reported that 158 East Germans were camped out in the West German embassy in Budapest, Hungary. Another 131 were in the West German consulate in East Berlin.[22] There were some consultations between the East and West German governments on resolving this problem, but no conclusions were reached. On August 24, 108 of the people in the Budapest embassy went to Austria using travel documents supplied by the International Red Cross. The GDR government referred to this arrangement as an organized campaign to smuggle people across borders and "reminiscent of the worst days of the Cold War."[23]

The other people had already left the embassy in Budapest to try and get to Austria on their own. They were sick of waiting on legalities when the border between Hungary and Austria in some places was already sitting there open.

The Hungarian government's policy wasn't real clear. It didn't mind having Hungarians travel, but to let GDR citizens out would mean breaking an agreement signed with the GDR government. The whole point was to allow orderly, legal travel between Hungary and Austria. The border was still patrolled to keep people from crossing where they shouldn't. According to agreements still in force between the GDR and Hungary, it was illegal for GDR citizens to leave Hungary without GDR government permission. Torsten and his friends had come to Hungary determined to get to Austria. They probably didn't have to worry about getting shot at the border, but if they were caught, they could expect to be sent back to the GDR as criminals. They went to 'visit' some Hungarian villages near the border. Every police officer or soldier they saw made them nervous. They tried to get the lay of the land, moving from one village to the next for lodging every night. When their vacation time was almost up, they finally worked up the nerve to try to get across the border.

After dark, the four of them set off in the direction of the border. They avoided the roads, walking instead through the fields. Since the barbed wire at the border had been taken down, they couldn't tell if they had reached the border yet or not. Suddenly they saw headlights coming their way. They made a mad dash for cover. The headlights belonged to Hungarian soldiers on patrol. The jeep stopped. They waited a long time for the soldiers to move on. When they finally did, the four of them continued walking. They were soaking wet from lying in the grass. They walked all night. As the sun came up, Torsten was sure they had made it into Austria.

They saw a border guard of some kind patrolling in the field. It was daylight now, so there was no point in trying to hide. The guard came towards them. Would he be Hungarian or Austrian? Oh, no, he was Hungarian! One could still see the disappointment in Torsten's face as he told our bible study his story several months later. In the confusion of hiding from the first patrol, they had lost their orientation. They had walked through the fields all night *parallel* to the border. Torsten and his friends were sent back home to the GDR. Trying to leave the country like that was illegal. Only the fact that the GDR government and the Wall fell in the next couple of months kept them out of prison.

The news that some people were making it into Austria from Hungary seemed to only encourage more people to try. By the end of August 1,400 East Germans overran the West German embassy in

Budapest. They waited in tents at various sites around the city for some kind of decision to be made.[24]

The Gap becomes a Flood Gate

The first week of September saw a flurry of diplomatic activity between the governments of the GDR, Hungary and West Germany. All the people holed up in the West German consulate in East Berlin agreed to go back home. They settled for the promise of legal assistance to push their applications for emigration. What they had really wanted was to be allowed to leave the GDR immediately. That was not allowed.

The number of people waiting in tents in Budapest, Hungary, for permission to go to the West grew daily. The Hungarian government made a statement that solutions that worked for a hundred people, like International Red Cross travel documents, didn't apply for thousands of people. They were really caught in the middle, with the GDR government demanding that its citizens return home and the West German government handing out West German passports to those same people. The GDR government declared an amnesty for anyone returning home from the embassy in Budapest. In addition, they were guaranteed their old jobs back, no matter how long they had been missing from them.

Of course, thousands of people 'extended' their vacations in Hungary in the hopes of getting to the West. The promise of their old jobs back wasn't what they wanted. A different solution had to be found. Shortly after midnight on September 11, the Hungarian government finally agreed to let GDR citizens cross the border to Austria if they wanted to. Almost 7,000 of them had been waiting for exactly that kind of decision. They left for Vienna and went on to West Germany.[25]

Before, the East Germans who were just on vacation in Hungary would have had to take a big risk if they would have decided to join the crowd waiting in tents for the opportunity to go West. If the Hungarian government changed its mind and sent them back to the GDR, no amount of promises on the part of the GDR government would have kept them from feeling repercussions in the long run. Now it was official though. Instead of going home after their vacation, they could simply drive on over to West Germany. That was still an awfully big step, since the GDR government regarded such action as illegal. Permission to return to the GDR on a visit to see family was routinely denied for at least ten years.

Most East Germans were not ready to make that radical decision at the spur of the moment. Those who were well established in life were not really interested in moving to the West. Parents who did their vacationing in the GDR while their young adult children went to Hungary were the ones who were now really on edge. Would their children come home? As I found out, Susanne didn't. What on earth did her parents think?

The GDR government protested the decision of the Hungarian government. A news story carried in the *Neues Deutschland* revealed the unofficial government response. The Hungarian government was accused of taking a bribe from the West German government to change its policies. In a bizarre allusion to the Bible, the alleged monetary reward for this betrayal was referred to as "pieces of silver".[26]

The GDR government soon put a stop to issuing exit visas to anyone who wanted to go to Hungary. They kept up their propaganda campaign about how terrible it was for West Germany to lure people over to the West. A long newspaper article described how one person had been 'kidnapped' in Budapest and transported to West Germany.[27] The article typified the way the government blatantly ignored the real cause of the exodus.

Since the people who desperately wanted out of the country could no longer get to Hungary, they went to Czechoslovakia. It was closer anyway and they didn't need a visa or passport. They could just show their GDR ID at the border. By the end of September there were almost 6,000 people crammed into the West German embassy in Prague. They were living in terrible conditions. People were parking their cars close to the embassy, abandoning them there and taking only what they could carry to what they hoped was a new life.

Although it was more difficult for East Germans to get into Poland, since the GDR government required exit visas to go there and didn't like to hand them out, a smaller group of East Germans also gathered in the West German embassy in Warsaw.

Finally on September 30, the GDR government agreed to let those people emigrate. The Warsaw group, about 600 people, would be flown out. The GDR government insisted, however, that the people from Prague leave by train. The trains would have to go through the GDR, so they could maintain the fiction that those people were emigrating under the authority of the government. 5,500 people made it to West Germany on that trip. This was accompanied by a statement from the government. Those people were released from GDR citizenship because they were the type of people who couldn't fit into GDR society.

"...some of these people are asocial, don't know how to work or how to live in a decent fashion. All of them have tramped on moral values through their actions and have cut themselves off from our society. Therefore, one shouldn't shed tears over their departure."[28]

Those individuals who had decided to leave were not asocial or criminal elements. They were largely young people looking for a better or different life. They left behind friends, siblings and parents. These people did shed tears over their departure. Since it wasn't clear when they could ever come back for a visit, it felt like they had just vanished from the face of the earth. It forced every East German to think about going or staying.

We're Staying Here!

Parallel to the pressure being put on the government by having so many of its citizens run away, pressure was growing from the people who wanted to stay and work for change. The various small opposition groups made plans to cooperate on a wider basis. At a gathering of opposition groups in a church in East Berlin, a nationwide movement was called for, a movement that would present an 'identifiable alternative'. The goal was to have such a group recognized on the ballot of the next election. In addition to making the necessary changes in GDR society, the hope was that by giving hope for change, the flood of people to the West and the disruption of lives in the East could be stopped.[29]

On September 9, 1989, two days before Hungary allowed GDR citizens to cross its borders, the foundation of a group called "New Forum" was announced. It was a group dedicated to justice, peace and democracy in the GDR. To achieve those goals, changes would be necessary in the GDR. The group issued a general appeal to the public to join up, to help make those changes take place.

This showed the complex interplay between the internal and external pressures. The internal opposition felt they needed to hurry up their confrontation with the state before so many people left the country that the whole society fell apart. The opposition thought the society could be transformed, that some aspects might be worth keeping while others had to be thrown out now. The general uproar of so many people leaving gave them some leverage. The party could no longer deny that the opposition was right in pointing out that something was amiss.

The people who were so determined to get out of the GDR seemed to be saying that there was no hope for the GDR. The only thing left to do was to leave the sinking ship while one still could. They only gave the state the option of locking them up or letting them go, there was nothing else to talk about. By trying to get some kind, any kind of dialogue going, the 'we're staying here' opposition perhaps helped give the 'we want out' opposition a little buffer from direct confrontation.

Other groups were founded; one called United Left previously on September 4th, Democracy Now on September 12th, Democratic Awakening on the 14th, after that there got to be more than one could keep track of. Even the Rock Musicians and Musical Entertainers union got in on the act with a resolution calling for change. New Forum applied for recognition as a legally allowed organization. They were turned down on September 21. The olive branch they had offered the government, to work for change inside the structures, had been turned down. It left the opposition little choice but to take their message to the streets, outside the power structures.

People inside the church had long been working on possibilities of change within legal structures. One of these attempts, the Monday night prayer services for peace in Leipzig, had a longer history than the new opposition groups being formed. This longer tradition, and the influence of the church as an institution, gave the services special significance as confrontation loomed.

In 1981, as a result of the increased tension between East and West, and between the governments of East Germany and West Germany, over the stationing of nuclear short-range and cruise missiles in West Germany, a youth pastor by the name of Johannsen, together with a group of young people, started holding weekly prayer services for peace at 5 pm every Monday in the St. Nikolai Church in downtown Leipzig. This prayer service sputtered along throughout the 80's; sometimes, when political events stirred up interest, with good attendance, sometimes with only a small core group of 5 or 10 people.

Events in East Berlin in January 1988 added prominence to the activities in Leipzig. At the annual official demonstration in Berlin that year to honor Karl Liebknecht and Rosa Luxembourg, leaders of the German Communist Party who were murdered in Berlin in 1919 and now served as martyr figures for the SED, some 'unofficial' people attempted to join the parade. The 'appropriate' slogans had been published in the papers several weeks in advance, and the party and its associated organizations made sure that people went to the demonstration with those slogans painted on their banners. The unofficial people brought along banners with unofficial slogans, the most memorable of which was "Freedom is always freedom for those who think differently", a quotation of Rosa Luxembourg's. This kind of activity resulted in over 100 people being taken in for questioning. Several key politically active people were arrested and eventually deported against their expressed wishes. In addition, several hundred people who had applied for permission to emigrate to the West, some waiting for years for a response, were suddenly told to leave the country on short notice.

The arrests and deportations in East Berlin deprived the opposition there of leadership and momentum.[30] It also helped give church-related activities that were addressing questions of East German life that could not be talked about openly, such as environmental and peace issues, the reputation of being good events to attend if one was interested in speeding up the process of being allowed to emigrate.

All of these factors made the prayer services in Leipzig more attractive and important. This increased interest resulted in some hefty political discussions using the open microphone there among those people trying get out of the country and those who wanted to change things. In March of 1988, it was decided that a pastor should always be responsible for the meditation part of the prayer service in cooperation with one of the special-interest groups that took turns preparing the service. A pattern of reading only those announcements which had been handed in ahead of time, the singing of a song at the beginning and end of each service and the unison reading of the Beatitudes was established. The service was well attended from then on and the regular attenders got used to this structure, although with many people being given permission to emigrate and new people finding their way to the services, the audience was different every week.

Throughout the spring and summer of 1989, massive police presence outside the Nikolai Church and people being taken in for questioning afterwards characterized the services. The local press, controlled by the party, demanded the end of the services. Church officials at all levels, down to that of the church board of the Nikolai Church, were pressured to suspend the services.

Those wanting to emigrate would gathered outside the church following the service to shout their slogan; 'We want out!'. On the Monday of September 4th a different note was sounded; the first cries of 'We're staying here!' were heard. This was a warning to the government that taking people in for questioning and then granting them their request to emigrate would not end the protests. The tension between those wanting to get out and those wanting to stay and work for change surfaced that day as well. Those seeking change were in the front of an attempt to start a demonstration through the downtown area. By breaking out into a more public area, their demands would come to the attention of more people. They ran into police opposition. Those further back saw the police coming and hung back. They wanted out. It didn't matter to them if the public knew about their demands. The police did and word would be passed on. Hopefully permission to emigrate would be granted soon just to get rid of the troublemakers. They only wanted to make as much trouble as was necessary to get the job done. Relations between the two groups weren't much better than between either one of them and the state.[31]

The following Monday, the church was completely surrounded by police after the church service. Numerous people were loaded onto trucks amidst much pushing and beating on the part of the police and were then taken in for questioning. About 20 were arrested and sentenced to jail. This brought even more people to the service the following weeks to show their solidarity with those prisoners. It increased the number of people attending who were committed to staying in the country.

On the Monday of September 25, several thousand people were able to mount a short demonstration. Although a dozen people were arrested, a precedent had been set. The next Monday, October 2, an additional church, the Reformed Church, was opened for a peace prayer service. This time there were fifteen to twenty thousand people who demonstrated. Many demonstrators and a few police were hurt in the ensuing scuffles.[32] Presiding Chairman of the Civil Senate of the District Court of Leipzig, Karl-Heinz Matheiowetz told the press "that such events require a permit. Since no permit was issued for the event on October 2, it was illegal. Demonstrations that take place without a permit can be dispersed by the People's Police".[33]

There was no longer any doubt that things were coming to a head. The pressure from people leaving and people demonstrating was increasing equally and dramatically. In the midst of this storm, the church kept advocating dialogue. Perhaps more importantly, the church kept advocating non-violence.

Chapter 9

Dona Nobis Pacem

By myself I have sworn, my mouth has uttered in all integrity,
a word that will not be revoked:
Before me every knee shall bow; by me every tongue will swear.
They will say of me, 'In the LORD alone are righteousness
and strength.'
Isaiah 45:23-24a, the Bible verse for October 9, 1989
according to the lectionary prepared several years in advance by
the Moravian Brethren Church of East Germany and used
extensively by Protestant churches there.

October 2 also marked the start of a scheduled 10 day prayer vigil
for political prisoners in the Gethsemane Church in Prenzlauer Berg, a
working-class and artist district of East Berlin. The vigil was
announced by word of mouth and mimeographed leaflets that were
barely legible. Even so, news of the vigil spread quickly among young
people, opposition groups and in church circles. In fact, the protests
that followed the arrests and expulsions at the Liebknecht/Luxembourg
demonstration in East Berlin in 1988 had been arranged in a similar
fashion. Those events served as a sort of dress rehearsal for what came
next.[34] This time, however, there was a sense of mounting pressure,
of things reaching a boiling point. Instead of the dozens of people
turning out for prayer services as in early 1988, eventually thousands
came out.

The leaflets had been printed up with the standard disclaimer 'For
internal church use only'. This made their printing legal. The leaflet
referred to the fact that in the last couple of weeks "people in Leipzig,
Potsdam and Berlin have been treated as criminals and arrested for
getting involved in society's problems and making use of basic human
rights". The vigil demand was "the release of those arrested, no

deportation against their will of those concerned, the halt of criminal proceedings against them and the lifting of all sentences and fines".

The leaflet concluded: "The use of police state methods will only make the current domestic political crisis worse and will not solve it. In addition, the largest flight since the construction of the Wall shows that it is not possible to shield a single country from the political changes in Europe, because a country that sacrifices its constructive potential to a rigid, dead-end state ideology is fumbling away its future.

Chapel services with up-to-date information are taking place daily at 6 pm in the Gethsemane church. ... Please bring candles, flowers, snacks, coffee and tea."[35]

The front page of next morning's *Neues Deutschland* had a large article about the greeting given to the Chinese delegation that had come to help celebrate the 40th anniversary of the GDR. A member of the SED Politburo was quoted as saying during a toast to China "we have unerringly the same position and expectations in the basic questions of our day. ... The GDR welcomes China's efforts to bring about less tension in international affairs and better arms control, to keep outer space free of weapons, your striving to solve conflicts peacefully...". This was about three months after the massacre on Tiananmen Square in Beijing.

Willi Stoph, chairman of the Cabinet, declared in a speech that day, October 3, that "the current campaign of provocation and slander by politicians and the mass media of the FRG (West Germany)" is "in no way coincidentally happening on the eve of the 40th anniversary of our Republic."[36] This was typical of the government's stance through the next week. All the problems that were cropping up were due exclusively to the activity of Western agents in one form or another.

Thousands of people had continued to gather in the FRG embassy in Prague. In response, on this day, the GDR government ended the practice of allowing its citizens to go to the CSSR without a visa. Before they could only needed to show their personal identification document to cross the border. Now they would have to apply for permission based on having business or relatives there. This shut the last door out of the country. Even many GDR citizens who didn't plan on going to the CSSR soon were indignant that this last bit of freedom had been taken from them.

I had been at a long weekend meeting of West German Mennonite theology students in Bad Dürkheim, West Germany. Now I was taking the night train back to East Berlin. I was just settling down for the night when a familiar voice greeted me. Cordelia, one of my fellow students, came into my train compartment on the train. She had been visiting relatives in the West and was on the way back. She was a little worried because her exit visa was only good for the rest of the day, but we wouldn't get back until 7:00 the next morning. We talked some about the exodus of 7,000 people from her country. She thought many people had wrong ideas of what they would find in the West. She had enjoyed her visit there, but couldn't image feeling at home there. Life was too fast-paced and superficial. Her daughter and boyfriend, her family and her apartment were waiting for her at home. She felt bad and a bit ridiculous for having to defend her returning to the GDR to her West German relatives. To her it was going home, why should anyone have to defend that?

The GDR press agency released a statement about the people in the West German embassy in Prague on October 4. "In agreement with the government of the CSSR, the government of the GDR decided that the people who are currently illegally in the embassy of the FRG (West Germany) in Prague will be deported through the territory of the GDR into the FRG. The government was most influenced by its concern for small children, who have been brought into a dangerous situation by their parents and who can't be held responsible for the irresponsible actions of their parents."[37]

In Dresden, there was speculation that those trains full of people going to West Germany would have to pass through the main train station there. Ten thousand people gathered there in the vain hope of being able to 'jump' on. The police attempted to clear the people from the station. Many demonstrators and some police were injured. Quite a bit of damage was done to the train station itself, which was pelted with cobblestones.

Typical of official response to that pent up frustration and anger is the following portion of an interview printed in the *Junge Welt*, the newspaper for young people. Maik Schmidt, a 23 year old riot policeman (most of whom are army draftees), whose jaw was broken by a thrown object, is reported as asking: "What kind of women are those, who push their babys in baby carriages onto the tracks to stop a train! What kind of mother is that, who withholds food from her three children to coerce her trip to the West by a hunger strike at the price of their suffering!"[38]

Also on October 4, numerous opposition groups got together in Berlin and released a statement about the "possibilities of common political activites". Their top demand was free and secret elections. This declaration found wide spread distribution in Berlin during the next several days. The protests were now not only against the old government, they were clearly *for* something as well.[39]

At our Bible study in the evening we talked about how to deal with people who lie to us, take advantage of us and actually need help. Thomas and Axel had some painful experiences in this area. For the moment these personal problems took precedence over the political events of the day. We also went over the changes the church board wanted in our letter inviting people to attend a young adults retreat our group was organizing. They felt Tim shouldn't be mentioned in the letter, since he lived in West Berlin and any kind of connection to the West could raise suspicions right then.

On Thursday, October 5, a big demonstration in Dresden again led to violence on the part of demonstrators and police. Fidus, the student from Wittenberg, wanted to go to the chapel service in the Gethsemane church. The news we got from West German media about what was happening in Dresden was a bit sketchy. She hoped to find out more at the chapel service. She was unsure about going by herself, so I agreed to go with her. We arrived a little ahead of the 6:00 pm starting time, but the church was already completely packed. We found seats behind a pillar, which blocked our view. The service began by singing a couple of songs. For a church full of people, one could hardly tell that anyone was singing. It seemed obvious that most people there were not regular church attenders.

The singing was followed by an informational part, which was mostly an eyewitness account of what had been happening this week in Leipzig. This was the first time that I heard eyewitness accounts of the kind of violence that had been going on in Leipzig since September. The names of those arrested and still in jail in a number of cities were read. A short meditation was given and then a prayer of intercession (*Fürbittengebet*). This was left open for people to come up front and prayed about their concerns. Each prayer was followed by everyone singing a short chorus of 'Kyrie elesion'. The service was closed out by singing the round 'Dona Nobis Pacem' in three parts. The singing of these songs was a little stronger than the hymns to start with, since they were more familiar even to non-church attenders. There were clusters of 2 to 5 policemen on every corner outside the church, but we had no problem just walking out. We went to visit friends of Fidus' who lived around the corner, they showed slides of their vacation in the Soviet Union. We also managed to talk them into providing us with supper.

The GDR's Birthday Party

"Greetings to all citizens in honor of the 40th anniversary of the GDR!" was the banner headline of the *Neues Deutschland* for the morning of Friday, October 6th. The first official festivities took place in the Parliament Building in the evening, Erich Honecker and Gorbachev each giving a speech. One hundred thousand members of the Free German Youth had been brought to Berlin and marched down the main street of East Berlin, Unter den Linden, past Honecker and Gorbachev in the review stand in front of the Humboldt University. They were all carrying torches, eerily reminiscent of the torch-lit processions that the Nazis had organized to celebrate their coming to power in 1933.

The second year Marxist-Leninist class was called 'Political Economy'. That day, our teacher, Frau Voth refused to let any discussion of the current political situation get started. Our once a week English evening at Uta's had been dropped since she was doing a pastoral internship for 6 months in the city of Perleberg, about an hour's drive northwest of Berlin. Knowing that there would probably be some excitement in Berlin on this particular weekend, she had arranged to come back for the weekend. We met at her place that evening and talked about the questions she had concerning some of the vocabulary in Steinbeck's 'The Grapes of Wrath'.

She also talked about the situation in Perleberg. Nobody wanted to become involved in the current upheaval, everyone was very afraid of saying anything openly. She had started a discussion about the *Neues Forum* in the youth group at church and had collected a few signatures on their petition to be allowed to exist. She didn't know how that would go over with the parents of those high schoolers or if it was right to put 15 and 16 year olds in the position of having to decide such things. Such a signature might well suffice to block one's entry into university.

Uta also mentioned she'd heard from a doctor friend of hers in Dresden that the surgical floors there were completely overfilled because of all the rioting that had taken place there. We went to the Gethsemane Church together after supper, so we missed the chapel service, but there were still a lot of people in the church reading the statements from different groups that were taped to the walls of the sanctuary. The whole church was like a big bulletin board. A friend of Uta's related the story that children from the elementary school down the street had been in the church during the day. When asked why they weren't in school, they said they were really supposed to be in PE class, but since the gym was completely full of riot police, PE class was cancelled. It seems the gym was being used as a holding area for a large number of police, in case the authorities should deem their help necessary.

I had made arrangements to meet Reimers, the MCC'ers from West Berlin, at my room in the Johanneum in downtown East Berlin at 9:30 am on Saturday, October 7. This 40th anniversary day of the founding of the GDR would be celebrated, as was the tradition, by a military parade on one of the main thoroughfares, starting at 10:00 am. I waited and waited, but Reimers didn't come. Finally I tried to call, but there was no getting through. I left them a note on the door of the Johanneum and went with Angelika, a fellow student, to see the parade. We got to Alexanderplatz, the main square of East Berlin, at 11:15, just in time to see the last formation of soldiers marching off. Usually the parade lasts much longer, but this year apparently the atmosphere was too tense in the country to merit a long parade. We looked around the food booths set up on Alexanderplatz a little, walked down Unter den Linden to the Brandenburg gate trying to find some excitement, but there just wasn't any. The streets were eerily deserted, it was a very strange atmosphere, not the kind of happy, relaxed scene one would expect for a major holiday. We finally gave up and went back to the dorm to do homework.

Tim came by and told us that the family had been turned back at Checkpoint Charlie. That was actually in violation of the Four Powers agreement that regulated visits to East Berlin, but when an East German border guard tells you there's no going through today, there isn't much point in bringing up agreements that are written down on paper. He'd taken the family home, then tried again at the crossing on Invaliden Street. They had let him through there. He had run into Micha, a student from my class, who had told him that there might be some activity at Alexanderplatz in the afternoon, related to the anniversary of the election fraud on May 7. Tim and I went there to see what was happening.

There was one big cluster of maybe 100 people gathered close to the World Clock, a clock that showed the time in all 24 time zones around the world and served as a meeting place on the plaza. There was a lot of milling around going on in the crowd. With a little imagination one could see plain-clothed Stasi agents trying to subtly push the people apart, but the people just going around them and crowding back together. Beyond that nothing was going on, so we decided to go to the vigil service at the Gethsemane church a little early so we could get good seats.

We ended up standing at the back of the sanctuary anyway, as there weren't any seats left. After singing a little again at the start, a number of reports were given from the cities where demonstrations had or were taking place. The most moving report was the one from Dresden. We heard about the large collection of people who wanted to "jump" on the train from Prague that was taking people from the West German embassy there to West Germany. It was supposed to go through Dresden. The train station was sealed off, a group of 150 young people tried to get in the main entrance, threw stones and pretty well trashed the place. Ambulances were reported coming and going from the back entrance. Whole families were inside, children and baby strollers were overrun in the action.

Tim drove me home after the service. In the dark we saw the silhouette of a tank parked in a side street near where I live.

I went to Igor's room, he had one of the few TV's in the dorm, to watch the West German news. It was full of reports of the demonstrations here in the East, they even ran a special on it. They showed the demonstrations that were going on right then in Berlin, one had apparently started from this group at the world clock on Alexanderplatz shortly after we'd left. They had tried to get to the parliament building where there was another official celebration with Honecker and Gorbachev. The streets in that direction had been blocked off by lines of police standing shoulder to shoulder, so the demonstration had done an about face and headed for the Gethesemane church, where the people who had come out of the church and just hung around on the street instead of going home constituted a demonstration of sorts as well.

Since I didn't even have a radio in my room, first thing Sunday morning I dug out some of my West German currency and went down to an Intershop, a store that only takes West currency, to buy one. Although the reports given on West Berlin radio stations were a bit slanted and, given the restrictions being enforced on Western correspondents that weekend, incomplete, it was still the only way to keep track of what was going on. East Berlin stations only brought reports on the official parts of the celebrations, which didn't really interest anyone. I heard reports that up to 1,000 people had been arrested in East Berlin the night before, amidst considerable police violence. Gorbachev had made the comment at an international press conference the day before that 'Life itself punishes those who delay'. He no doubt meant to encourage Honecker to start loosing up some. It was at the same time great encouragement for those hoping to force change in the GDR.

The rest of the morning I worked on typing up and printing out our letters of invitation to a youth retreat weekend. It had been agreed that the pastor, Knuth Hansen, would sign the letters to give them a little more of an official status. Angelika went with me to the Mennonite church service in the afternoon. Knuth talked about a lady who'd called him all upset because the Protestant church service she'd wanted to go to that morning had been changed into a political discussion. He implied that that was a misuse of the church that shouldn't be tolerated. There didn't seem to be much danger of that in the Mennonite church that Sunday, there were only 3 people there under 70 years of age. As was customary, we had a time of fellowship with cake and coffee after the service and Knuth signed our letters of invitation. That was over in time for us to get to the vigil service at the Gethsemane Church.

The church is at the corner of Stargarder and Greifenhagener streets. It sits at a 45 degree angle to the corner. It has a double stairway, one flight coming up from each street. They meet in a landing in front of the final steps that go into the church itself. A spire with bells towers above the entrance way. There is an iron fence all the way around the church, with iron gates at the foot of each stairway.

A banner exhorting to 'watch and pray for all those unjustly imprisoned' was hanging above the entrance. There were candles atop the gates, along the wall between the gates, on the walls that go up along the stairs to the landing where they meet and on the wall around the landing itself. A solemn, eerie feeling took hold of me as soon as we rounded the corner from Schönhauser Allee and saw all the candles flickering at the end of the block with the church tower soaring above them.

We were sent up to the balcony because the downstairs was so full. The reports given after the meditation listed 700 arrested in Berlin last night, some had already been sentenced to 6 months in prison in accelerated trials, most had been released. A note was read from a mother who hadn't heard from her 15-year-old daughter since last night and was unable to get any information out of the police. The calls for non-violence and statements that there were no reports of violence on the part of the demonstrators were greeted with very enthusiastic applause. A call to sit down and exchange experiences with the police and Stasi brought considerably less applause and a number of catcalls. We closed by praying the Lord's Prayer and then all joined hands and raised them to sing 'Dona Nobis Pacem' in three parts. The two guys in dark suits standing right in front of us didn't sing along or join hands with anyone so we knew they were working for the Stasi. The rest of the church, four or five thousand people, was swaying, singing softly and reverently.

We started shuffling out. A few minutes later, when about half the people were out, the crowd stopped moving. It was announced that we should all back up and stay away from the entrances. We stood around on the balcony for a little while, waved across the way to some other students from our class on the other balcony. After about five minutes we got bored and decided to try to get out the back door.

We got out with no problem. Once we got on Greifenhagener Street, we discovered that the bridge at the end of the street that went over the subway tracks was blocked off by a solid wall of police three or four deep. We walked up to the front of the church, where a couple hundred people were milling around. We went out into the intersection and looked in turn down each of the other three streets. At the end of each was the same solid wall of police. Just then a police loudspeaker announced: "Citizens of the city of Berlin, leave the area immediately and individually in the direction of Pankow". The crowd yelled out their opinion of this; "leave us alone", and "why don't you leave?".

We joined a small group of people who went towards the subway bridge, which was the direction of the district of Pankow. Another group of people, large enough to span the whole street, were already standing there, talking to the police and trying to get out. We talked to a couple of people coming back from there who said there was no getting out there. Meanwhile the noise and activity in front of the church, just 70 yards away, was picking up.

I started thinking about China, and we decided we were both pretty scared, so we went around to the back of the church and tried to find another way out. It was all a dead-end. The back side of the church was surrounded by apartment buildings and courtyards. We started looking into the courtyards in hope of finding one that led out onto another street. In one of them we met a middle-age couple who apparently lived there and were just coming down the stairs. They told us that in an adjacent courtyard there was a wall we could crawl over. They showed us the way to it. We found about 20 people working on crawling over a 9 foot wall. They had pushed a large trash container up to it. Since it had wheels on it, somebody had to hold it to make sure it didn't roll away when the person crawling over the wall jumped up from it to get to the top of the wall. A guy from an apartment overlooking the courtyard saw our predicament. He brought his ladder down and set it up on the wall for us. We kept asking the people going over what was on the other side. No one would answer. Finally someone said it was a long drop, but we'd be alright. We helped a 50 year old lady over this

9 foot wall, she wanted out and didn't care how undignified she looked. Angelika and I were the last ones over. Someone had found a pallet to lean up against the other side of the wall, so we could climb down onto it and didn't have to drop all the way down.

We discovered we had landed behind a grocery store. We went out to the street, Pappelallee, and discovered we were on the other side of the police line sealing off Stargarder Street. A small crowd had gathered on that intersection as well, mostly to gawk at that many police all lined up. The crowd in front of the church a block away could barely be heard.

Angelika pulled at my sleeve. "Let's get out of here."

"What for? We're not surrounded here."

"I don't care about that, I've got to go."

"What?"

"I have to pee! Bad!"

"Good grief!"

We walked up the street away from the cops looking for a bathroom. The streets were quiet and dark. There was no indication that only a few blocks away hundreds of police and demonstrators were facing off in great fear. It seemed like we were in a different world now. We walked past a tiny park nestled among the tenements.

"I don't care any more, this is good enough. Make sure no one comes along here."

The street lights were dim anyway. I stood guard for Angelika, then we decided to take the streetcar home and watch the rest of the action on the evening news.

Late in the evening, Katharine and Katrin, two of the students we had waved at in the other balcony, came and told us what they had experienced. As it turned out, we had just gotten too nervous. After about 20 minutes they were able to walk through the police line over the subway bridge. They couldn't fathom *their* police doing anything as stupid as the Chinese, so they weren't at all worried. They decided to take in a show at a nearby movie theater, the Colosseum, on the corner of Stargarder Street and Schönhauser Allee. While they were in there, demonstrators had gathered on the outside of the police lines there, so that wall of police who were surrounding the church were themselves surrounded. They called in reinforcements to surround these demonstrators. The new encirclement took in the Colosseum, so that when they came out after the movie, they found themselves trapped again. They went to the middle of the street and up the steps to the platform of the above-ground public transportation system. From there they could watch the police with riot sticks and dogs try to clear the streets. They saw a line of police that went all the way across the six-lane street, Schönhauser Allee, moving up towards their station. When they looked up the other way, they saw a line from that direction coming towards their station too.

As soon as they figured out that those two lines would meet right at the station, they realized they were in trouble. They decided to ride the next train, which they could see coming down the tracks, right on out of there. It pulled into the station and didn't even slow down. Now they decided to get as worried as Angelika and I had been before. They tried to run down the stairs that connected the above ground train with the subway. The door at the bottom of the stairs was locked. The police were starting to come up the stairs on the outside. In the nick of time an employee of the public transportation department unlocked the door. They were able to get away and arrived home a little shaken and very angry. (See the Scrapbook page 178 for more accounts of this evening.)[40]

Unknown to us at the time, the tension had already started to ease in Dresden on the evening of the eighth. There too police had completely surrounded a group of demonstrators. They sat down on the street. A couple of church officials managed to get a conversation started with one of the ranking Stasi officers. There was finally agreement that talking was better than more violence. The demonstrators were asked to list their demands. They were 'voted' on by the level of applause received; freedom to travel, freedom for the press, conscientious objection status for those desiring an alternative to serving in the army, legalization of 'New Forum', open and non-violent dialogue in society, free elections, the right to peaceful assembly and the release of political prisoners. A group of twenty people were selected more or less at random to represent the demonstrators in continuing dialogue with ranking party members in Dresden. It was a spontaneous town hall meeting of sorts. No word of this beginning of looking for a peaceful solution got out to the rest of the country though.[41]

"On the evening of October 7, rowdies attempted to disrupt the Volksfest in celebration of the 40th anniversary of the GDR. In cooperation with Western media, they gathered illegally at the Alexanderplatz and surrounding area and yelled slogans hostile to the Republic. The composure of the protective security forces as well as of the participants in the Volksfest was responsible for preventing the intended provocations. The ringleaders were arrested."[42]

This little article in the *Berliner Zeitung* on Monday, October 9th, was the official comment to the events of the weekend. The party paper, *Neues Deutschland*, made no mention whatsoever of all difficulties in the country, instead the whole Monday edition was dedicated to the successful weekend celebrations. One headline was 'Good mood from the coast to the forest of Thuringia'. It was almost as if they were determined to report the *exact* opposite of what the truth was.

Only half the people showed up in Latin class that day. The teacher, Herr Güpner, liked to make asides about pertinent aspects of history and culture related to Latin. Today his off-hand comment about the prison and torture tactics of the Middle Ages upset Micha, a fellow student. He started talking about what he had heard from a friend of his who'd been in jail the night before last. He had been made to stand for a long time with his face to the wall, many others arrested had been beaten or kicked. Herr Güpner stuck strictly to the lesson for the rest of the day.

They Blinked!

It was Monday; as everyone knew, the day for demonstrations in Leipzig. In a system where the ideology dictates that nothing can possibly be wrong, a demonstration of any kind is deadly to the state. At the same time, people were hopeful that the location of the GDR in the heart of Europe and the need for stability in such a sensitive area would help deter a Chinese solution here. "This is the middle of Europe, we're not in China" was the common wishful thinking among students over the weekend.

"We are all prepared, and willing, to effectively defend that which we have built with our own hands, in order to put a stop to these counter-revolutionary activities once and for all. If it has to be, with our weapons in our hands." This letter to the editor was signed by a Commander Günter Letz of the GDR equivalent of the National Guard, which had units in all the larger factories and offices in the country. It was published in the *Leipziger Zeitung* on Thursday, October 6.[43] It was clear that the biggest confrontation would be in Leipzig, but the demonstrations would need to be squashed in all cities eventually. From the escalation of heavy police presence on Saturday to surrounding the church on Sunday, it felt like things were coming to a head. With fear and trepidation, Angelika and I went to the vigil service in the Gethsemane church again. I would have quite frankly been too scared to go by myself. Going with someone else, someone who lived in the country, made the fear bearable.

Turning the corner into Stargarder Street, I was once again impressed with all the candles in front of the church. Today, however, it wasn't only the church that was lit up. Many of the windows in the turn-of-the-century tenements also had candles in them to show support. This was in itself a risk, the Stasi were surely noting exactly which windows had candles in them. The subway train that went thundering past on Schönhauser Allee tooted its horn. We turned around in time to see its lights flickering on and off, another obvious and dangerous sign of support. No police were to be seen on the way in. In spite of the intimidation of the party press, indeed the perception of maybe even risking one's life, more people had come than the night before.

The first thing said in the welcome was that it would be difficult to leave the church following the service. The church was fuller than ever, standing room only, there wasn't a speck of floor space left anywhere, not even around the altar. Not every one had been able to get in. Several of the leading church officials were there, including Bishop Forck and General Superintendent Krusche. We were standing behind a pillar on the balcony, so we couldn't actually see anything.

During the informational part of the service, it was reported that in Leipzig two additional churches were being opened for peace prayer services. Parents there had been ordered to pick up their children from day-care centers at 3:00 pm. Many factories and offices were ordered to close then as well. The med-evac system had been put on full-alert, doctors had been given passes to get through police lines because the inner city was completely sealed off. Instructions were given to deliver any injured people straight to prison hospitals. In factories and offices, workers were warned not to go to the inner city, which led to numerous unanimous decisions to go there together. Someone had counted 27 army trucks full of soldiers going to the inner city, where a special army camp had been set up. One of the buildings on the exhibition grounds had been prepared as a morgue.

A 50-year-old man, who had been arrested the previous night around midnight near the Gethsemane church, was given the opportunity to tell about his experience in order to prepare us should we experienced anything similar. He had been taken to Rummelsberg, a notorious Stasi prison named after the city district it was in. All those taken in with him were suppose to stand spread-eagle with their noses to the wall, but the lower-ranking police officers told them to go ahead and sit down. They whistled when an officer came by, so they could stand back up in time to make it look good. Those arrested were questioned about an hour and a half each. The police seemed particularly interested in if they had seen any violence or aggression on the part of the demonstrators. Before he was let out, he talked with a couple of middle rank officers who pleaded with him to make sure the demonstrations didn't get violent and agreed that some changes in the system were necessary. He got out just a couple of hours before this vigil service started.

The service was starting to wind down about 7:20, but we were too impatient to wait, so we left a little early. It took a little while to get out the door, other people had had the same idea.

To our great surprise there wasn't a policeman to be seen anywhere. The feelings of relief and joy were indescribable. We laughed and skipped right on over to the street car stop. The party, embodied by the state and protected by police and the Stasi, and demonstrators, who were mostly just fed up, literally and figuratively stood eyeball to eyeball that weekend. On Stargarder Street that Monday night, it felt very much like *they* had blinked and we had won! We rode the streetcar home. We were keenly interested in finding out who had blinked in Leipzig.

When we got back to the dorm, we talked for a while in the stairwell with a couple of students. They told us about a fellow student, Danny Fink, who had also been at the Gethsemane Church the past night with his sister. They had seen what was happening, managed to get through police lines, went home and talked their dad into coming back with them. Professor Heinrich Fink was the head of our theology department at that time. Danny had challenged the police before, but his father seemed to have a hard time believing him, so Danny wanted him to see the police in action first hand. They got caught in the police action. The police ordered them to get on a truck. Heinrich started to protest and wanted to show his ID that would prove he was the head of the theology department. The policeman started swearing at him, calling him names and roughing him up. Danny got an even worse beating. It was only after they were on the truck that Heinrich was able to get someone to listen to his story. It was not possible to become head of the theology department at the Humboldt University without having some good contacts to high places, an elementary fact that the police officer on the truck immediately recognized. Heinrich and his children were allowed to go.

The students relating the story found it amusing that Heinrich Fink got a first hand look at police violence. They felt that he had otherwise been much too accommodating of the state, so it was only fair that his beloved state beat on him. His doctor ordered him to take a week off from work to recover. Danny was on his way to Leipzig.

Watching the 10:30 pm West German news in Igor's room, we were amazed to see that everything was going peacefully in Leipzig (see the Scrapbook page 183 for accounts of what was said in the churches that night). Fifty thousand people had shown up in Leipzig for the demonstration in spite of, or perhaps, because of, the psychological pressure applied to stay away. That demonstration had been allowed to take place and disbanded peacefully as well. The slogans of the day in Leipzig were 'Wir sind das Volk!' (We are the people!) and 'Keine Gewalt!' (No violence!). In the GDR there was a People's Police, People Owned Corporations in place of corporations with stock holders, even the parliament was the People's Parliament. All of those institutions were controlled by the party in its own interests, not the people's interest. The cry '*We* are the people' jolted the nation's consciousness of that fact, long buried under the half-truths of the party.

At some point on this Monday, a decision was made by the party to give up the attempt for now to violently suppress the demonstrations. The courage of those East Germans who had decided they wanted to stay and work for reform, who gathered for demonstrations on that Monday in the face of great fear and uncertainty was breath-taking.

A blink, alas, is in the eye of the beholder. It seemed to me that the demonstrations would not end until radical changes were made in the GDR or shots were fired into the crowd. The fact that the party, for whatever reason, blinked, seemed to make the prospect of shots being fired more unlikely. All the same, the front page of the *Neues Deutschland* the next day, October 10th, greeted its readers with the headline "Erich Honecker receives the leader of the delegation of the People's Republic of China". Amidst mutual toasts to the respective stability (!) of each other's countries, was this little veiled threat. "The delegations agreed that at present an especially aggressive anti-socialist attitude on the part of the imperialistic class enemy can be observed, with the goal of turning around the socialist development. Thus one of the basic lessons to be learned from the counter-revolutionary activities in Beijing as well as from the current campaign of slander against the GDR and other socialist countries, is always to remain true to the basic values of socialism and at the same time to continue to perfect the socialist society. This can only be accomplished by enforcing the leading role of the working class and its party."

We made the third page, under the heading "politics". That whole page and page four were dedicated to reports from various cities that tried to show that the demonstrations were organized by news services in West Germany looking to boost their ratings. This was accompanied by letters from citizens calling for the police to enforce law and order; a letter writing campaign organized by the party as part of the orchestrated raising of tensions.

An officer of the People's Police speaking about the 7th of October said: "We found the hard core people in the Schönhauser Allee. There had been a chapel service in the Gethesemane Church, with hardly any religious content. And even though church leaders tried to talk reason and we kept ourselves in the background, some hot heads broke iron rods out of the fence. In such a situation we had to get a little more physical to get at the ringleaders."

Of course, I knew that was lie, but that paper sure didn't look like much of a blink. Perhaps the euphoria of the night before was a little premature. In addition, less than one percent of the population of East Berlin had taken part in the demonstrations. While most people didn't believe what they read in the paper anyway, only those who were actually there would know that the party had blinked at least once.

The events of the weekend left me with many questions, most of which I can't even phrase. If only 5,000 people had demonstrated in Leipzig, the results might have been much different. If it seems that only large numbers help, does it make sense to demonstrate non-violently when only small numbers turn out? Should I, as a representative of North American Mennonites, have stayed at the demonstration to get beaten up or not gone at all in the first place? What does it mean that mostly non-Christians carried out a successful non-violent weekend campaign? Should we have believed East German police who say they want to avoid violence? How should we have related to those people? How should North American Christians react if they are open to Jesus' teaching to love our enemies and also don't ever want to experience communist rule? Do we love communist policemen who beat up our friends? Do we pay taxes to keep a strong military? Isn't that military in large part responsible for the respect my American passport brought me there?

I was attending a Russian class at a community college. It met Tuesday and Thursday evenings. Frau Lehmann, a heavy-set women in her late 40's, was one of the students. She was the kind of person who would bring cookies along to class on her birthday, was always friendly and interested in many things, but beyond her family, nothing seemed to really touch her. She was brushing up on her Russian in anticipation of a vacation in the Soviet Union with her husband. At class that evening she talked about all the overtime her husband had had to work over the weekend. He was a policeman assigned to the local police station in that neighborhood, quite a distance from the scene of the demonstrations.

"There were all kinds of rowdies out this weekend, they were putting leaflets in the mailboxes and my poor husband had to run around and try to catch them. I don't know what ails those people."

I didn't know Frau Lehmann very well, I didn't know what to say, so I said nothing. Not for the first time that year I wondered, who is my neighbor? Who is my enemy?

Chapter 10

Breaching the Wall

In retrospect, it has been pointed out by numerous observers of the East European Revolutions that 'peaceful Revolution' is a bit of an oxymoron. Revolutions are almost by definition violent. Once the dust settles, only a few decisive moments are remembered, usually the most violent ones. The revolution in the GDR certainly had decisive moments. Just as important, and not to be forgotten, it was carried by a sustained growth. The story of the GDR from the 9th of October to the 9th of November,1989, is the story of an ever-expanding circle of people facing and overcoming their own fear. It is the story of a peaceful revolution.

On October 11th the Party started its counter-attack. A statement of the Central Committee finally admitted that problems existed, a victory of sorts for the opposition. That was about as much of a concession as one was going to get though. The rhetoric changed from the defiant 'not shedding tears over those who left' to a more conciliatory 'Socialism needs everyone'. All the same, they couldn't resist pointing out that many of those who left were being misled by a conspiracy organized in the West to undermine the GDR.[44]

There were still veiled threats against those who thought Socialism should be ended in the GDR. However, the newspapers had taken on the tone of a shrill school teacher instead of the menacing thug of only a few days before. This was coupled with a flurry of high-profile, carefully arranged visits by ranking party men to talk with workers at various factories around the country. One got the impression of a party awakened from its dreamy sleep, based ultimately on Soviet tanks, now rubbing its eyes to confront a dangerous people. Like the opposition, they were very much winging it. Unlike the new groups contending with them for the people's attention and loyality, their years of lies, lies and more lies had worn away any chance of people listening to their half truths. Of course, this view of things depended on one's vantage point (helped out here, no doubt, by hindsight). The biggest shift in vantage point came as each individual found the courage to bring their private thoughts out into the public.

The biggest manifestations of this continued to be in Leipzig on Monday evenings. For the next Monday, the 16th of October, sources talked of 100,000 demonstrators or roughly double the number of the week before. It's easy to imagine that for the half of the crowd who had been there the week before, it was a relaxing, joyful celebration of the new found freedom to protest. For the other half of the crowd, getting involved publicly for the first time, it must have still been very scary. The Monday demonstration in Leipzig even got coverage in the GDR press. "Following peace prayer services in five Leipzig churches, tens of thousands of Leipzig citizens as well as people from the surrounding area gathered for a demonstration. The discretion of the security forces and the other ordinance forces as well as the reserve of the demonstrators is to be thanked for preventing any disturbances."[45]

Once the shock of initial success had worn off, the small opposition groups started formulating new demands of the government. The continually growing demonstrations backed up these demands. For theology students, the first demand started right at home. It had to do with the Free German Youth (FDJ).

FDJ Gets The Boot

The FDJ was the only legal youth organization in the country. It was to represent the interests of the students. Every department in the university was required to have its own FDJ organization. In our department, each of the five classes was expected to 'elect' two representatives to a governing council. In most other departments, where students were more carefully screened than in ours, that never presented much of a problem. A number of students in our department, however, weren't even in the FDJ. That ruled out their participation in student government. It became more a matter of finding two volunteers per class who were willing to volunteer for the governing council and go through the motions of pretending the FDJ represented student interests. There were a couple of real benefits to this arrangement. Students representatives of the FDJ got access to department meetings where information about internal going-ons came out, (certainly not where decisions were made). More importantly, one of the student representatives had the right to sit in on the oral exams common in German higher education. They could take part in the subsequent discussion of the grades to be given and report back on the discussion to the students.

Several of the more outspoken students had been trying for about a year to establish an independent student organization that would recieve official recognition. The whole issue offers a microcosm of the dilemma of living in the GDR. At first I thought, if the system is so silly, why don't the students just refuse to go along with it? The answer was actually equally obvious. Every class more than likely had someone who was reporting to the Stasi. If things got too carried away, the ringleaders could thus be easily identified and kicked out of the university. If by some miracle the students all stuck together, the professors might well put them under pressure as well, since they themselves would certainly feel the pressure from above. The easiest answer to the whole mess was simply not to get involved. Hence the task of finding ten volunteers in the 120-member study body to go along with the charade of a FDJ student government was almost as difficult as trying to change the system.

Enough of the theology students had been at the Gethsemane church to realize that now the time was ripe. A meeting of the students was called for Monday evening, October 16. The first order of business was quickly dispatched; the FDJ organization for the department was thrown out. Second item of business: what should replace it?

Have you ever thought about what would make the ideal (student) government? That question is only rhetorical in the West, the answer assumed or given. Now my friends were asking it for themselves, in a real way, for the very first time. Sixty people jammed into the classroom; again a microcosm of the discussion that would break out all over the GDR in the coming weeks. How can we make sure all the various opinions are fairly represented? Are votes taken still valid if less than half the student body is present? (Quorum and a host of other terms were not even present in their vocabulary.) And most important, how can we maintain control over whatever kind of new officials we elect? They had been burned so badly by authority that there was little consideration of trusting fellow students who might get into positions of even this very limited power.

It quickly became clear what they wanted; participatory democracy and a smaller council empowered to act on short notice. The discussion on how to set it up went on and on and on. I sat in the back of the room and tried to recall a few rules of parliamentary procedure from high school. I finally offered a suggestion from the 'real existing democracy' (at least they laughed at my joke). I outlined some of the ways questions of quorum and majority versus 2/3 votes are handled back home. Particularly the suggestion to allow a petition drive to call for a referendum on any decision the officers made seemed to alleviate their fear of losing control. There was more debate, but finally most of the suggestions were accepted. After a three and a half hour meeting, the theology department of the Humboldt University had its first democratically elected student representation since 1933. No one knew if the professors would accept its representatives on their committees, or how the FDJ or the state would react to this technically illegal act.

It was so interesting to see otherwise intelligent people struggle to run a simple meeting on democratic principles, something that is second-nature back home. They could trick the bureaucracy out of an apartment, laugh or just shrug at the mention of the Stasi, but they couldn't run a meeting. It was like finding out a friend who otherwise functions normally doesn't know how to tie shoes. Or maybe it was finding out how a society defines what's normal.

Typical of the way the circle of discussion broadened was the discussion the next afternoon at a university-wide gathering of students. Fidus went and reported back full of enthusiasm. Six thousand students were there, it was a continuation of a discussion from October 12th about creating new structures for student representation for the whole university. In that big of a group, it was much harder to reach radical decisions, like just throwing the FDJ out. FDJ representatives were there, Fidus said it was obvious how they were trying to channel all the reform energy into acceptable channels they could then control. They were pretty much ignored, but did manage to confuse the whole situation. Still it was exciting to hear things said in public that would have meant expulsion from the university only a week before. The Stasi faithfully filed a report for the highest government officials (see Scrapbook page 189).

Expanding Circles Of Protest

When things are looking bleak, it never hurts to have someone to blame, and things were certainly looking bleak for the SED. They selected Erich Honecker as their scapegoat and he handed in his resignation 'for reasons of health'. I was very excited to hear the news, my friends just rolled their eyes at my ignorance. Egon Krenz had been appointed to take Honecker's place. My friends were quick to point out that he had been in charge of the election commission that must have falsified election results. In addition, he led a delegation to China after the massacre on Tiananmen Square and praised the Chinese leadership for their handling of the 'problem'. They were better than I was at spotting the lie around the half-truth. Certainly Honecker was largely responsible for how the GDR turned out, but to blame him for everything was hardly realistic. East Germans had started demanding changes in the *system*. Switching people around at the top was not going to change that.

All the same, revolutions are not the kind of things that surrender the final word to a careful analysis. There's the soul-searching, the fear and trembling, the quieter, accidental ways of revolution. Uta told me the story of how the revolution came to Perleberg. It has a long-standing tradition as an army town and had a Soviet garrison of around 15,000 soldiers.

The first prayer service had been planned there for Thursday, October 26. Of course, everyone knew that an evening prayer service really meant an opportunity to address political grievances. Information was still being passed along by word of mouth, what the East Germans called *Buschfunk*, or wilderness radio. Unfortunately, the signal got a little garbled, perhaps there had been 'interference' from Leipzig. At any rate, most people recieved the message that the prayer service would be on Monday, October 23.

So on Monday night a crowd of people went to church and found themselves standing in front of locked doors. After milling around for a while, a few people decided to go downtown and somehow everyone else just kind of followed. About 600 people ended up 'demonstrating', or walking en masse, downtown. The local police and party officials were completely befuddled about how to handle this. They finally ended up just letting the people walk around. Another 600 East Germans had liberated themselves from the fear of the past, had discovered a new reality and soon turned to the task of now shaping that reality. Does it take more courage to demonstrate in a small town where you and the police know each other by name? On that night in Leipzig 300,000 people demonstrated, according to the rough estimates; a number equivalent to half the population of the city.

At the actual meeting then on Thursday night the church in Perleberg was packed, something that otherwise only happens at Christmas. The local party officials were there. Uta was pressed into duty as minute taker, saying something about her status as an outsider. Perhaps it said even more about her status as a church leader at the time. The public had a lot of pent up anger to spew at the officials. Any attempt they made to respond was whistled and booed down.

Back in Berlin, a group of actors from a theater called *Berlin Theater* started calling for a mass demonstration. Their union backed them up. They applied for permission to stage a demonstration on

November 4 in Berlin. Church prayer services and public meetings of the actors union were used to publicize it. The Stasi listening in on phone conversations reported that the word was being spread throughout the country. The demonstration also got mentioned in a couple of newspapers that were not as directly under party control.[46] Perhaps most important for setting the tone for November 4 was the fact that the government issued a demonstration permit. Official permission took away the remaining fear. It turned into the kind of joyous festival that the government had tried to organize for itself on its birthday on October 7. Except that this was a festival of protest.

The estimates ran from 500,000 to 1,000,000 demonstrators, in a city of 1.1 million inhabitants. A number of prominent actors, authors and opposition leaders spoke, as well as some party members who tried to pass themselves off as reform-minded. The home-made banners that many people had brought along were what made the biggest impression. One pictured Egon Krenz in bed wearing a grandmotherly nightcap and a hugh toothy grin. "Grandma, why do you have such big teeth?" was the caption. It so captured the mood that day that it entered East German folklore itself. No account of the demonstration in the following days was complete without describing it. Many of the banners were collected and displayed at the nearby Museum of German History.

This huge crowd gathered on Alexanderplatz, the center of East Berlin, at the base of the TV tower. It was about a mile down the main street of Berlin, Unter den Linden, from the Brandenburg Gate and thus the Wall. The security forces were very paranoid about a million people making a rush at the Wall. That tension was still in the air, as it was at every demonstration, but it had been almost a month since the People's Police or the Stasi had resorted to beating demonstrators. The completely peaceful demonstration would have been amazing for a crowd that size anywhere in the world. It symbolized the ripple of revolution that had started at the middle of the pond as now having reached the shore. It touched everyone in the country. Comparing the experience report of this demonstration found in the Scrapbook on page 191 with those of the previous chapter makes the point more elegantly than I could here.

During this whole time, the leaders were also under heavy pressure from the continued emigration of its citizens. Not only were hundreds of thousands protesting in the GDR, tens of thousands were protesting by going to West Germany. In addition to the thousands who were being let out with official (i.e. arbitrary) permission, starting November

1, the ban on travel to the CSSR without a visa was lifted. It only took two days for 4,500 to gather once more in the West German embassy there. This time they were simply allowed to emigrate to the West. Soon there was a steady stream of East German cars taking the shortened end-run around the Wall through Bohemia, instead of having to go all the way down to Hungary.

On November 5th the Czechoslavkian press agency announced that 13,000 GDR citizens had emigrated to the West through Czechoslavkia over the weekend. Two days later the rate given by the West German border guards was 300 East Germans an hour, 24 hours a day. In rough figures 100,000 people had left the country since Hungary opened its border to Austria on September 11. The next day the figure was up to 300 cars per hour, plus people taking the train. On the 9th of November it was announced that 225,000 people had left the GDR so far in 1989.[47]

East Germany had around 16.7 million inhabitants. That meant well over one percent of the population had emigrated. That's 1 out of every 100. It was discovering that your mailman was gone, the checker in your grocery store, several co-workers, a fellow church member, a friend, a son, a daughter; all gone. Since it wasn't clear when those who had left illegally could come back for a visit, it felt like they had vanished from your life. It forced every East German to make a conscious decision; should I go? should I stay? The answer to that question coupled with the anger that a friend had left, and the fear that a son or daughter might, was one of the most powerful drives behind getting 50,000 people together in Leipzig and ultimately a million on the streets of Berlin.

In the midst of all this turmoil, the church struggled to address all the issues. As people found their public voices out on the street, the meetings in the churches lost some of their importance. Many of the speakers on the public squares of the country were preachers, however. Less overtly religious when speaking in those settings, they still saw their messages based on the eternal truths of the Bible; freedom, truth, light, concern for the oppressed. They warned not to be taken in by the illusion the party was trying to present of changing itself. On the other hand, the humanity of those on the other side, the police, the party members and the Stasi did start to receive some mention as the mood swung from fear of them to anger to raw hatred.

Typical of the civil war mood of the country was an incident in our Marxist-Leninist class the end of October. The students managed to turn the lecture into a discussion. Frau Voth, our professor, used her authority and experience in fielding questions to keep the upper hand. What I really remember about that class session was her remark at the end that she hoped her son would make it home OK. He was serving his army time with the riot police unit in the town of Neuruppin. Many of the students in that class had faced riot police in much different circumstances. The idea of thinking of them in terms of having mothers just struck me as odd. These tensions, plus the trials of ordinary, everyday life and some attempt to make sense of it all were addressed in a variety of ways in church services. (See Scrapbook page 192 for two examples.)

Crossing The Wall In The Other Direction

Still trying to ride out the storm, the Party had the government resign, and they reorganized the Central Committee. A press conference was called for 7:00 pm on November 9th to talk about the decisions of the new Central Committee. It was broadcast live on GDR TV. The decision to allow travel to the West was announced. Startled journalists asked for confirmation and when the new regulations would go into effect. Eight o'clock the following morning was the answer.[48] The Germans have a word to describe such events and they used it often in the next days; *Wahnsinn* (craziness!).

Given the nature of GDR TV news, it's amazing that a few people were actually watching it. A crowd gathered at the border crossing at Bornholmer street and when it got large and boisterous enough, the guards apparently let them through just to keep the peace. By the time the West TV news came on at 10:30 pm, the first East Germans who had made it through were being interviewed on the streets of West Berlin!

Doors were knocked on and people thrown out of bed to be told the unbelievable news. All rushed to the nearest border crossing, some still in pajamas, to test the truth of this incredible rumor. As for the Johanneum, Ekkehard knocked on my door and asked if I wanted to go along to West Berlin. Matthias and Fidus were ready to go along, we also talked Angelika into coming. Nobody really believed it could be true, but what if it was? It wouldn't be the first non-rational (miraculous?) event in the last month.

We walked to the Friedrichstrasse station, the public transit gateway to West Berlin for all nationalities, a five minute walk away. There wasn't hardly any line, but there was great confusion. A police officer came out and announced that we would have to go to the travel agency located at Alexanderplatz and get a visa stamped into our ID's there. He assured us that they were going to open just for this occasion in the middle of the night. We would be able to get visas right away. We talked about going to the Bornholm Street border crossing, the one shown in the TV report. I objected, since it was only for West Berliners and I knew they'd never let me through there. The East Germans could get through the Wall easier than I could now. Since we didn't want to split up, we all got on the S-bahn and went to Alexanderplatz. There was a line of about 100 people lined up in front of the darkened travel agency. As we joined the line, we noticed cars pulling up on the nearby street. People jumped out and sprinted to get in line. After the parking spots were all full, people just started leaving their cars parked on the street in order to get in line quickly.

The rumor circulated that this was a trap to find out who wanted to leave the country (still a criminal offense at this time). We looked around nervously to see if police trucks were coming to arrest us. After 15 minutes some officials came and opened the travel agency for business. They let the first ten people in. By this time the line had grown very large and taken on a life of its own. The people at the back started pushing like crazy, up front we were so squashed we could hardly breathe. After waiting 28 years, they didn't want to wait another minute. I finally wiggled my way out since I didn't need a visa stamp anyway. When the first ten came back out and the second ten went in, we decided I should follow the first group back to Friedrichstrasse to see if they would really get across.

There was quite a line there now. The same police officer who had sent us away before now was telling all comers "Just get in line, you'll get through, calm down, children, just get in line". When I asked him what was with the song and dance he had given us about getting a visa stamp, he just shrugged his shoulders and looked away.

Back I went lickity split to get the others. In the meantime, Angelika had managed to get inside. The press of the crowd was so tight that it would probably be a while until anyone else from our group would be able to get in. Once Ekkehard, Fidus and Matthias found out they didn't need a visa stamp, we decided that I would try and fish Angelika out of the building somehow and they would go hold a place in line for us at Friedrichstrasse. After trying for half an hour, another guy, who had the same dilemma, and I managed to get his way talked past the policeman guarding the back door. This other guy got his girlfriend and Angelika out. He just stood in the room and yelled her name until she came over to talk to him. It was after 1:00 am by now. The S-bahn had quit running, so we had to walk almost a mile to the Friedrichstrasse station. By now there was no line, they were waving people through. It was obvious that this whole thing was sort of happening and was not being organized from the top.

It was *Wahnsinn* to see my friends walking through the control booths, the 'air-locks', with me. *We just walked through the Wall!* In February a young man had gotten shot and killed for trying to do the same thing. *Wahnsinn!* Fidus had been to the West once before to visit relatives. Ekkehard, Matthias and Angelika had never been there, although we all lived but a five minute walk away. *Waaaahnsinn!!*

I got the usual careful going over from the border guards. The others ID's were hardly glanced at. I had to stop and buy a S-bahn ticket for West Berlin By long standing agreement, East Germans fortunate enough to make it to West Berlin could ride for free. They didn't have any West money to pay for it anyway.

We went up to the platform for the S-bahn to Bahnhof Zoo, the center of West Berlin. The public transit authority had quickly organized overtime work crews, the trains ran all night. When the train finally came we all crowded in, as tight as possible. As soon as it start moving, everyone cheered. The windows were completely fogged up, so we couldn't see the Wall as we drove through it. The platform of Lehrter Stadtbahnhof, the first stop in the West, was full of West Berliners who cheered as the train pulled into the station. We stayed on until we got to Bahnhof Zoo. Once we got out, we realized we had no idea of what to do next. We hadn't even brought along a city map. We joined the crowd on the main street of West Berlin, Kudamm. The street was almost completely blocked by pedestrians. The East German Trabis and Wartburgs were mixed in with the West German Mecedes and BMW's. All were stuck in a traffic jam of pedestrians.

After gawking around for a while, we decided to go visit Fidus' boyfriend, Olaf, who was a theology student in West Berlin. We found a bus headed in roughly the right direction and climbed aboard. It was a double-decker. We got the front seats up top. The bus inched its way across Kudamm, giving us a nice view of the crowd.

Once we got to the end of the line, the driver told us we were still a half hour walk from our destination. Finally we just flagged down a taxi. We told him we were from the East, and ask for a ride. I kept my mouth shut so he couldn't hear my accent. He took us right to Olaf's front door for free.

It was a bit of an odd dating relationship. Every time he wanted to talk to her, he had to invest the 25 DM ($15) in the required daily exchange rate of 1 to 1. She could never go to see him. Fidus was so excited she was literally bouncing up and down. Olaf didn't seem to mind being thrown out of bed at 4:00 am! After the initial celebration, we went for a walk along the nearby Teltow canal. In that corner of West Berlin it formed part of the border of East Germany to the West. As we stood in the dark, looking through the mist across the water to the well-lit guard towers and death strip on the other side, we talked about the murders of Karl Leibknecht and Rosa Luxembourg. In 1919, their bodies had been found near where we were standing. I sensed the sort of surreal bending of history that made for Germans like Kafka or Marx or, well, for that matter, Fidus and Olaf. To celebrate as great a triumph as the fall of the Wall was also to contemplate equally profound German tragedies.

I called Tim around 7:00 am. Angelika and I got ourselves invited for breakfast, Tim came and picked us up. Again, it was the thrill of being able to return a visit. The Reimer's children couldn't figure out what Angelika was doing at *their* house. I went home to sleep. Most other East Germans went home in time to go to work. My theology student friends spent the day in West Berlin looking around. The professors back in East Berlin were undoubtedly a little lonely in their classrooms.

Wahnsinn!

Chapter 11

What do we do now?

The trash cans out on the street proved it was not a dream. The next morning they were overflowing. There were a set number of trash cans and usually only so much trash. That had changed over night. People had spent some of their carefully hoarded West Marks on Coca-Cola, bananas, Mars or Snickers candy bars. After all those years of watching commercials on West German TV, they now for the first time had the chance to buy those goods for themselves. And on the East Berlin side, every trash can within blocks of a border crossing proved it. How out of place those candy wrappers, banana peels and pop cans looked in East trash cans!

That first weekend 2 million East Germans poured into West Berlin, almost *doubling* the population of that city. They bought out much desired items such as citrus fruits, ketchup and coffee. East German TV gleefully showed empty selves in West Berlin for a change.

It was a time of high emotions. The seemingly impossible had happened overnight; it took us mere human beings a little longer to adjust our thinking. Angelika's brother, Thomas, had been fed up with his job and life in general in the GDR for quite some time. The opening of the Wall was the opportunity he had been waiting for. Together with a friend, he just took off for West Germany. When he didn't come home from his job at his usual time, his mother figured out what happened. During all the years she was raising her children, to go to the West meant never being able to come back. When she called Angelika, she was so distraught Angelika could barely get the story of what had happened out of her mother. Of course, it was now possible for Thomas to come back home as often as he wished. There were a few days of great heartache in the family until that new reality sank in, mixing with the euphoria that the Wall was now open.

Twenty-eight years after the Wall was erected to save the GDR it had been opened in a desperate bid to save the party's rule over the

GDR. This was the butt of many jokes and much bitterness. A display in a local bookstore of the memoirs and writings of various party officials who have been sacked in the last several weeks was accompanied by the small hand-printed sign 'All for nothing'.

The opening of the Wall culminated a long series of concessions the government had made to the opposition so far. In fact, so many concessions had been made so fast, that the question on everyone's minds became 'what should we do now?'. Should we try to rebuild East German society or would it be better to seek unification with and a society like West Germany? This question dominated life in the GDR for the next couple of months.

The party's answer was to continue juggling leadership and making concessions in the hope of keeping itself in power. On November 13, just a few days after the Wall opened, Hans Modrow was proposed as the new head of government. He had served the last 17 years as the top party official in the district of Dresden. However, he had never been accepted into the Politburo, the center of Party power. That made him seem like a bit of an outsider. He talked about a 'democratic innovating' for the GDR. The old garde of party leadership was completely removed from power and eventually even banned from the party. Some were arrested on criminal charges of corruption. Not all of them adjusted quickly to the new reality either. A fellow student reported that the top party official in her home county had committed suicide. There were several other suicides, other party leaders were admitted to hospitals for psychiatric care.

The overwhelming reaction of the people was to travel. On weekends cars were lined up for many kilometers at the border. In West Berlin, the city doubled its population every weekend for the next couple of weeks. The West German government had the policy of giving 100 DM ($65) 'greeting money' to any East German who made it to the West for a visit. Now they were all coming. They each got their 100 DM, almost a month's wages at black market rates. There were long lines in the banks, making it difficult for West Berliners to get their banking tasks done. There were also huge crowds in the grocery and department stores. The store owners complained that the East Germans were just looking and not buying anything. Most did, in fact, tend to horde their new West money. I went on 'shopping' excursions with some of my friends, spending a whole day just looking at the variety offered in the large department stores. Most of my friends didn't want to actually spend their West money, since they didn't know when they'd get more. They window shopped, looking wistfully at the goods on display.

The East Germans also kept demonstrating. They were still afraid that given half a chance the party would try to reassert its control of the GDR. There were weekly demonstrations in most larger cities now. The ones in Leipzig continued to be the largest and set the tone for the demands in the whole country. The demand to delete the 'leading role' of the party from the constitution was an expression of this fear of the party. The newest, and eventually most insistent, demand of the Leipzig demonstrations came with the shift from the slogan *Wir sind das Volk* to *Wir sind ein Volk* (We are one people).

That was a call for unification with West Germany. For some people this was seen as the ultimate guarantee that the Communists had forever been banished from power. For others, the demand for unity was based on the desire for a dramatic improvement in the standard of living as quickly as possible. The new battle cry was *Deutschland, einig Vaterland* (Germany, united fatherland), taken from the lyrics of the GDR national anthem. It was on account of those words that the singing of the lyrics had been forbidden after Honecker came to power in 1971. West German flags and calls for unification were the main features of the Leipzig demonstrations by the end of November.[49]

The streets, subway and S-bahn lines, phone lines and even the sewers had been cut by the Wall. Now they were starting to be reconnected. The GDR border troops were tearing down the Wall, starting at the street crossings. Quick temporary repairs were made to the street surface, a few border guards were posted to check passports and collect money from West Germans wanting to enter.

West Berliners and the many visitors pouring into West Berlin from West Germany, Western Europe and the US all decided to help tear down the Wall. People brought their own hammers and chisels, or rented them from enterprising individuals who were applying some free market principles to meet this new demand. A new term was coined, 'Wallpeckers' (*Mauerspechte*). Indeed, long stretches of the Wall, particularly those close to the Brandenburg Gate, were swarmed by 'Wallpeckers'. Hundreds of people diligently pecked away at the Wall. At first, they only dared to do it on the West side. Occasionally the West Berlin police would come by and confiscate the hammers and chisels.

In a few weeks, however, holes large enough to walk through had been carved into the cement. Now people were even venturing into the death strip. Hot dog stands, pop vendors, even 'pieces of the Wall' vendors for those too lazy to swing a hammer, gave the Wall the atmosphere of a county fair that went on for weeks.

Of course, I couldn't resist taking a few licks at the Wall myself. I wanted a few pieces to keep as mementos. None of my friends could understand why anybody would want a reminder of anything so stupid, so offensive. Once again it became plain to me that the Wall was not really my reality, but it sure was theirs.

The Third Way

With the government making so many concessions, the opposition groups soon found themselves in the embarrassing position of having all their demands met. Things were changing so fast it took a lot of energy just to keep informed. I would literally spend half of my day reading newspapers and listening to the radio to keep up with the changes. News that would have been worth a front page all to itself a month earlier might now buried in a small column on page 3 of the *Neues Deutschland*. Newspapers, instead of being ignored, were intently scrutinized front to back.

The opposition set about formulating new demands. Ending the 'leading role' of the party and free elections were at the top of their list. Many opposition leaders were not so sure about unification with West Germany though. They were idealists. They had protested the oppression of the GDR government at a time when that seemed a foolish thing to do. Back then, more staid GDR citizens considered the opposition leaders to be nothing but rabble rousers and trouble makers. The ideals they had struggled for certainly included freedom; freedom to travel, freedom to say what one thought, freedom to hold real elections. As those ideals were realized, some of the other ideals of the opposition leaders came to be stressed.

These other ideals were based on some of the same ideals as the communists espoused but had never realized. They wanted the new society being formed in the GDR to *really* make sure everyone had a job, that everyone *really* had enough to eat, adequate health care and a decent, affordable apartment. Looking at West Germany clearly showed that these ideals had not been realized there either. Thus, the search was on for a 'third way', for a societal structure that would guarantee individual freedoms as in the West and grant the peace of mind of social security as in the East.

Various leaders of the plethora of new opposition groups talked about keeping a separate GDR. Typical was the remark by Bärbel Bohley, one of the leaders of the New Forum. "The New Forum wants to preserve the GDR and change its contents. There are many social policies that are worthwhile and should be maintained, for example, the fact that there is affordable day care for every child. The children should, however, no longer be coloring pictures of army tanks there."[50]

Many East German citizens who were travelling to West Germany and seeing the great wealth there were not particularly interested in joining in on the search for a 'third way'. They liked what they saw in West Germany. That became their key demand.

At end of November two plans for the future of both Germanys were announced and competed for attention. Chancellor Helmut Kohl of West Germany called his a '10 Point Plan'. He outlined steps for cooperation where possible, but made it plain that extensive economic aid and cooperation would have to wait for 'basic reforms in the economic system'. The political unity of Germany was reiterated as the ultimate goal of his government. The reforms in the economic system were taken to mean that the GDR would have to fully adopt capitalism in order to proceed towards unification. Kohl portrayed this as being the wish of the majority in the GDR in addition to being the only reasonable alternative. Opposition leaders saw it as a direct threat to their search for a society that was better than both existing German societies, East and West. Their plan from the end of November called for developing a "socialist alternative to the Federal Republic".[51]

The opposition leaders were, after all, idealists, since realists would never have dared to take on the party's power. Their idealism had, in fact, proven to be a realistic challenge to that power. That didn't settle the issue, though. The struggle between 'idealist' and 'realist' positions was continued in the debate among my fellow students of what should be done next. We spent one of our English conversation classes debating what the future GDR society should be like. Only a few people had showed up, the general excitement kept attendance low in all classes.

We started debating who should decide if the society should take a third way or follow in the footsteps of West Germany. To my surprise, most of the students were skeptical of doing whatever the majority votes for. Things got so heated up that we switched back to German pretty quick.

"What if they vote to do the wrong thing?"

"Ha, there's no doubt they'll vote for the wrong thing!"

"What", I asked, "is this 'wrong thing'?"

"To just sell out to West Germany and do everything like it's done there!"

"But what if that's what the majority of the people want to do?"

"Well, it's just wrong!"

"So if that's what most of the people want to do, but it's wrong, how should the minority impose its will on the majority? Isn't that sort of what we just had?"

"Well, I don't know, but unemployment and homelessness and poverty are just wrong!"

The debate was settled for us by the course of events.

Working Together

On December 1 the party leadership made another concession to the opposition and the demonstrators. The 'leading role' of the party was removed from the constitution, but the GDR was still defined as a 'socialist' nation. Since Modrow had been installed as head of government, the party's direct influence on politics had been somewhat reduced. Usually decisions had been made at the highest level of the party and then carried out by the government, whose leaders were those highest party members. Now the new head of the party, Gregor Gysi, didn't have any government post. Modrow's suggestions were debated and voted on in the *Volkskammer*, the parliament. Of course, Modrow and a majority of parliament members were still members of the SED, so the lines of decision making had only become a little grayer. In order to break through this SED monopoly on power, the demand for a Round Table was raised by the opposition at a time when it was clear many of their other demands were being met. Now it became a question of power.

The proposed Round Table was loosely modelled after what had been done in Poland. There leaders of Solidarity had sat down with leaders of the Communist Party to work out the details for somewhat free elections and an agreement on governing the country in the meantime. GDR's precedents for this type of arrangement could be found in the 'Group of 20' in Dresden and the six people who made an appeal for non-violence in Leipzig on October 9. The leaders of the various opposition groups met already on October 30 to get this process started. It was largely the same group that had met together in Berlin back on October 4 to formulate an appeal for free elections. They asked church leadership for assistance. The suggestion of a Round Table was made to the government on November 21 by the opposition group Democracy Now on behalf of a wide range of groups. On November 30, the Federation of Protestant Churches of the GDR issued formal invitations to all the old and new political parties to come together at a Round Table meeting. The proposed meeting date was December 7.[52]

The mistrust of the government was so deep that they were forced to take this proposal seriously. Joining forces with the opposition would give the government some badly needed credibility. All the old political parties sent representatives to the first meeting. It was held in the *Dietrich-Bonhoeffer-Haus*, a church office building around the corner from the Johanneum. The street was jammed with people yelling slogans. If I opened the window of my room I could hear them. I kept it shut and turned on the radio so I could get some studying done.

The job of chairing the round table was passed around between a Protestant leader, Martin Ziegler, a Catholic priest, Karl-Heinz Ducke and a Methodist paster, Martin Lange. They started work on a new constitution for the GDR. More importantly, they called for national elections for a new parliament on May 6, 1990.

By the end of December, the government was willing to give the Round Table even more official status. They were invited to use a larger government meeting hall. They were also asked to send representatives to the Volkskammer to take part in the debates there, although they were not allowed to vote. The momentum was clearly still with the opposition.

There were a couple of gestures made by the GDR government right before Christmas as sort of Christmas presents to all Germans. On December 22, two big holes were knocked in the Wall on either side of the Brandenburg Gate. The one on the north side was for going 'out', the one on the south was for coming back 'in'. The Brandenburg Gate, located in the middle of the death strip, had been the symbol of Germany's division. Now it served as the symbol of the new coming together.

On a more practical note, it also gave nearest access from the Johanneum to West Berlin phone booths. The number of phone calls being made across the two parts of the cities had grown so fast that the few existing lines were completely swamped. It was impossible to get through. Now, however, it was only a five minute bike ride to a West Berlin phone booth. That made it much easier to keep in touch with the Reimers.

Tim had been working on getting an official invitation from a GDR church organization. This would provide the basis for getting a business visa and save him the $15 daily exchange fee every time he came to East Berlin. After trying for months, he finally got word from the Christian Peace Conference that they would be willing to do the paper work for him. He asked me to pick up his visa for him from their East Berlin office, saving him the $15 day visa fee. It would go into effect on January 1. That coincided with the other Christmas present of the GDR government. On December 24 the daily exchange fee was dropped. Now West Germans could go visit their relatives free of charge. Tim got his business visa when it didn't matter anymore.

As that experience of Tim's illustrated, all the changes going on in the GDR took away people's ability to plan ahead for their lives. When it takes several hours every day to keep up on what's changing, how can you plan anything? It was becoming clear that the GDR economy would not fare well in competition with the West German economy. One couldn't necessarily plan on keeping one's job. Subsidies on food, rent and utilities would be dropped sometime. Would wages or unemployment benefits keep up with the new rates? There were many reports of corruption on the part of high-ranking party officials. For those who identified with the old government, that news brought a sense of betrayal and dismay. For those who had never identified with the old government, it brought great disgust and anger.

The SED was certainly working to change its image, if nothing else. On the day that the *Neues Deutschland*, the main party paper, carried the news that the 'leading role' of the party had been taken out of the constitution, it also carried a new subtitle. It had dropped the 'Central Committee' from its official title as the 'Paper of the Central Committee of the Socialist Unity Party of Germany'. Two weeks later, the party gave itself a new, hyphenated name, the SED-PDS, the latter part standing for Party of Democratic Socialism. On the day of that announcement, December 16, the subtitle of the *Neues Deutschland* became simply 'Socialist Newspaper'. The call above the title 'Workers of all Nations, Unite' was dropped as well. The party tried to get on board the opposition's band wagon of appealing for a third way, knowing they'd have no voice whatsoever in a united democratic Germany. Typical of the cynicism shown by the party in this campaign to gain respectability was the printing of the GDR national anthem in *Neues Deutschland* on January 8. The party had been responsible for the ban on those lyrics for almost 20 years because they included the phrase 'Germany, united fatherland'

The beginning of January, our Marxist-Leninist classes were cancelled outright. Even Frau Voth agreed that it was pointless to continue. A teacher friend reported confusion in her grade school. The Pioneer's Salute used to start the day had been dropped. Now the teachers were unsure how to communicate to the children it was time to settle down and get on with the business of learning. In the high schools, especially in history, they were no longer even sure of what they should teach. At least they no longer had to go to school on

Saturdays. So many students had been skipping school on Saturdays so they could go with their parents to visit in the West that Saturday school was dropped as abruptly as our M/L classes.

Finals week was looming at the end of January in our department. Students gathered to write petitions asking for the cancellation of some finals and the postponement of others. Who could study with all the commotion? Besides, it was argued, participating in the demonstrations, in the reshaping of society, was more educational than going to classes, and certainly more important. A few students pointed out that it was actually at best a large minority of students who had actively demonstrated, but that point was ignored. The professors were amenable to most of the proposals. Some finals were simply dropped, since the whole course of studies was to be reformed.

As a sophomore class, the time for us to do our training in civil defense or the army reserves was looming. That was, of course, one requirement foreigners were excused from. Now we were informed that the whole class would be sent to work as orderlies in hospitals for the five weeks. The couple of students who planned to risk expulsion by refusing to participate in army training were very relieved.

It was reported that 343,854 East Germans had emigrated to West Germany in 1989[53], that's over 2% of the population, half of them gone since the Wall opened. You couldn't plan on who would stick around and who would go. Demonstrations, people leaving, anger, uncertainty; living in the GDR, it seemed the whole world had started spinning. What would life be like when it stopped? And would any of us be left standing?

The Mediating Role of the Church

At a time when the state was collapsing, many in the church in the GDR realized anew what a blessing the separation of state and church was. It had liberated them to take a fresh look at the Bible and to rethink old positions. That is how they found their message of peace, of non-violence and of looking out for the disadvantaged in society.

The church had amassed considerable good will by her conduct during the peaceful revolution. Indeed, the demonstrations launched from peace prayer services were exactly that, peaceful, at least as far as the demonstrators were concerned. The church had adopted a stance of reconciliation between oppressed and oppressor. There was a distinct bias in favor of the down-trodden, although admittedly never so much sympathy as to get the church in serious trouble. Still, church leaders were well prepared to take over the mediation of the round table in

Berlin, as well as the scores of local round tables that sprang up all over the country. In many cases key figures of the opposition were pastors or lay church members. And the stature of the church, based on its support and shaping of the opposition as well as its long-standing practice of limited cooperation with the state, give it the appearance of stability needed to make that mediation acceptable to all parties in this spinning society.

The church leadership did not just join in the political game of hardball. Many of the sermons that I heard in those couple of months admitted guilt on the part of the church, that none, in fact, were guiltless. Only two weeks after the Wall opened, the sermon in the Castle Church in Wittenberg noted that 40 years of Communism had not kept some people from going to church. The pastor lamented that now with the first chance to buy cheap bananas, some otherwise loyal Christians had gone to the West to go shopping instead of going to church.

In an official announcement on December 8, the church leadership acknowledged what many pastors had been saying from the pulpits (Scrapbook page 195). "Nobody, ourselves included, can claim complete innocence. Speaking as the Protestant Church, we freely admit this. We spoke openly already years ago, when many were quiet. But we were also silent at times when we should have spoken up."[54]

The calls grew for revenge against the party leaders who had robbed the people of their freedoms for all those years and left the country completely bankrupt. Soon anyone who had been a member of the party feared for their safety. In keeping with their stance of siding with the oppressed, the church called for judicial justice, not mob justice. One sermon in January talked about the Stasi as being the tax-collectors of society. It was exactly those kind of people that Jesus had sought out.

Uta reported from Perleberg that the pastor there had written a letter to the editor of the local paper stating that former Stasi employees should be given a chance to start over. He received a threatening anonymous phone call the same day.

The church was losing influence. Once the opposition could gather in the street for demonstrations, the protection of meeting in a church building was no longer needed. The church services were as poorly attended as a year ago. The policy of the church showing special interest in the down-trodden brought it great support during the brief span of time when people felt free enough to go to church and still down-trodden enough to appreciate it. When a new group of down-trodden appeared, party members and Stasi employees fearing for their lives, the church raised its voice to point out their worth as human beings, in spite of their great failings and the need to bring them to justice. Many East Germans had gone from feeling down-trodden to being very angry and uncertain of the future. The church's popularity started to faded almost as quickly as it had soared.

Chapter 12

Storming Stasi Headquarters

The Stasi didn't exactly go willingly. Most were completely unrepentant, they felt they were only doing their jobs. Some were in fact still at work. The question was, what were they doing? Were they still spying on the opposition? Were they still plotting to roll back the changes? Opposition groups occupied some of the district Stasi offices in cities outside of Berlin, but the national headquarters was apparently still in full operation. This in spite of government plans that had been announced to close it down. The New Forum and other groups finally decided more drastic steps were necessary to close down the Stasi.

A new mass demonstration was called for at the gates leading into Stasi headquarters. Those headquarters took up a whole oversized city block. Buildings that were eight to ten stories high were all the way around the outside. High metal gates made it impossible to see what was going on in the courtyard of those buildings. The whole building complex was referred to by the name of one of the streets that bordered it, Normannen Street. By now leaflets announcing demonstrations could be printed on real printing presses and distributed indiscriminately. Leaflets calling for a demonstration flooded the city. The final suggestions of the appeal were: "Write your demands on the walls of the Normannen Street! Bring your own paint and spray paint cans! We'll close the gates of the Stasi! Bring your own bricks and mortar!" The demo was scheduled for January 15, 1990 at 5:00 pm.

When I got there at 5:30, I had already missed the most exciting part. There were a couple hundred people milling around the gates to the complex on both Normannen and Rusche streets. The symbolic 'wall' they wanted to build to lock in the Stasi only got three layers high. People were just stepping over it on their way in and out of Stasi headquarters. One guy was painting a slogan on the wall of the tunnel leading into the courtyard with a can of paint and a brush. He spelled it out one huge letter at a time, I H R   H A B T   M A T T H I

A S D O M K E E R M O R D E T ! (You murdered Matthias Domke!) Three People's Policemen just stood and watched him, the German grammatical rule of putting verbs at the end of the sentence adding suspense to the painting ceremony. There was more graffiti inside the courtyard. Two police cars were also parked inside. One was letting people from the crowd use its loudspeaker to give speeches, the other had a small knot of people standing around it who were talking with the police officers.

A couple windows had been broken out of the courtyard side of the third floor of a building along Normannen Street. Every so often handfuls of paper would come flying out, fluttering to the ground in the breeze. The people had stormed Stasi headquarters!

I followed the stream of people going in a back entrance of that building. Like a river in reverse, the stream went up several flights of stairs, people branching out on the various levels and down different hallways. Some of the hallways were blocked off by New Forum volunteer orderlies trying to stem the destruction of property. Graffiti was painted in the hallway where the windows were broken out. Some people were carrying off electrical equipment, old tape recorders and such. One man was trying to cart off a VCR, but he was too drunk to figure out it wouldn't follow him home unless he unplugged it first. Some of the bystanders finally convinced him to leave it there.

I wandered into a repair room next door, with tools on the walls and spare parts on shelves around the rooms. There was no looting going on here, the rows of wenches above the workbench were still complete. People were merely looking over the assortment, as if to reassure themselves that the Stasi fixed broken toilets just like real people. The next stop was a big auditorium. Whatever picture had been hanging at the front of the room had been torn down and the spot where it used to be had been spray painted with a slogan comparing the Stasi to the SS. The foyer to this hall had a nice stain glass window incorporating the slogan 'Workers of all nations, unite', with a bust of Lenin, a couple of doves and soldiers of the National People's Army.

I followed the crowd on down the only hallway open to us on that floor. We came to a book storeroom, apparently for a bookstore for Stasi employees. People were picking over the books, helping themselves to the more desirable ones. Marx's writings were being conspicuously ignored. The books were all standard literature that could be found in most bookstores. The special attraction was that they were now free of charge.

My most vivid memories of that evening are of this book storeroom. There were picture books of the GDR, novels and how-to manuals. There were works by Lenin and Honecker's memoirs. And there were children's books. The Stasi had children! The faceless minions of this organization that caused so much fear, mistrust and brokenness were also fathers and mothers, who brought books home from work to read to their children.

The New Forum orderlies started going through the building systematically to clear it of demonstrators and spectators. On the way out, we went past a grocery store and a cafeteria. The adjoining walk-in refrigerators had double doors and simple labels, like Meat, then 10 yards further, Fruit and Vegetables and so on. We had seen only one small part of one building, which in turn was only a small part of the whole complex.

Once I was back outside, I stopped to look at the papers that had been flung out of the building. They were only blank custom declaration forms and the accompanying explanation brochures. They looked much more glamorous fluttering in the breeze than they did lying on the ground.

Now that most everyone was out of the building, people were just milling around the courtyard. There didn't seem to be much interest in breaking into other buildings. Hans Modrow, the prime minister, and some of the opposition leaders had come straight from their Round Table meetings to try and 'restore the peace'. They set up a platform and Modrow gave a little speech calling for the continuation of the non-violent principles of change. It a least helped distract the crowd from its growing boredom. I went home.

A Power Struggle

The State Security Service, the Stasi, was the structure that embodied the power of the party and secured its rule. They had amassed files on 6 million people, roughly one out of every three GDR citizens. After the Wall was opened and before free elections were held, it was the focus of attention, fear and anger about the injustices of the last 40 years. There was still no guarantee that these injustices had stopped.

About the same time as government leadership passed from Krenz to Modrow, the goals of the Stasi seemed to change as well. They had referred to themselves as 'the sword and shield of the party'. Now the party's domination of society was shrinking and the government, although still composed of party leaders, was becoming the dominate power of the land. Thus the Stasi concentrated its efforts on self-preservation and trying to create a new role for itself serving the government. As part of this campaign, the name was changed from

State Security Service to Office for National Security. The people weren't buying it, however. The nickname was simply changed from Stasi to Nasi (from *Staatssicherheitsdienst* to *Amt für Nationale Sicherheit*).

Already on December 5 the Stasi building in Dresden had been occupied by opposition groups. They wanted to prevent the Stasi from destroying all the files, which would wipe out any hope of finding out for sure who had worked for them as spies. Similar actions were taken to protect Stasi files in district capital cities, like Suhl, Gera and Erfurt. The next day the New Forum called for the complete abolition of the Stasi.

In the districts of Gera and Neubrandenburg, the process of evicting the Stasi was begun a few days later. The buildings they had occupied in every larger town and in every county seat were to be used as retirement homes, day cares or other community uses. The head of the Stasi for the district of Gera released a statement to the press expressing his regret that his department was being shut down since the GDR needed law and order now more than ever.[55]

In order to gain a measure of control over the disbandment of the Stasi, on December 17 Modrow's government announced the formation of a 'Control Committee for the Disbandment of the Office of National Security'. At the same time, it was announced that a new spy service with dual responsibilities of gathering information from foreign countries and watching out for domestic dangers would be formed. The domestic wing was to be called the 'Constitution Protection Service' (*Verfassungsschutz*). It was apparently to be modeled on the *Verfassungsschutz* in West Germany, which is in charge of gathering information on any groups deemed to be a danger to the constitution. The government was in effect saying, all governments have spy services, why shouldn't we? The idea of just changing the name of the agency and otherwise leaving the same people in charge of spying had the opposite effect. Instead of people agreeing with the government that a spy service was a good idea, the resolve grew to get rid of the Stasi once and for all.

On December 28, unidentified persons spray-painted anti-Soviet and pro-Nazi slogans on a monument in the Treptow area of Berlin that was dedicated to the liberating Soviet army . The party paper, *Neues Deutschland*, ran front page appeals for people to come to an anti-Nazi demonstration in the park close to that memorial on January 3. At the demonstration, which *Neues Deutschland* claimed was attended by

250,000 Berliners, speakers called for the establishment of a new *Verfassungsschutz* to combat the danger of a return of Nazism.

That call started to make a little sense to me, after all, just about anything would be better than letting a Nazi organization get off the ground. It took a couple of conversations with GDR friends to bring me back to earth. They pointed out that some of the graffiti was so far up the monument that the perpetrators must have used a ladder. It was ludicrous to think such an important monument was so poorly watched by the police that they wouldn't notice people sneaking around in the middle of the night with ladders. As far as my friends were concerned, it was all a plot to stir up sympathy for the idea of a new internal security apparatus. They were angry and a little afraid.

About the same time, a member of the GDR Mennonite church board related a story about the Stasi that confirmed their knack for self-preservation. He owned a large house that had several apartments for rent. The Municipal Apartment Agency had sent a person over that was to move into one the apartments. This person was being forced to leave his former apartment because it was a company owned apartment and he had been laid off. The company he had worked for was the Stasi. The fact that he was getting a new apartment so quickly, instead of waiting the usual three or four years, was proof that the old connections that favored the Stasi at every turn were still in good operation.

The first confrontation between the government and the opposition over the Stasi came at the Round Table meeting of January 8. The opposition groups were not happy with the Control Committee for the Disbandment of the Office of National Security's inability or refusal to answer questions the opposition raised about the continuing activities of the NaSi. They decided to boycott the Round Table until later in the afternoon, at which time they demanded that Modrow, the prime minister, appear before the Round Table to answer their questions. Did the Round Table have the authority to order the prime minister of the country around? Since there was no general agreement on this issue among the opposition groups and the old guard political parties, it was decided to postpone the whole issue for a week, until January 15.

In the meantime, the opposition printed its leaflets and called for the demonstration at Normannen Street. In retrospect, it's obvious why we were able to storm Stasi headquarters. A little looting would help the government make its case for needing more law and order. The headline of the next day's *Neues Deutschland* was "First stormed, then trashed", accompanied by a picture of people crowding through a broken glass door. According to the government statement the events on

Normannen Street showed that "the democracy that is beginning to develop is in great danger".[56]

On the other hand, New Forum claimed that the "gate to the Normannen Street was to be blocked off by New Forum orderlies. ... The speed with which the gates were opened from the inside allowed the orderlies to be overrun. They were no longer able to prevent people from entering the premises. It remains unclear how the gates were opened."[57]

So in a sense everybody won. The government got its 'looting' and could make a fuss about internal security. The opposition was able to occupy Stasi headquarters, ending all activities there. Even more important, they had forced Modrow to come report to the Round Table. It was the last real test of power the opposition had to make. The party's and the government's power was broken for good. Only free elections could resolve the question of power now.

What were the Stasi up to?

Amidst the general chaos that had become life in the GDR, one heard constant revelations about the role of the Stasi in maintaining the status quo of the old regime by whatever means necessary. The storming of Stasi headquarters, as we have seen, had been quite a while in the making. It was just one milestone in the continuing unmasking of the people who worked for the Stasi and the role they played in the events of the fall of '89. Many people, myself included, had never been directly confronted by the Stasi. We were all curious, however, about what the Stasi had been up to and why. We were curious about what on earth those people were thinking.

One of the focal points of this curiosity in Berlin was the "Investigating Committee into the Events of October 7/8". Actually two committees had been formed concurrently and independently of each other at the end of October. One committee was official in nature, appointed by the City Council and included prominent opposition leaders and authors as well as high-ranking police officials. The other committee was unofficial, having been formed by the opposition leaders who had been in contact with the demonstrators who had been beaten on that weekend. The two committees agreed to work together, provided that the police representatives were not granted voting rights. That would have been too much like the fox guarding the chicken coop.[58]

The Investigating Committee met about once a week from the beginning of November until the end of January. They interviewed all the ranking police, government and Stasi officials, including Erich

Mielke, the former Minister of the State Security Service. What most people assumed was quickly confirmed. The Stasi had perpetrated the worst of the violence on that weekend. The weekly hearings kept the Stasi in the news.

The questions quickly centered around the issue of who gave the command for the violence. The Stasi officers interviewed maintained that they had never ordered beatings, at worst a few individuals had gotten a little carried away. The opposition leaders who had been on the receiving end felt that all the activities had been carefully planned out and that the Stasi officers were covering up the facts to protect each other from criminal charges. This impasse, particularly the lack of progress in finding out who was to blame, contributed to the atmosphere of urgency in completely shutting down the Stasi. The rising level of frustration in the general public in turn gave the government reason to warn about potential unrest and thus the need to keep the Stasi.

There were two aspects to the question of who gave the commands. The first was concerned with structures, who could give orders to whom between the party and the Stasi. The second issue was what the leadership had done to mentally prepare police to be ready to beat up on peaceful demonstrators.

The issue of structures was very confusing. The wide spread perception was that the Stasi were a 'state within the state'. The theory was that their wide-flung network of informants gave them such power that they could do whatever they pleased. This theory was intended to shift blame for all the problems in the GDR from the party to the Stasi.

In fact, the Stasi were known internally as the 'Sword and Shield of the Party'. The Politburo was the boss, the Stasi supported party leadership policies. Mielke put it this way, "The resolutions of the party are our law."[59] One of the opposition citizen's group that was investigating the matter broke the Stasi's work on behalf of the party into three parts. The Stasi were first to appraise the various situations as assigned. That information was then distilled and passed on to the party officials along with recommendations. Finally they were to take steps to 'maintain control'. As the party leadership lost its ability to admit to and address problems, the final phase of maintaining control encompassed more and more of the Stasi's work. They would perhaps file criminal charges for defamation of the state or attempting illegally to emigrate in order to get 'troublemakers' off the streets. Or they would use informants who were close to the 'targets' to attempt to influence their behavior.[60]

Informants, called Informal Co-workers, IM's for short in German, were in many cases the only source of information for the first phase of assessing a situation. There were three main categories of motives that the Stasi looked for when recruiting IM's. The first, "Positive convictions of a world view, moral, and political nature", which meant people who were willing to cooperate with the Stasi to help preserve the socialist system of the GDR. Sometimes IM's were recruited for patriotic duties like counter-espionage, then turned against other 'targets'. A second motive was "personal needs and interests". This was a nice way of saying that some IM's did their spying in order to secure promotions, entrance to a university or a little pocket money. The final motive was "restitution efforts". This was a arrangement whereby people agreed to become IM's in exchange for having a criminal sentence dropped. (See Jürgen Fuchs' poem in the Scrapbook. page 199)

There were IM's for specific areas, like a factory or an apartment block. There were IM's with 'direct enemy contact', who were to infiltrate opposition groups. There were IM's to serve as couriers and even as leaders of other IM's. IM's generally signed a commitment to serve the Stasi. From that point on there was no turning back. Breach of contract was, of course, a legal offense.[61]

By the late 80's, there was a new motivation for some Stasi and IM's. They hoped to bring about change by working through the system. Like the general population, there were differences of opinion among the Stasi about the need for reforms based on the model of the Soviet Union. In addition, the Stasi who complied the data from all the various sources were well informed about the extent of the difficulties facing the GDR.[62]

A friend of mine related how a member of her church young adult group had confessed to reporting on the group to the Stasi. It was a heart-breaking revelation. After much discussion, the IM remained in the group. They accepted his argument that he was only trying to tell the Stasi how bad things were in order to convince them to join in demanding changes.

One opposition group went so far as to suggest that the whole peaceful revolution had been masterminded by the Stasi. After all, they had IM's working for them in all the major opposition groups. Peter Zimmermann, one of the six signers of the plea for non-violence that was so important in Leipzig, had been an IM. IM's even provided leadership for a couple of opposition groups. The files were actually found to show that in the district of Neubrandenburg the Stasi office there had developed complete programs to be used at opposition sponsored peace seminars![63]

The Enemy is Everywhere

Figuring out who the IM's were and what role the Stasi played in GDR society was puzzling enough. A second puzzle was, what were the police and Stasi thinking when they indiscriminately beat up peaceful demonstrators? Where they acting under orders? Or was it more a matter of mass hysteria?

The head of Humboldt University's theology department, Heinrich Fink, had originally been appointed to the official Investigating Committee into the Events of October 7/8. He offered a seminar class for Spring Semester 1990 based on the way the police had been trained to think about their enemies. I decided to take the class.

Michael Römhild, a police sergeant who had been on duty that weekend and was also a member of the Investigating Committee, told our class about the preparations the police had made for the 40th anniversary celebration of the GDR. Back in March 1989 they started training with riot gear. There was intensive political schooling held for all the security forces. From childhood on, they had heard about an 'enemy' that wanted to destroy their country. There was no doubt that Western intelligence agencies were operating in the GDR (just as Eastern agencies had spies in the West). The new schooling turned the focus of the fear of the 'enemy' from beyond the borders to the 'enemy' within. The police and other security forces were repeatedly told that the 'enemy' would try to disrupt the birthday celebrations. The only reason given for the disruptions were Western intelligence agency influences. There were no other problems in the GDR.

There was no doubt about who this enemy was. There was even an official definition. (Scrapbook page 200) The people who met in prayer service for peace and change in the GDR fit this definition. Since the opposition met in churches, the local pastor was to be thought of as the 'arch-enemy'. The goal of this training in thinking about the enemy was clear. "Concrete knowledge about the enemy is the basis for the deep feelings of hatred, disgust, disaffection and mercilessness towards the enemy, which are extremely important requirements for a successful conclusion of the struggle against the enemy."[64]

Another reason the police and security forces learned to hate the opposition was that every national holiday meant extra security was needed. All that overtime meant that the 'fruitcakes' out demonstrating for change were keeping security forces from enjoying time off with their families.

Police and their families were also closely watched. They were among the civil servants not allowed to have contact with Westerners. Until the late 1980's they were not officially allowed to watch Western TV. If they did so, they had to be on guard to act ignorant when conversations turned to the latest antics of Alf or JR Ewing. They certainly would never have actually talked to a pastor or bothered to find out what the opposition really wanted.

The ideological indoctrination hit its high point on the weekend of the October 7 and 8. Rumors were spread among the police force that demonstrators had called for hanging police from the street lights. The police were told that the counter-revolution had taken to the streets and that this treason was to be stopped by whatever means possible. The police had a very different impression of what was going on than the demonstrators did. There were also apparently Stasi agents dressed in leather jackets mingled in with the demonstrators in order to instigate violence against the police. Under those circumstances, when the two sides met, it was no wonder the police were so willing to use their riot sticks to beat peaceful demonstrators. One policeman described what he saw that night at the Gesethmane church this way: "On Stargarder Street, people all over the place, candles all over the place, flickering lights..., absolute chaos - the gates to hell. I didn't know that that's what the counter-revolution looked like."[65]

Creating Reality

Not only did the system create a separate reality for the security forces, the Stasi in turn were part of an attempt to create a certain reality for all of the GDR. The image they projected was that of being everywhere and checking everyone. In fact, apathy, fear or agreement with party propaganda made the majority of East Germans no threat to the government. Thus, they were, in fact, not bothered by the Stasi. It was only the people who challenged the system who were actually spied on and harassed. This was to make it clear that some forms of criticism were simply unacceptable to the Stasi and thus shouldn't be made, regardless of how necessary the criticism might have been.

The Stasi did indeed have the network stretched out everywhere to catch those who misbehaved. One of the newspapers printed a special edition that was a list of the over 10,000 addresses of apartments or buildings used by the Stasi. Everyone could check to see if the Stasi had been using an apartment in their building for secret meetings with informal co-workers. That was the case for the post office across the street from the Johanneum. In addition, one whole floor in that building had been turned over to the Stasi department in charge of listening in on phone calls. In the dorm for foreign students where I lived in Storkower Street two of the dorm rooms made the list of Stasi apartments.[66] This corresponded with the fact that the resident director there, Frau Ronsch, was demoted to laundry lady. She had probably only gotten her director position by agreeing to cooperate with the Stasi. It was embarrassing to go turn in dirty sheets to her knowing what she had done. What do you say to a lady like that?

It took awhile for people to adjust to the new reality of doing things that used to be illegal but were now allowed. A psychologist, Jürgen Fuchs, who had been arrested by the Stasi and eventually deported to West Germany, described it this way. "After the Wall opened, whole shifts of workers went to West Berlin, just to look, just to see if they could. They could! There was a group of such people, a young lady said 'Man, this is great, unbelievable, we're just running around here'. And then she looked at her colleagues and said 'So when are they going to nail us?' That reaction, when are they going to nail us, is a typical sign of trauma. Security, in the sense of protection, isn't present, state security in the sense of repressive overkill is. Real security, spontaneity, breathing easy, trusting, all have to be practiced before they become real."[67]

For the opposition the question of a 'created Stasi reality' came down to the question of how one changes it. Just as some informal co-workers hoped to affect change by working inside of Stasi structures, some of the people working for change hoped it would come through party reforms and government changes, as had been the case in Hungary and the Soviet Union. For others the system was the problem, so they wanted it all thrown out. That is, they worked for change outside of and against the system, more analogous to the Polish situation.

Typical of this debate were the discussions between students of the theology department of the Humboldt University and the *Sprachenkonvikt*, a nearby seminary that had been completely financed by the church and thus not as tightly controlled by this system. As part of the merging of those two seminaries in March 1991, there was opportunity for the students to reflect on how they had decided where they would prefer to study theology.

"The reason I decided to study at the *Sprachenkonvikt* is that I wanted to get out of the ideology swamp the party had sunk society into. I wanted a chance to think for myself without the pressure of having to take Marxist-Leninist classes."

"The reason I decided to study at the University was to face up to reality. I couldn't see much sense in hiding from Marxist theory. It was everywhere anyway. As a future pastor I wanted to learn how to handle communist officials in my village. You had to talk to those people in order to improve things."

"There you go, you can see how the Stasi influenced your thinking. Don't you see that the main job of the Stasi was to *create* a new reality? Even trying to talk to those people reenforced their false reality. The only thing to do was to retreat to a stronghold where one could still think clearly and tough it out until better days arrived."

"Oh, make me puke! I can't stand it when cowards in the church now try to play the martyr!"

Opposition leaders who are now in positions of government power in the united Germany are still hashing out this debate. The current governor of the new province of Brandenburg, Manfred Stolpe, used to be the chief administrator for the Protestant church in that province. As such he had frequent contact with the Stasi. He tried to keep the Stasi from going after the opposition too eagerly and the opposition from getting too far out of line. He tried to keep the peace at the cost of pushing for reforms. Other opposition leaders who are now members of the Brandenburg provincial parliament resented his half-hearted approach and now question his ability to govern because of it.

There is no end of the personal conflict in the former GDR because of the evil of the Stasi. As those who had been spied on gain access to their files, they discovered which friends, in some cases, even that a spouse, were delivering information to the Stasi. That poses a lot of big questions about human weakness, forgiveness, guilt and reconciliation.

There are still a few voices calling for learning from the whole sad episode. If the Stasi taught that (false) knowledge about the 'enemy' was key to creating the atmosphere of hatred necessary to destroy human lives, perhaps efforts to gain accurate knowledge of future 'enemies' in a spirit of love is a path to peace.

(A former IM, Monika Haeger, tells of her experience with getting to know the enemy in the Scrapbook. page 201)

Chapter 13

Election Time

There were lots of other things going on in the GDR at this time besides the agony with the Stasi. The Monday demonstrations in Leipzig continued to serve as a barometer of the mood in the country. Fred Fransen, a MCC volunteer in Brussels, came to visit and we went to Leipzig to see first hand what those demonstrations were all about.

By mid-January the demonstrations had acquired a much different reputation than the one they had originally. They had become a forum for demanding immediate unification and improvements in the standard of living as well as a place for the various political parties to campaign. Most of the leading West German parties had found corresponding groups in the East to support for the March 18 elections. The anti-foreigner party, the Republicans, were considered especially scandalous because they were outlawed in the GDR. Their campaign posters and stickers went like hot-cakes.

The demos were also marked by calls for bringing the old guard to justice. Since the prosecutors and judges were still part of the old guard and many of the 'crimes' of the party leadership had in fact been legal under GDR law, there was little progress on this front. The uncertainty of what the economy would do fed this search for scapegoats. There was considerable concern that the demonstrators would resort to mob justice. All of this seemed a far cry from the original spirit of the demonstration and the prayer services for peace, so we weren't sure what to expect when we got to Leipzig on Monday, January 29.

We went to the Nikolai Church, the place where the prayer services had started. We had trouble getting in. The church was filled to overflowing. The doors were locked to keep it from getting too full. We managed to sneak in when someone else came out. At least the content of the meditation hadn't changed. The pastor called for tolerance, patience and a continued commitment to non-violence.

After the church service we went to Karl Marx Square. Loud speakers had been set up, a big crowd had gathered already. The crowd up by the speaker's platform was loud and boisterous. The West German flags were all congregated up there. These were symbols of demands for quick unification. Once we went to the back of the Plaza, the shouting was completely gone and the crowd was very orderly. The crowd was huge, the estimate of 100,000 seemed right. One speaker related that last week left-wing demonstrators had been chased by right-wing demonstrators. He plead with the crowd to stick with the non-violent tradition of the demonstration. Another speaker warned about rents going up once apartments were privatized. The alternative she suggested sounded too much like socialized housing for the crowd up front. They booed and whistled so loud that she was unable to finish her speech.

After about 45 minutes worth of speeches, the whole crowd took off for a walk around the inner city ring. This was precisely the activity that had been so dangerous to the government's control of society. Now that that control had been broken, it was just a nice walk around town. The demonstration must not have been too violent in the past, cars were still parked on the streets where the demonstrators walked. Thousands of people streamed past these cars on the sidewalk and in the street, but the owners were apparently not worried about them getting scuffed up.

Along the way there were booths where all kinds of campaign material were given out or sold. The other source of entertainment was to shout slogans. *Schwarz, Rot, Gold, Wir sind das Volk* (Black, Red, Gold, We are the people, the colors coming from the German flag) and *Deutschland, Einig Vaterland* (Germany, united fatherland, a line from the GDR national anthem) seemed to be the favorites. There was also a catchy little song that was sung between slogans about *Keiner will die SED* (No one wants the SED).

Rounding one corner we came upon a small cluster of people having an argument. It appeared to involve right-wing West Germans and left-wing East Germans. Some of the people standing at the edge of the crowd started yelling *Nazis raus* (Nazis out), meaning the right-wing people. Others misunderstood and picked up the chant as *Stasi raus*. The two favorite groups to hate seemed to be facing off. The argument heated up. It looked like a fight was about to break out.

Just then people dropped out of the flow of demonstrators going by. They started chanting one of the original slogans of the Leipzig demonstrations, *Keine Gewalt!* (No Violence!). More people stopped and joined in that chant. Soon the small knot of angry people was surrounded by people chanting 'No Violence'. I don't know if they drowned out the argument or if they actually got the people ready to start a fight to thinking, at any rate the cluster of people eventually broke up. Violence was avoided. The fledgling tradition of non-violence still had power on that day. The same procedure was repeated a few more times along the demonstration route.

For all the reports in the newspapers of the danger of mob justice breaking out and the few arguments we saw, the whole atmosphere on that day was more a rowdy celebration of victory than anything else. Unfortunately, the demonstrations continued to deteriorate. With a higher sense of purpose gone, it became not much more than a good excuse to get together and look for trouble. By February 27, all the original organizing groups withdrew their support because they felt the demands for Germany unity and strength coupled with a strong right-wing Neo-Nazi presence gave the whole event a 'Nazi flavor'. Those who had won the peaceful revolution had hoped for a different outcome.[68]

March 13, the last Monday before the elections, was the last Monday evening demonstration in Leipzig. Even though they only lasted 6 months, one could say it marked the end of an era.

Transformations

In other areas of life the rate of change was picking up. It was as total and far-reaching as the transformation of the Leipzig demonstrations had been.

The party realized that they would have to do a lot of things differently to win votes in the March elections. They had some of their cabinet members step down to make room for opposition leaders in the government. They were probably hoping to spread some of the blame around for the nose dive the economy was in.

The party also worked hard on creating a new image. The old party emblem was dropped the end of January. Party members had formerly worn it pinned to their lapels in order to show off in public. Those pins had long since disappeared from view. Now the extra large version of it hanging on the party headquarters building downtown was removed. Only the outline where the bricks had weathered differently remained.

The beginning of February the SED-PDS became simply the PDS (Party of Democratic Socialism). The old name was now gone, although the ideal of Socialism was clearly retained. In an attempt to repair the party's image of having been the exploiters in the old system, some three billion marks ($2 billion at official exchange rates) were transferred from party bank accounts to help out government finances.

Even the most important party paper, *Neues Deutschland*, revamped its look again, adopting a new style of print for its heading, as if that would make up for the years of lies in its reporting. Some of the new advertising the paper took on signaled at least a little change of heart. They ran several half-page advertisements for a Billy Graham crusade that was coming to East Berlin!

Another transformation was the increased contact with things Western. Fidus, for example, finally got to go visit her boyfriend's parents. When Fidus and her boyfriend dropped in unannounced one time, his mother promptly apologized for not having any bananas in the house. Many West Germans assumed that East Germans were starving for that fruit. Breaking down stereotypes was a two-way street.

My favorite comment that East Germans typically made on returning from trips to West Germany usually went something like this:

"I've never been so mortified in all my life! I looked all over that stupid toilet for the flusher. I couldn't find the dang thing. I finally had to ask the lady of the house how it flushed! Of all the strange contraptions those West Germans have!"

East German toilets either had a tank up high with a drawstring to pull or a knob protruding from the tank behind the stool that had to be pulled up. West German toilets did in fact have numerous different flushing mechanisms. This type of conversation was especially hilarious if a larger group of East Germans was swapping 'West toilet horror stories'. A remark about the softness of West toilet paper always served as a footnote to such conversations.

At the same time numerous changes were taking place at the university as well. Marxist-Leninist classes had of course been dropped fairly quickly. The sport and Russian language requirements were the next to go. I was now allowed to move into the Johanneum officially. The discussion about revamping requirements for graduation was so intense that the list of classes being offered for second semester was released only a few days before the semester began.

The ritual of going through the Wall had changed considerably as well. All paperwork requirements had been dropped for West Germans at Christmas time. As an American, I still had to fill out a little card every time I crossed the border. That was finally dropped at the end of January. Now I was waved through the border crossing points as fast as anyone else.

The real adventure was trying to talk my way past border guards at the crossings meant only for Germans. The Brandenburg Gate was one such a crossing. It was also the nearest crossing for me to get to a West Berlin phone booth. I worked out a pretty good story about being a student in East Berlin and having residency status there. For awhile I even carried a newspaper clipping from *Neues Deutschland* that stated that foreigners with residency in the East were eligible to cross at 'Germans only' crossings. Things printed in the *ND* carried a lot of weight with East German officials. Fortunately for me the system was so complicated the border guards never realized that the law stipulated that student visas didn't qualify as residency. It's hard to describe the satisfaction to be derived from talking one's way past an East German border guard.

The beginning of February, whole segments of the Wall were offered for sale. The street that ran past the Mennonite Church in East Berlin was reconnected with West Berlin. A metal fence replaced the Wall around the Brandenburg Gate. The border guards had lost their old enthusiasm. During a border crossing the end of February, I was getting ready to start the standard argument about why I should be let through a 'Germans only' crossing when the border guard *apologized* for his mistake and waved me through.

Rapid change made life seem uncertain. Political jokes disappeared. The politicians were changing faster than new jokes could make the rounds. Life had somehow become too serious for jokes anyway. The upheaval was visible on the office index posted in the town hall of Perleberg. Uta gave me a tour of it when I was there visiting her. Some municipal government departments had been closed, their office numbers taped over. New departments, like environmental affairs and water management had been opened. Their office numbers were merely written in with pencil.

People continued to move out of the GDR at an alarming rate. In January 1990 56,177 people left the country.[69] If that pace kept up, by year's end it would mean four percent of the population had left.

Unemployment became a reality for the first time as well. Fifty one thousand people had applied for the newly created unemployment benefits. Many of them were laid-off Stasi and government workers.[70]

Things seemed to be spiraling out of control. People were looking for someone to blame, someone to punish.

Homeless Honecker

There can be no doubt that Erich Honecker was a good person to blame. The structure of the party and GDR society was very much that of following orders from the top down. As the head of the party and leader of the country, Honecker was one of the people clearly responsible for the dismal shape of the economy and the years of repression.

Honecker and many of the other top leaders had lived near Berlin in an exclusive housing development called Wandlitz. The houses were modest in comparison to Western political leaders homes. However, the stores there had Western consumer goods for low prices in East money. The hypocrisy of the leadership living with Western imports while exhorting the masses to do without enraged East Germans when it was revealed. The housing development was closed and the former tenants kicked out.

Already on December 5, 1989, investigations were started into criminal activities that Honecker might have been involved in as head of state. Since he wrote the laws, the investigation to prove he did something illegal promised to be tricky. In addition, his doctors said that he was physically unfit for questioning, much less imprisonment.

An independent doctors commission was formed to examine Honecker. They reached the same conclusion, adding that a kidney tumor needed operation soon. Any questioning would have to wait until he recovered sufficiently from that operation.

The beginning of January, Bishop Forck, head of the Protestant Church for the area of Berlin and Brandenburg, reported that the government had asked the church to help look for a new home for Honecker. He had been kicked out of his old government home in Wandlitz and would more than likely be declared physically unfit to stand trial. Since he wasn't going to jail, he would, in effect, be homeless. The government was worried that no matter where they found him an empty apartment, the neighbors would lose little time in organizing a lynch mob. Bishop Forck agreed that it would be possible for the church to find room for Honecker and his wife, Margot, in one of the large church institutions. He encouraged the government and the SED to look a little harder before coming to the church.

Finally the Attorney General of the GDR announced on January 29 that charges of high treason were to be filed against Honecker and several other former high-ranking officials. They had disregarded the constitution on numerous points in order to usurp power. Honecker was transfered from the hospital to prison. His doctor attested to the fact that he was physically unfit for trial.

Sure enough, the next day Honecker was released from prison and taken to a large institution for mentally handicapped adults that was run by the Protestant Church[71]. It was called Lobetal or Praise Valley.

Uwe Holmer was the pastor who was the administrator of Lobetal. Twelve hundred senior citizens and mentally handicapped people lived in this church institution, so large that it was more of a church village really. He had been approached already the end of 1989 by church leadership about the possibility of taking in Erich and Margot Honecker. After much discussion, the Holmer family and the board and administration of Lobetal agreed to take in Honeckers, if no other housing for the couple could be found.

The original plan was to put them up in an apartment that was temporarily available, in the expectation that their stay would not be all that long. There was some opposition in Lobetal to that plan. The opposition was especially strong, though, in general public opinion. The idea that Erich and Margot were taking up living space, a commodity their policies had kept all too scarce, would simply not go over. So Pastor Holmer and his wife invited Honeckers to come live in their own home.

They were given three small rooms in the upstairs of the house. One was fixed up as a kitchen, so that the couple could prepare their own food. Margot was only 11 when her mother died, and had taken care of her father's household after that, so, as Pastor Holmer noted, "she was a very practical lady" when it came to housekeeping.

When they were together, they mostly talked about Honeckers' daughter or granddaughter or Erich's 10 years in a Nazi prison. They never talked about political or spiritual things. Pastor Holmer noted that the political events, and especially news reports of the great hatred in the general population against the Honeckers personally, really bothered the old man, even physically affected his health.

Pastor Holmer was asked what connection there was between his Christian faith and his family taking in the Honeckers. "Meditation, prayer, the word of God, including obedience to the main principles in the word of God are my most important priorities. And this word of God says 'Forgive, as you have been forgiven'."

A further statement of his, when talking about the difficulties his family had in dealings with the state, makes his attitude all the more remarkable. "It came time for my own children to take part in the socialist youth dedication (*Jugendweihe*). Naturally I resisted that. The consequence was that our children were not able to get into any university."

Margot Honecker was Minister of People's Education during this time, she and her husband were directly responsible for denying Pastor Holmer's ten children higher education and they found welcome in his home in time of need![72]

Pastor Holmer still felt that the Honeckers must be tried for the injustices they had caused and punished, if found guilty. He had, however, found a way to combine the Biblical motifs of justice and forgiveness. That was not the prevailing mood of the country. In fact, there was quite an uproar.

Church leadership was deluged with phone calls and letters protesting this action. A few people even quit the church. After all the terrible things Erich Honecker had done, he did not deserve to be taken in by the church. Bishop Forck finally felt compelled to release a statement explaining the church's action. He outlined the course of events leading up to the Honeckers' move to Lobetal. The government had asked the church four separate times to help find housing for them. The Honeckers themselves had asked for the church to help them, since that was the only place where they "would feel relatively safe". The church was not standing in the way of the criminal justice system, nor were the Honeckers taking housing away from anyone.[73]

The Honeckers' fear was borne out when the government attempted to move them into a government retirement home in small town of Lindow. A crowd gathered quickly to protest their arrival. The Honeckers were forced to return to Lobetal.[74] They finally left there on April 3. Erich was admitted to a Soviet army hospital close to Potsdam. Later the Soviet government flew them to Moscow, ending attempts for the moment to put the couple on trial.

Election Fraud Part II

At the same party meeting on January 20 when the SED-PDS decided to get rid of the old party emblem, a plan to include opposition leaders in a new coalition government was also approved. A few days later, the Christian Democratic Union (CDU), a former partner party of the SED, announced that its cabinet members were resigning their posts to make more room for the opposition. CDU was also the name of the ruling party in West Germany. The West CDU had put pressure on its namesake party in the East to withdraw from the GDR government. The government's credibility was so low that its only hope of survival was to 'borrow' some legitimacy from the opposition. At the same time, such 'borrowing' was sure to speed up the dissolution of the old government's power structures. The West CDU hoped having the East CDU pull out of the government would speed the demise of the GDR altogether.

On January 28 agreement was reached on a new coalition government between opposition leaders and the government. A new date for parliamentary election was also set, March 18. It would be the first free election in that part of Germany since 1933. The new coalition government would rule until then.[75]

The basic question facing the GDR only three months ago was if changes would be allowed. Then the question became if the changes would be reversed or not. Now, the question had become, what new course do the citizens of the GDR want to chart for their country? It was harder to form a consensus on this issue. There was consensus on having East German citizens make that decision in their new role as voters in elections that offered real choices. There was an array of options offered to the voters by the parties.

The PDS (Party of Democratic Socialism), the old party, had little new to offer. They continued to hammer away on the evils of capitalism, like unemployment and homelessness.

The SPD (Socialist Democratic Party) was a brand new party in the East. The old East SPD had been forced into a shotgun wedding with the Communist Party in 1946, giving birth to the SED (Socialist Unity Party of Germany). The new SPD quickly established links to the West SPD, the leading opposition party of West Germany. Their platform was roughly similar to that of the West SPD. They were in favor of a slower paced unification. Many of its leaders came from opposition groups or the church.

The West German FDP (Free Democratic Party) had found allies in two new parties in the East, the Alliance of Free Democrats (BFD) and the German Forum Party (DFP). One of the old GDR parties, the Liberal Democratic Party of Germany (LDPD), also joined this alliance, giving the others instant access to office space and a grass-roots party organization all over the GDR. The Free Democrats viewed themselves as being politically in the middle of the road, between the SPD on the left and the CDU on the right. The West FDP usually got between five and ten percent of the votes. Its cooperation was usually necessary to make a coalition government work in West Germany, giving it influence out of proportion to the votes it received.

The CDU (Christian Democratic Union) was the right-of-center ruling party in West Germany. Its sister party in the East had been a junior partner in the GDR government but now was coming around to the West CDU's positions. The East SPD caricatured the East CDU as "the only party to have done two about-faces in the last three months." The CDU also picked up support from two new parties. Democratic Awakening (DA) had been founded by several leading opposition leaders. The German Social Union (DSU) was a party to the right of the CDU, founded only after the dust of the peaceful revolution had started to settle. All of these parties joined forces under the title of Alliance for Germany. They favored a very quick unification of the two Germanies.

The main opposition groups had the most difficulty getting organized. Their anti-establishment origins made many of their members question the wisdom of turning their groups into parties. Political parties were seen as part of the problem, not the solution. In addition, they were virtually the only groups still debating a vision for the GDR that did not necessarily include unification with West Germany. Finally some of the main groups, the New Forum (NF), Democracy Now (DJ) and the Initiative for Peace and Human Rights (IFM) agreed to form a coalition, called Alliance '90, to stand together on the ballot. In addition there were a number of smaller opposition groups who formed their own parties.

All of this not only sounds confusing; it was confusing! It was certainly a different type of election than the old 'fold up your ballot without looking at it' routine of last May. Fortunately, a little of the old East German sense of humor was making a comeback. To show their disdain for the new establishment, a couple of nonsense parties were founded. One was the German Sexual Union. The other off-beat party was the German Beer Drinkers Union (DBU). The latter even managed to get on the national ballot!

In a way, I was thankful that the changes in laws had taken away the right for foreigners to vote. It would have been difficult to gather enough information on all those parties to feel I was making an informed decision. Many East Germans felt the same way. Instead of thinking of the campaign as charting the future course of their country, one issue came to dominate the campaign.

The end of February the new GDR coalition government started talks with the West German government about converting their relatively worthless East German currency to the West German mark. The East Germans now had an issue to focus on. What would happen to their money? Most of the parties were calling for an exchange rate of 1:1. The thing that seemed to make the biggest difference was that the CDU was in power in West Germany. They would have to tap the government budget there to finance whatever agreement was made. It was obvious that they would be most willing to work with a CDU government in the GDR.

A poll from the beginning of February showed that 80% of the electorate was planning on voting. Of that 80%, 54% were planning to vote for the SPD, 12% for the PDS and 11% for the CDU[76]. A month later it was 34% for the SPD, 17% for the CDU, 4% for the LDPD, 2% for Democratic Awakening and 1% for the New Forum and Democracy Now parties[77].

Prominent West German politicians were the main speakers at election rallies. It was revealed shortly before the election that West Germany taxpayer money had been funnelled to party foundations in the West, who in turn used the money to help their respective partners in the East. The CDU received roughly $3 million and the SPD and FDP about $1 million each.[78] Of course the PDS and the former opposition groups got nothing. The PDS had plenty of money left over from their days in power. It was the former opposition groups (and the partner for some of those groups in the West, the Greens Party) that got left out of taxpayer campaign money.

Scandals rocked several of the parties. The biggest one concerned one of the leaders of Democratic Awakening, Wolfgang Schnur. He was a lawyer and had defended many opposition leaders in the GDR court system. Four days before the election, it was revealed that he had informed on all of his clients to the Stasi.

In spite of the scandals, the questions of things Western, especially West money, seemed to be the most important concern. Some parties became known for the Western consumer goods they passed out at their rallies. DA booths had stacks of Coca-Cola; the DSU, bunches of bananas; the SPD, coffee. The other leader of DA, Rainer Eppelmann, a pastor and prominent opposition leader, recalled hearing a child's voice at a rally. "Lookie there, it's the pastor from the Coca-Cola Party!"[79] On March 14, Helmut Kohl, prime minister of West Germany and leader of the West CDU, made a forceful statement that East German money would be exchanged 1 to 1 for West German marks for 'small savers'.[80] It was not clear what he meant by small savers, but it was the kind of assurance that undecided voters were looking for.

The ballots were cast and counted. The CDU pulled off a surprise victory. In the last couple of weeks they had gone from 17% to a final result of 41%. The SPD was second with 22%, the PDS third with 17%, the DSU, 6 %, the FDP coalition, 5%[81]. Alliance '90, the largest concentration of opposition leaders, received only 3%.

Apparently most voters had either lost or never shared their vision of a new and improved GDR, separate from West Germany.

The East CDU began the task of setting up the coalition needed to gain a majority for passing new laws and the two-thirds majority needed for making changes in the constitution. At the same time, negotiations continued with the West Germany government about adaptation of the West German Mark as the new currency. Soon after the election, government officials in the West German banking industry started talking about an exchange rate of 2:1, cutting savings, salaries and debts in half. This would have undoubtedly come closer to the East economy's value measured against the West German economy. The psychological impart on East Germans was devastating. Once again demonstrations broke out, including over 100,000 people in East Berlin.[82] Many of the banners referred to such talk as being 'election fraud' on the part of the West CDU. In fact, Kohl had only promised 1:1 exchange rates to 'small' savings accounts. The voters own wishful thinking had translated that into 1:1 across the board. The large majority of voters had chosen parties that presented unification with West Germany as the future of the GDR. It would take much longer for those same voters to understand the West German system at all levels, including mistaking nuances in fulfilling campaign promises for election fraud.

Chapter 14

Charting the Final Course

The first freely elected parliament in the history of the GDR had a large majority in favor of making sure it was the last parliament of the GDR. A new course had been charted for East Germany; to make it like West Germany as quickly as was reasonably possible. That was certainly not a bad goal. It was, however, difficult for the idealists of the revolution to admit that their dream of making a substantially different, and thus hopefully better, society was now dead. And although everyone knew where the ship of state was headed, it was not clear how it would get there, or how rough the ride would get.

Only a few days after the election it was announced that the currency union with the West German Mark would be ready to go before both parliaments went on summer vacation. During the whole month of April, this topic dominated East German life, overshadowing the building of the coalition government.[83]

The specifics of the negotiations on converting to the West German Mark were finally made known the end of April. The date for this transaction was set for July 1. Each individual would be able to exchange 4,000 East Marks at a rate of 1 to 1 for West Marks (roughly $2,700). After that, the rate would go to 2:1, meaning that savings accounts above 4,000 Marks would be cut in half. Salaries and pensions would be carried across 1 to 1, although the later would in some cases be adjusted according to a complex formula based on a percent of the average earnings during the years of employment. Following a few more negotiations, the final agreement was announced on May 2. Now children up to age 14 could only exchange 2,000 East Marks at 1 to 1, people between 14 and 59, 4,000 and people age 60 and up could exchange 6,000 East Marks to West Marks 1 to 1. Any amount above that would be cut in half.[84]

Changes

With so many changes still going on, people were struggling to find their bearings again. Would they be able to keep their jobs once East German companies were exposed to Western competition? Would the apartment building or house they were living in go back to a former owner, who might raise the rents or try to evict them?

A holding company of sorts, called *Treuhand*, was formed. Most businesses had been owned by the "people", really the government. These were now given to the *Treuhand*. It was to sell the business as best as it could to the highest bidders in order to reprivatize the economy. The proceeds would go to the government. Unprofitable companies were to be shut down and their assets liquidated. Although this process was actually quite slow in unfolding, there was no doubt that a tremendous shift in the economy was underway. Unemployment figures rose steadily.

A similar process was underway for all the government owned apartment buildings as well. They were being grouped and turned into companies that still recieved government subsidies. But one day they might be expected to pay for themselves. That would mean raising rents and handing out eviction notices, if necessary. Again, this program was being implemented slowly, but no one knew what its final form would be or how high the rent would go.

The circle of changes had expanded to affect every aspect of life. An elementary school teacher friend of mine worked primarily in directing after school homework sessions for children whose parents were both working. The West German school system had no similar positions. Once the transition to that system was complete, she would be laid off. Adding to the uncertainty was the fact that at the end of the school year, all the principals in the whole country were to be fired. Almost all of them had been party members and were not trusted to move forward vigorously enough with the reform of the education system.

Ulrike, a high school senior who attended our young adult Bible study, invited me to visit her high school. That would not have been possible for me before as a Westerner. Now the history teacher invited me to come back in a few weeks to teach the class about the influence of Enlightenment ideas on the U.S. Constitution! The old history books had been thrown out as being inaccurate and inadequate. Instead of studying the history of the SED, the usual senior year fare, they had started over with the history of Europe. In addition, the history class only met two out of three weeks. The teacher went to week-long seminars in West Germany to learn the material to be taught for the next two weeks, came back to teach it, then the cycle was repeated. I dredged up what little I remembered from my own high school U.S. Government class and a few weeks later indeed taught a class in the Henningsdorf High School on the outskirts of East Berlin about the U.S. Constitution!

The middle of April it was announced that all border controls would be dropped on July 1, the same date that the currencies of the two Germanies were to be united. Since the Wall opened the border guards concentrated mostly on trying to stop the smuggling of goods and currency. Once the currency became the same on both sides of the border, there wouldn't be any point to having border guards.

One advantage of the coming lack of border guards was that all of the old public transit stations could be reopened. Right up the street from the Johanneum, city workers ripped up the sidewalk and dusted off the old stairs down into the Oranienburg Street Station. We could finally catch a ride on the S-bahn that was shaking our dorm without having to walk over to the Friedrichstrasse Station!

The Wall was dismantled fairly quickly during this time, providing a new type of employment for the border guards. The Allied control point Checkpoint Charlie was removed on June 22. Two days later I drove through the East German installations there. Since the guards had loosened up so much in the last months, I struck up a conversation with the one who was checking my passport and car registration.

"So, will Germans be allowed through here after July first?" (Only non-Germans were allowed through the 'air-locks' of Checkpoint Charlie.)

The guard grunted and shrugged his shoulders. "They never tell us anything."

"Well, its really no big deal, but it would be kind of handy for Americans and Germans who want to drive into East Berlin in the same car. Of course, its a bummer for you guys not knowing if you'll get to keep your jobs."

"That's the one thing they did tell us. On July 2nd I'll be standing in line down at the unemployment office." He laughed bitterly. "That's what we wanted, I guess."[85]

Students were also unsure of their future. Their monthly stipend was being raised from 200 to 495 Marks a month ($130 to $325), but prices were rising fast too. ($325 was the minimum pension for senior citizens, who thus faced the same problem as students, but were not given to demonstrating.) With rising unemployment, part-time jobs would not be easy to find. Perhaps the main issue was that part-time work had never before been necessary for students. They organized demonstrations at the parliament building down the street from the university. The newly elected government had the police barricade off the parliament building to keep the demonstrators out of ear-shot. The same police faced many of the same students as in the previous fall. This time there was not as much of a threat of violence and the students found very little sympathy among the general population. The demonstrations slowly faded away during the summer.

The fact that municipal and county election were held on May 6, almost a year to the day from the last municipal elections, was a small footnote to the events of the summer. The voters were starting to get tired of elections, although voter turnout was still eighty percent. Most of the parties in the coalition lost a little ground as voters vented their frustration over the way the negotiations for unification were going. No other party's alternative vision seemed very attractive, so there were no big gainers either.[86]

Out with the Old, In with the New

On May 18 a treaty was signed between East and West Germany to regulate the 'economic, currency and social unification' of the two countries. On this historic occasion, West German prime minister Helmut Kohl stated that 'nobody will be worse off' after the new currency is introduced; a quote that would come back to haunt him.[87]

Detailed instructions on how to get one's money exchanged were now printed in the newspapers. Each person had to fill out a separate application form. Only one account for each person would be converted, so people with more than one account had to consolidate accounts. The money could be paid in until July 6. After that date, all bills and any coins larger than 50 Pfennig would become worthless. The 50 Pfennig coins and smaller would be kept as legal tender for the time being. Applications could be handed in starting June 1. At the time of application, a receipt would be issued to be redeemed on July 1 for West Germany money. Since the banks would be closed the entire first week of July, everyone was suppose to request a large enough sum of cash to get them through the first week.

I waited until the end of June to worry about getting my money exchanged. The lines at the banks were always incredibly long. I hoped everyone would be done before the deadline so I could just sneak in. Of course it didn't work out that way.

I found out from the University's Office for Foreign Students that my money would qualify for a 1 to 1 exchange rate if I could prove that I would be staying in the country for at least the next six months. I had quite a stash in my bank account, about 2,500 Marks. The original contract had called for me to get 500 Marks a month. I was also required to adhere to MCC spending guidelines, which helped me keep my spending well below that rate. I also got money from Reimers on occasion, who had been forced to exchange more money than they could spend in a day every time they came over. In addition, MCC'ers who had left the GDR a year before I came had built up a tidy surplus which the Mennonite Church had kept for MCC until I arrived. So even though I had been able to renegotiate my university contract back in January to end the forced money exchange, I was glad I would be allowed to exchange MCC's money back at 1 to 1.

A few days before the deadline I went to my bank to hand in my application. I knew I'd have to kill a couple hours in line, so I went well before closing time. There were two huge lines, going way out on the plaza that the bank was located on. When I went to join one of the lines, I discovered that there was a bank employee at the end of each line. It was their job to keep people from joining the lines, since they were already 3 hours long and that would take them well past closing time. I asked the line guard if it would be possible to sign up after July 1. He assured me that my application would be accepted until July 6, but it would not be possible to get West marks until after July 6 if the application was turned in after July 1. Since I had always had access to West marks, I decided to hand my application in after July 1. I at least had the option. The East Germans had to stay and stick it out in their lines.

That last week shelves got pretty bare in grocery stores. People bought up cheap, East German goods faster than they could be supplied. Going shopping with money that would be worth only half as much if you didn't spend it turned out to be a remarkably good way to remove most people's inhibitions against going on wild shopping sprees. Going to the grocery store had been getting more exciting all along, since more and more West goods had been showing up, albeit at very high prices. The last days the retailers, however, didn't see the sense of selling West goods for East money when they could wait until after the weekend to sell the same thing for West money. The stores even ran out of toilet paper.

The weekend of June 30 and July 1, I was visiting Angelika's family in Klettwitz. Talking with Angelika's grandmother helped keep things in perspective. "Well, here we go changing money again" was her comment. It would be her fourth currency. Hyperinflation in the '20's and the devastation of Germany in WW II had wrecked the first two, now the third one was going too.

I was still full of eager anticipation. "Tomorrow will be the most exciting day of your life", I told Angelika.

"No, that was already the 9th of November", was her instant reply.

I still wasn't thinking like an East German.

West Mark day arrived! We went to the bank in the morning. Klettwitz being a small town, there was only a small line. We heard there had been a near riot in East Berlin at the one bank that had opened at midnight to pass out West money. Since the old money could be paid in until Friday, the offering at the church service was all East money. The usher we talked to said it was more than they usually got. Most of the village stores had people working to restock the shelves. Surprisingly, there were not many West goods. It was mostly East goods that had been hard to find the previous week, including toilet paper.

The magic slips of paper were finally here. For East Germans the issue was no longer *what kind* of money they had, a concept difficult for Americans to understand. The question was *how much* of it did they have, a way of asking the question that seems more familiar to us.

And More Changes

July 1 was the date for a number of other changes. The myriad subsidies for everything from bread to children's shoes to books by Karl Marx were dropped on this date. The only subsidies left were those on housing, mass transit and energy. With subsidies gone, the prices in the East became similar to those in the West. For staples like bread and milk that meant a large jump in prices. For consumer goods like color TV's and cars it meant a sharp drop. Another factor in setting new prices was the switch from the old state monopoly to a new private monopoly in a suddenly capitalistic system. For this reason, prices were suddenly higher on staples in the GDR then they were in West Germany. Many people in East Berlin took to shopping for groceries in West Berlin, causing traffic jams and a temporary shortage of goods there. East Germans who lived further from West Germany, and thus from Western competition, had to learn to pay higher prices or go without. The large grocery store chains of West Germany eventually started putting up new stores in large tents in the East. After several months, prices started stabilizing at West German standards.

Also on July 1, the special subsidies to help out East Germans going to West Germany were dropped. These people were no longer counted as 'refugees'. They were simply people moving from one place to another. Statistics were no longer complied as comprehensively on this movement, downplaying the fact that the number of people moving remained high even though any political motive for doing so had disappeared. The exodus was now entirely economically driven. Over 190,000 people, more than 1% of the population, had left the GDR during the first six months of the year.[88]

Erich Mielke, the former head of the Stasi, had his office at the heart of the building complex on Normannen Street. This office complex became the scene of political struggle again in the fall of 1990. Some of the idealists of the opposition were upset when they heard government plans for the old Stasi files stored there. The GDR government said they would agree to let West German intelligence and internal security agencies look at the files to clear up unresolved cases in the West. This included especially cases of West German terrorists who had been aided by the former GDR government. No one else would be allowed to look at the files, not even their own. At the same time, the opposition knew that those same agencies might be interested in looking at the Stasi's files on them, since they would still count as opposition in the coming unified Germany. They argued that no one except those who had been spied on should be allowed to look at those files.

To press this demand, a few of the leaders occupied several rooms in the former Stasi office complex. A daily rally was held at 5 pm outside the gates that had been 'stormed' earlier in the year. As was the case with the student's demonstration, this demonstration failed to find much sympathy in the general public. The number of demonstrators rarely topped a couple hundred people. Now however, some opposition leaders were in positions of government power. They were able to eventually negotiate a deal whereby government agencies access to the files was limited and victims would be allowed to look at their own files.

The protests there required a police presence that kept people out of most of the buildings. The building that we had 'broken' into on the night in January was still open though. I went in to see what had all changed in the last seven or eight months. The grocery store that used to be only for Stasi employees had been taken over by a West German chain and was now open to the public. There was a restaurant and cafe open to the public as well. The East German railroad company had been given most of the rest of the building to use as office space.

The huge flood of minor and major changes transported East Germans to a different country without them even having to leave home. A way of life was dying.

The influx of Western consumer goods was so striking that a book was published with page after page of pictures of East German products, in order to hold on to those images of what GDR store shelves used to look like.[89] Talk was started of what to do with the old communist statues. Lenin, Marx, Engels, Thälmann and others dotted the parks of the GDR. For some it didn't seem possible to enjoy a picnic under their stony stares anymore. Others had grown accustomed to them and didn't want to see them go.

Unification

The final stretch of the road to unification was not without its potholes. On June 17, 1990 the DSU made a motion in the GDR parliament that the GDR declare itself part of West Germany immediately, on that very day. June 17 was celebrated in West Germany as the day of German unity, to mark the June 17, 1953 uprising against the GDR government. Unifying the two countries on that day would have made for some nifty symbolism. More importantly in that political setting, it was the DSU's way of reminding everyone that the unification was now only one parliamentary vote away. They hoped this tactic would translate into public pressure to accelerate the unification process, a key plank in their platform. What it actually showed was the chaos inherent in a government trying to negotiate its own non-existence.

In addition to all the internal tension about the hows and whens of unification, both the GDR and West Germany needed to worry about international relationships. The Soviet Union was still very skeptical of allowing its best Warsaw Treaty partner to go over to the other side by becoming part of NATO. On the other hand, the Soviet Union had few options. Helmut Kohl met with Gorbachow to work out the details. The new united Germany would reduce the size of its army and help finance the movement of Soviet troops from the GDR back home to the Soviet Union. During the three or four years granted for those troops to leave, no NATO troops would be stationed on GDR territory.

The West German government also was talking with the other victors of World War II, the U.S., French and British governments. It was agreed that when Germany was unified, all Western Allied rights still in force would be ended. The unified Germany would finally be fully sovereign.

On August 23, the GDR parliament approved a plan for the GDR to become part of West Germany on October 3. At this point, negotiations with the Allied countries had still not been completed. The parliament could only hope that a treaty with them could be signed in time. The GDR government was having trouble coping with the enormous task of restructuring the economy. The sooner the GDR joined West Germany, the quicker the latter's vast resources could be brought to bear.

At that same time it was decided to change the internal political structure of the GDR. The government had broken up the five old states in 1952 and created fifteen new districts. Now those five states would be recreated. Elections for the new state governments would be held on October 14. In addition, new national elections in both parts of Germany would be held on December 2. That would be the fourth election for East Germans to participate in during 1990.

To mark the actual event of unification, a very dignified ceremony had been worked out for midnight of the night from October 2 to October 3. All the political dignitaries gathered at the Reichstag. A large platform was built for them out to the west side of the building. To the side of the platform was an extra large flagpole.

Three spot lights had been set up behind the Reichstag, sweeping the night air. Each one was surrounded by police vans and water cannons. The strands of German history seemed to bend together there on that night. The spotlights as they might have been during the war, searching for enemy bombers, the massive police presence a reminder of the urban unrest and political division of contemporary Berlin. They were parked on the former death strip of the Wall, behind the German parliament building that symbolized the birth, death and now the rebirth of German unity.

At midnight, an extra large West German flag was brought out to the flagpole, carried by selected teenagers from East and West Germany. The flag was slowly hoisted to the tune of the West German national anthem, reaching the top exactly at midnight. A fireworks display lit up the sky. From that moment on, there was to be no more West German flag or national anthem, no more East or West Germany. Now there was simply Germany.

A way of life was dead. The GDR was gone. Few were all that sorry to see it go. Still, it doesn't seem to be the way of countries to lower the flag one last time and march off to the footnotes of history books. Perhaps that's why a small group of theology students gathered at the end of the hall past my room on Unification evening. They were determined not to set foot out into the streets. If they did, someone might mistake their presence for celebration. They looked so glum I didn't figure they had much to worry about in that regard. They drank cheap GDR red wine and stared at the flickering candles scattered across the room.

Some would say only those who had been privileged in the GDR could mourn its passing. That comes close to the truth. Students could have been counted in that group since access to higher education was so limited that getting a university degree propelled them into more privileged positions. Theology students though, by the very nature of their commitments, had suffered varying degrees of persecution, harassment and limits on their choices of vocation from the very state whose passing they now mourned. It seemed to me that something more complex than loss of 'privilege' was at work here.

The most immediate reason given for mourning the end of the GDR was the death of their ideals for a better society, something closer to the kingdom of heaven here on earth. Lurking under the surface, I also sensed a fear of the unknown, triggered perhaps by the anti-capitalist indoctrination they had soaked up in schools and at church youth meetings that had a strong social concern element. One could see the rising unemployment, homelessness and criminality since the demise of socialism. That fit the accusations of their teachers about the shortcomings of capitalism.

The most interesting insight for me was the mirror image of hopelessness they held up for me of democratic capitalism. I, along with most Americans, had always assumed that socialist countries like the GDR never changed. Life there seemed to be one gray, hopeless affair. Living there showed me that vast changes had taken place in the way of life even under the communist government, not to mention the astonishing events of the last year. My friends had not been people without hope. Now these students felt they had been thrust into a system that offered only a hopeless, materialistic life, very colorful no doubt, but offering no real chance to work for their ideals. The activities of civil rights and peace movements in Western countries were too slow and ineffective in achieving results to give them hope. They were embarking on a journey in the opposite direction of the one I had started only a year before, leaving many aspects of their culture behind as many aspects of my culture overtook them. It had been my choice to switch, they had no choice.

There were certainly many positive aspects to unification. East Germans had access to one of the world's most powerful currency.

They could travel, read formerly banned books, breathe more freely without worry about who was watching. When I pointed out to East Germans that their former way of life was dead, I didn't mean it as a judgement on good or evil. I thought it was a statement of fact that was worth thinking about, mourning over, looking at in order to see where new hope might come from. The changes of the past year had been so intense that I was amazed all East Germans hadn't check themselves into a counselling program. Recognizing how much the ground had shifted under one's feet amidst all the hoopla and dancing was for me the start of dealing with the intense pressure of change.

East Germans were not the only ones who needed time to sort out the significance of recent events. The week before unification I realized that some Americans had also not kept up with the times.

Time-Delayed Reactions

Andre and Cathy Stoner were MCC'ers in West Germany. They worked at establishing contacts between the West German peace movement and American soldiers stationed in West Germany. Those two groups viewed each other with a fair amount of suspicion. One of the forums that Stoners were able to use to facilitate communication between them were special chapel services organized together with Army chaplains on the bases.[90]

Friedrich Schorlemmer was an outspoken East German pastor who belonged to the 'elite' group at the very top of the Stasi's list of trouble-makers in the GDR. He was a pacifist and committed to a vision of a society based on Biblical principles of shalom and justice. He had been involved in the East German peace movement for years, a leader of peaceful demonstrations in the town of Wittenberg and was one of the founders of the new party, Democratic Awakening.

It was a mutual acquaintance that brought the Stoners and Schorlemmer together. Eva Löber was active in Friedrich's peace group in Wittenberg and had met Andre through that work. She and her husband, Lothar, convinced Friedrich to plan a trip to West Germany to speak at a special chapel service on Hahn Air Force base on Saturday, September 29, just days before German unification. That U.S. Air Force base was home to 72 F-16's with nuclear capability and an estimated 150 nuclear bombs.[91]

Andre and Cathy's involvement with West German peace protestors at a nearby cruise missile base had resulted in their base visiting privileges being revoked. Since they were unsure if or when they might be reinstated, I was asked to come and do the translating at the chapel service.

A small group of about 30 service people and several West German peace movement people gathered in the chapel. Andre and Cathy did manage to get on the base to attend the service as well. The East German guests were amazed that they were able to get on to an American Air Force base, an unthinkable event at their Soviet counterparts. The three took turns explaining their work for peace in the GDR. Their work started in earnest in 1983, a time when short range nuclear missiles were being introduced in both Germanies. They took pains to explain that they had wanted all missiles removed, not just the American missiles. That led to conflict with GDR authorities. They talked about the non-violent demonstrations they had organized to throw out communist government. Lothar described one demonstration that threatened to do violence to people working in the Stasi office in Wittenberg and how he, along with a few other leaders, had been able to persuade the crowd to depart in peace.

Friedrich summed up the events of the past year. "The Holy Spirit came to visit us in the GDR for six months. It was a powerful experience. Now it seems the Spirit has left our country, the churches are empty again and we are under a new occupation."

It was difficult enough just translating the words from one language to the other. There still seemed to be something missing in the exchange. The life experiences of the Christians gathered in that chapel were so different, I wondered if we really connected with each other. At one level, all the people there were happy to be rid of the communist government of the GDR. They had, however, pursued radically different paths to achieve that goal. The Americans probably didn't understand the concept of Western capitalism and democracy as a new occupation. The three East Germans felt it was an overwhelming force that kept them from having the time and space to talk about a 'third way' for GDR society. The East Germans didn't understand the mix of religion and nationalism they found in that chapel, or the multitude of motivations of Americans who join the armed forces that seemed so menacing to them.

Perhaps the ultimate irony of that meeting was the fine print on the Air Force announcement of the event. Since listening to the East Germans constituted contact with the enemy, Air Force personnel who attended the chapel service were advised that they were required to report that contact to the local counter-intelligence officer.

Chapter 15

What Remains?

As people caught their breath after a year of intense change, one question was asked over and over. What remained of their lives as they had been in the GDR? Were those forty years wasted, empty time? And what were they going to do now?

Having become West German citizens, many (now former) East Germans looked to West Germany to provide answers to these questions. The West German government was doing a reasonable job in shoring up the social net and adapting the planned economy to the capitalist West German model. In that model, though, there were clearly to be winners and losers, those who became wealthier and those who become poorer. The latter group included the hundreds of thousands of new unemployed. Prime Minister Kohl's words of assurance that 'no one would be worse off' now rang hollow.

Although government policy was more or less reasonable given the difficult situation, no policy could address the issues of West Germans and former East Germans just getting along. Those relationships moved past the initial stages of cultural shock and 'where is the flusher on the toilet?'. Now West Germans were coming to the former GDR to 'help' out. Many former East Germans found their advice to be condescending, as if they were little children who hadn't done anything in the last forty years. Many West Germans couldn't understand the apparent utter lack of gratitude on the part of the former East Germans for all the money and expertise being poured into their part of the country.

The field was ripe for the return of political humor. The new comic characters were *Wessi* and *Ossi*, archetypical West and East Germans respectively.

Wessi asks: '*Ossi*, what are you most impressed with, my boundless willingness to help or my brilliant intelligence?'

Ossi replies: 'By your boundless sense of humor.'[92]

The number and conduct of new businesses opened in the former GDR by West German corporations raised former East German suspicions as well.

Wessi to *Ossi*: 'I must insist that under no conditions are you to tell anyone how much I'm paying you'.

Ossi: 'Don't worry, I'm as ashamed of it as you are.'[93]

It was not really surprising to find that bosses and employees had trouble getting along across East and West German cultural lines. The whole question of getting along was actually quite difficult, even among people of good will from both sides. I think we were all surprised to find out how difficult it was to merge or even coordinate the two youth groups of the East German and the West Berlin Mennonite Churches. These congregations had been split by the Wall in 1961 and merged back together shortly after the Wall came down. In that time, youth work had developed two different styles in the two congregations.

Both congregations were so small and scattered that there wasn't really enough youth for a regular group. In West Berlin, the high-school age young people participated in camps and retreats organized by the Mennonite conference in West Germany that the congregation belonged to. In East Berlin, we had revived a defunct youth program by reaching out to non-Mennonite young people and including both high schoolers and career people in one group. Our youth group had developed into a small and committed group of friends. We had organized our own retreats for junior and senior high aged young people of Mennonite background who had lost contact with the church.

We had several preliminary discussions and even a meeting in East Berlin to talk about ways of working together, particularly to coordinate future retreats so that they were held on dates mutually agreeable to all. There was no shortage of good-will and willingness to work together. And yet we couldn't seem to find agreement.

We scheduled one more meeting in June of 1991. At Tim Reimer's suggestion, we would have a picnic supper on the grass in the former death strip under the shadow of the Brandenburg Gate. That way we would be on neutral ground. We all brought something along and spread our supper out on the grass. The rabbits who had formerly led such a peaceful life in the death strip sat up on their haunches to observe the latest intruders.

We talked about the different age structures of the two groups, the different operating styles, the long distances to be travelled (an hour each way for some) if we were to meet together. No matter how things were done, there would have to be substantial change for everyone involved to be able to work together; more change, on top of all the other change of the past two years. The result of our meeting was that the goal of working together was just not worth more change at that time. We were all disappointed, I think, and surprised to discover how defensive change made all of us feel. Dealing with feelings of change was a struggle for all Germans now, particularly for former East Germans.

Very Personal Struggles

As part of wrapping up my studies at the Humboldt University before coming home in September 1991, I tried to get my academic records in order. I realized that I had neglected to get a required signature from Frau Maihorn, our freshmen year Marxist-Leninist professor. That department had ceased to exist already the year before, but I was able to track down Frau Maihorn's home address. I found out that Fidus needed her signature as well, so we called her up and made arrangements to meet her. I didn't think I would ever need academic credit in that course, but I was curious to hear what Frau Maihorn had been doing since getting fired and what she thought now about our class and life back then.

We met in the cafeteria and got our signatures. Frau Maihorn told us she had found work in a private social services agency in West Berlin. She was now getting on the job training in family counseling and domestic crisis. She had not had any experience in this field. She thought the people at the agency were so amazed to have a person with a doctorate in Marxist-Leninist philosophy apply that they decided to give her the job. She seemed to be less open about talking about the past, so after we parted ways, Fidus and I talked about inviting her over for cake and coffee sometime so that we could visit in a more relaxed atmosphere. Frau Maihorn agreed to come. It was only a few days before I left Germany.

We sat down to cake, coffee and pleasantries at 4 pm. We talked more about her new job. Standard Marxist teaching says that domestic crisis is the result of the economic tension inherent in capitalism. I asked Frau Maihorn if she had any trouble reconciling her new job with the realization that broader societal structures need to be changed to provide real help.

She admitted that bothered her. Her training told her that change needed to be affected at a higher level to make her work more effective.

She would work with families to build up rapport and help them deal with the conflict in their lives in a healthier way. Then something would go wrong at work, someone would get laid off or fired and all the progress seemed to be wiped out. Still, she said, she had come to admire and respect those people and their struggle. Her enthusiasm about her clients made it plain that they had become real people to her, not just objects in a class struggle.

We went on to talk at great length about how the changes affected her only child, a high school student. We talked about the old animosity in our class, the old system and its failings. Our afternoon coffee became a late night bull session. It was 11 pm when we finally broke up.

Frau Maihorn had done a lot of thinking about her life in the last two years. She seemed to have made peace with herself and her past. She was still determined to make an impact for the better in her world.

Shortly after the two Mennonite congregations had reunited, a weekend retreat was held for all the people from the former GDR who had been in the Menno-Heim as children and had not had the opportunity to come back since. About twenty people came, only a few had been active in the church in the GDR. For most of them it was the first contact with the church in years.

The point of the retreat, besides getting to know each other again, was to discuss the future goals of the church, especially for those Mennonites who were living so scattered in the former GDR. Some of the West Berlin leadership tried to keep the discussion focused on the future amidst much reminiscing. It became apparent that many in the two groups had two different expectations about the weekend.

After a short break for coffee, the air was finally cleared when one of the 'new' visitors from the former GDR talked about her vision for the church.

"I haven't been a church-goer for almost twenty years now. I raised my children, 18 and 11 years old now, as atheists. I didn't know what else to do, where else to turn. I can't answer your questions about the future of the church because I don't even know what the future of my own faith is. That's the question I hope to be able to answer."

For her, and many others there, it had been thirty long years, as long as the Wall stood, of being shut off, of shutting themselves off from the church. What anguish to admit to living like that. Accusations would bring only defensiveness, not healing. Still, the Mennonites who had been active in church in the GDR all those years felt betrayed by the insinuation that only in the West was one able to be a Mennonite.

No final conclusions were reached at that weekend retreat. The only achievement was to put a name to the fear that many had. A long, arduous rebuilding of trust, of recommitment of lives to God is now underway in the Mennonite congregation of Berlin. So far progress seems slow and is hard to measure at any rate. Hopefully what started as many very personal struggles can become a struggle for the congregation to share with each other.

Getting to Know the Enemy

Surrounded by people asking the question of what to 'take with them' from their old homes in the GDR to their 'new homes' in a united Germany, in my last year there I often asked myself what lessons and memories I wanted to take home with me from my stay in the GDR[94]. I had arrived with two suitcases and a boatload of ignorance. I was to leave with multiple suitcases full and some new understandings. I felt I might even have started to find an answer to one of the main questions that brought me to the GDR in the first place.

Some people will point out that in the Sermon on the Mount, Jesus was more likely talking about enemies in the local neighborhood than the distant boogie man of our Cold War. On the other hand, the political enemy of Jesus' day, the Roman occupation forces, lived close by, whereas some of our enemies today live far away. It seems to me that the difference in distance does not absolve us from the question of how to love our enemies, near and far.

I had gotten to know the enemy. To say that seems a bit trite, but it was a lesson I had learned experientially and not academically. Only then could I think about what it might mean to love them. At that moment, 'they' ceased to be enemies. I still abhorred the GDR government, but I could honestly say I had come to love East Germans.

Unfortunately, like all experiential learning, it's a lesson that can't be passed on, only learned anew by people on similar pilgrimages. I am convinced, however, there is much we could do to help foster such experiences.

I suggested to both of the informal English classes I was helping teach that we invite an American soldier who was a professing Christian to talk with us. I hoped it would help share the experience I had of breaking down the walls between people of such different backgrounds and experience. Both classes responded enthusiastically. I made contact with an Baptist congregation in West Berlin comprised mostly of American Armed Services people, explaining our interest. This was in the summer of 1990, before unification. It was still pretty complicated for service personnel to visit the GDR privately, so nothing came of it. After unification, I renewed the invitation. One of their members, Ed, agreed to come and share with our two groups.

Both groups agreed to meet together this one time. Ed came to my room in the Johanneum. That gave us a chance to visit alone a little bit first. Ed was curious about what kind of East Germans he would be meeting with. After answering some of his questions, we went to the apartment of one of the students, Antje, for supper and our meeting. Ed was still a little apprehensive about the whole undertaking, although our conversation made it apparent to me that it was more the fear of the unknown than thinking of East Germans as enemies.

Our meeting was on January 17, 1991, right at the start of the bombing in the Gulf War. That topic dominated our discussions. The East Germans, with grandparents' stories of the devastation of war lurking in the back of their minds, could not comprehend the idea of a Christian being a member of Armed Services that had started bombing runs. Ed offered no easy answers, admitting his own struggle with the issue. He talked of his deep, personal relationship with God. He felt that God had called him to join the military and had not yet called him to leave it. He worked in the Public Relations Department of the Army. A friend of his from the same department had made a quite a splash that week by writing an article in opposition of the war for a left-wing West Berlin daily newspaper, *die tageszeitung*. My friends were acquainted with that article and wanted to know more about how Ed related his faith to his work.

Ed's work in the PR department meant that he had learned fluent German. That greatly aided the discussion. And the defensiveness was definitely not a one-way street. My friends all had a more liberal, intellectual understanding of faith as opposed to Ed's experience of a more personal faith . Ed quite correctly pointed to differences in culture that supported these differences in understanding faith. Since the East Germans had little experience with and no understanding of American Evangelical culture, the discussion stalemated on this point.

As with the meeting between the East German peace activists and the American Christians at Hahn Air Force base, the gap was too large for one meeting to bridge. The lively discussion with Ed helped my friends confront their need to get know their own enemy, the way they thought about the people in the U.S. military. In a small way, it helped deepen my relationships with them as they became more aware of the vast distances I struggled to bridge in my own life, living among them.

It seems to me there are no easy answers when trying to pass on the experience of learning to know the people we once thought of as 'enemies'. There are some definite barriers that can be identified; language, distance, the amount of time and effort required to have a meaningful encounter with people across those barriers, and the fear of losing something precious by examining other options. There are many steps that we can take to reduce those barriers in the hope that the grace of God will effect the miracle of understanding between estranged peoples. Learning a foreign language is a good start. Exchange programs can play a key role here, programs like MCC's International Visitor Exchange Program. Already before the Wall came down, MCC was looking at ways to include East Germans in this program. Ulrike, the high school senior who was such a faithful member of our young adult Bible study, left Germany a few weeks before I did as one of several participants from the former GDR in this program. Perhaps most important is admitting to ourselves that God is so much bigger than we are. God can work with other people in ways that we would never expect God to work with us.

I think I have also gained a new appreciation for the difficulty of such undertakings. Not everyone who undergoes such experiences finds the same insight. A few individuals are so evil and repugnant that loving them may well be beyond human ability. The animosities amongst East Germans (and North Americans) seems greater than that between the two distant groups. Yet having experienced the profound joy of making friends among previous unknown 'enemies', I can only hope that this book passes on some of that knowledge, some of that joy, as an inspiration to keep striving for the goal of following in Christ's footsteps of loving all people.

Non-Violence

When I returned home to the U.S., it struck me how difficult it was to pass on the experiences that I had been part of. It was amazing how much life seemed to be business as usual on questions of military spending and national security. Apparently what happened in the GDR and in the rest of Eastern Europe hadn't sunk in yet. Sure, there were pronouncements that the Cold War was now over. The only image that seems to have significance for North Americans is the opening of the Berlin Wall. To East Germans, that was only one of many significant events. The Wall was *our* symbol of the Cold War, not the East

Germans. We are so wrapped up in the powerful symbolism of the Wall coming down that it seems few stop to ask the question of how it became possible. The question of *how* the Cold War ended doesn't seem to get much discussion. Most people are content with the knowledge that *we*, the West, had won it!

Had we offered our bodies up to the hard rubber batons, the police dogs, the water cannons, or as was the case in Moscow in the fall of 1991, the tanks of the powers that be in Eastern Europe? Did our churches agonize over serving God first and the government second? Did our pastors preach the Biblical principle of non-violence week after week to eager listeners who went out on the street to practice what was preached? Did *we* win the Cold War, or was it won for us?

The world is too complex a place for one side or one group to claim all the glory while another gets all the blame. Breaking Communist Parties' lock on power in Eastern Europe was a highly complicated series of events. No doubt a more balanced, nuanced explanation is needed than I can offer here. Nevertheless, having *experienced* the power of non-violence to bring down structures once thought unshakeable, I cannot contain my astonishment at how little attention the non-violent East European contributions to the end of the Cold War receive.

There are many disheartening examples that non-violence is not an easy solution; Romania, Yugoslavia, ethnic tensions and battles in the former Soviet Union, Northern Ireland, Somalia, and elsewhere. While these examples do not speak for the success of non-violence, neither can they be called examples of success for violence. Above all, they are an urgent call for us to learn to know our enemies before fear and violence limits our options.

Only days after unification, violence exploded again in East Berlin, in November, 1991. A group of young people, many of them from West Berlin and West Germany, had taken things into their own hands to solve the chronic shortage of apartments. They had simply occupied abandoned tenements. They fixed them up to suit themselves. They didn't always bother to pay rent, but under the chaotic circumstances in the East, it was hard to tell who the landlord would end up being anyway. Their activities were, however, illegal. The West Berlin police were well practiced in clearing out similar problems in West Berlin. Since the city was now one, they had jurisdiction in the East as well. They moved in with great numbers, with armored vehicles and water cannons. When it was over, the violence on both sides, ironically mostly by West German police and demonstrators, had exceeded that of the demonstrations that had overturned the communist government. Neither side was now interested in what the church had to say about non-violence. It was an unhappy omen for the end of the division of Berlin.

I frankly don't know if non-violence can always be called the best alternative. I am merely suggesting that its powerful success in the GDR and elsewhere in Eastern Europe makes including it in any discussion on solving global problems necessary for the integrity of the discussion. Friedrich Schorlemmer said it well.

"The people went on the streets with 'chinese' fear in their bellies. I went through that in Leipzig. Was the city ever under siege! You can't imagine it.

In this threatening situation something wonderful happened. Three church-related groups in Leipzig passed their Appeal for Non-Violence, which was then read in the churches. People who had been pressured and spied on for years by the State Security Service confessed to their fear in that statement, including their fear *for* those in uniform and warned that violence solves no problems and is inhuman. Violence cannot possibly be the sign of a new, better society."[95]

Consciously building a better society was the goal that drove the leaders of the GDR's peaceful revolution. They realized that violently overthrowing the government might bring them to power, but not to their goal. Christians were at the center of this movement and their ideals came from the Bible, from the great hope of serving God by working for the Kingdom here on earth. The politics of a secularized society prevented them from phrasing their goals in Biblical language. In fact, when the voters had a choice in the March 1990 parliamentary elections, they thrust the idealists back out of power before it was even really in their grasp.

With all our nuclear weapons, peace training seminars, laser guided bombs and demonstrations, we still don't know how events will turn out in this world. I can still feel the tension in the pit of my stomach from the confrontation with the People's Police at the Gethsemane Church. Will the bullets fly? As Christians we have to ask an additional question to the one about what will produce the better society, or what will build up the Kingdom. We have to ask what actions will be faithful to our God. To rely either on violence or on non-violence is a statement of faith. With my friends in the East of Germany, I can only say that my faith is in the Prince of Peace.

Scrapbook

Odds and Ends of East German life

Leadership of Young Pioneer Groups, a textbook published by the Academy of Pedagogical Science in the GDR.

Young Pioneer Groups must be led in a manner that increases the importance of political goals in the life of the Pioneers and creates a desire on the part of the Pioneers to base their actions on the examples of Communists.

It is easy to see that this must be the most important principle for the leadership of the Pioneer Groups.

But how can concrete goals be set for the pedagogy of the Young Pioneers in this direction? How can we shape the political profile of Pioneer activities at such a young age?

One of the most important tasks is to activate the interest of Young Pioneers in political events, to fulfill their wish to take active part in the life of the society and to create the experience of the whole society depending on and approving of the actions and deeds of the Young Pioneers.

Pages 20-21

<u>The direct preparation of the children in first grade for their initiation into the Pioneer Organization.</u>
... Thälmann Pioneers (4th - 7th graders) take on the assignment of presenting one of the Pioneer Commandments in an interesting and understandable fashion to five or six of the children. ... Following are some suggestions for these common activities of the Thälmann Pioneers and the first grade pupils.

The commandment "We Young Pioneers love peace".

Main points of emphasis:

- Song: Little white peace dove
- Why do we need peace?
- Who are the friends of the children?
- *Who is an enemy of the children?* (my emphasis)
- Celebratory poem and musical piece.

... We should pay particular attention to the following elements of the initiation ceremony when working to prepare the pupils of the first grade:

... *Pioneers' Greeting and bearing during the presentation and retirement of the flag.* The children can perform the Pioneers' Greeting precisely, using the correct hand. Their bearing during the presentation and retirement of the flag is to match the given commands.

... *Handing out of the scarf and membership card.* The children hear their names called and line up in that order. Afterwards they return to their places together.

... The day of initiation has arrived. It should be a day of dignity and celebration, the day when the children receive their blue scarves and first membership cards.

... The Young Pioneers experience their first great day as members of the Pioneer organization; they wear their blue scarves with pride, they explain and show everything that distinguishes them as Young Pioneers. That is the beginning of a new chapter in the pedagogical work with the youngest members of the Pioneer organization, in that we build on that joy and enthusiasm and help the children to keep Pioneer pledges as promised.

Pages 45, 48, 49, 51-53

Best of Friends

1. Soldiers went marching by just now in per-fect
2. *The captain who now leads the march, we know him*
3. A lieuten-ant leads on the next group with joy that
4. *The flank man up in the first row with hel-met*
5. Soldiers went marching by just now, the whole big

rows with song. As Pi-o- neers we know them all and
ver-y well. He used to lay red bricks right here, he
fills his chest. As our teach-er not long a-go his
and M G.[1] was a milk-er in the co-op and
com-pan-y. And when we're grown up we'll be soldiers

happ-'ly go a-long hur-rah! As Pi-o-neers we
built our hou-ses swell-ell-ell! He used to lay red
les-sons were the be-e-est! As our teach-er not
bus-y as a bee-ee-ee! was a milk-er in
just you wait and see-ee-ee! And when we're grown up

---

[1] MG stands for machine gun.

know them all and happ - 'ly go a - long! Chorus:
bricks right here, he built our houses swell!
long a - go his les - sons were the best!   Best of
the co - op and bus - y as a bee!
we'll be sol - diers just you wait and see!

fri - ends,   best of fri - ends, best of   fri - ends are in

the ar - my now.   They guard our home - land well on

ground in air and on the sea, hur-rah! They guard our home

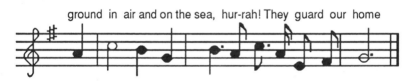

land well   on   the ground, in air, and   on   the   sea.

The Rise of Christianity
from the sixth grade history book

The life of slaves, farmers, work crews and craftsmen became more and more difficult during the Roman Empire. They suffered from the decline of the economy and as a result of the failure of all revolutions, they despaired of ever having a better life. They were looking for a way out of this situation.

At this time some people in the Roman Empire came forward and promised relief from the misery. Since they didn't think relief was possible in this life, it would come after death. Faith in that would help people forget their terrible lives.

There were many religions in the Roman Empire. One of them gained more and more popularity as time passed, the Christian religion. It developed in the first century in Palestine. It was easier to understand than other religions and appealed to slaves as well as to non-slaves, indeed to all people around the Mediterranean. "There is no difference between Greek or Jew, male or female, free or slave". The poorer classes and the slaves, especially in cities, felt attracted because early on, Christianity was critical of wealth and profiteering. One saying went, "it is easier for a camel to go through the eye of a needle than for a rich man to get to heaven"!

Followers of Christianity reported that God had appeared in human form in the carpenter's son, Jesus. They were drawing on age-old ideas that the salvation of humankind from suffering and oppression would come from a Chrestos, in Latin Christus. That means one elected or similar to God. The teaching that a divine child would come to bring wellness and blessing as well as the teaching of a god dying and being resurrected were well-known in the near east from ancient stories.

People who believed in Christ were named Christians. Their teachings were later gathered in writing, called the New Testament or Bible. In the first century the Christian congregations decided for themselves how to organize their church services and who should be the pastor.

However, very soon representatives of Christianity connected their religion with the slave society. Christians should be obedient and not take part in revolutions. They should be loyal subjects of the Emperor. In the Bible it says, "everyone is subject to the authorities, there is no authority that is not from God". Christianity never demanded the end of slavery. The slaves were to remain slaves and not try to escape their masters. The oppression of the poor and the inhuman exploitation of slaves was only to be made a little easier to bear.

(Question for reflection: Did Christianity offer the oppressed a real solution to their problems?)

The Roman Emperors created their own religion about the same time, a cult of the Emperor. The Christians refused to participate in this religion. There was conflict with the authorities and Christians were persecuted.

Rich and prosperous Romans became Christians. The wealth of Christian congregations grew. The power and influence of the bishops, the leaders of the Christian congregations, increased. They wanted to reconcile themselves with the Roman state. The ideas of early Christianity, that all are equal and one should struggle against the rich and their wealth, were gradually forgotten.

Christians created an efficient organization, the church. Since Christians taught that there is only one God, the gods that the Romans used to worship had to be gotten rid of. Their temples were often destroyed by Christians and many monuments of ancient art and many old writings were lost in this way.

At the end of the 4th century, Christianity was made the state religion, which meant that all Romans had to become Christians if they wanted to or not.

The spread of Christianity enabled the ruling class to use religion as an effective means of oppressing the exploited classes; in that slave society as long as it lasted and in the other types of societies that followed.

Christianity was originally a religion for the poor and exploited. It intended to offer them comfort. In time, however, the rich Christians made sure it supported the Roman state. The Emperors realized that Christianity, which had spread throughout the Empire, could be useful in ruling the Empire. Therefore, they made it the state religion.

The office of the city youth pastor encouraged and coordinated the collection of eyewitness accounts of police brutality on the nights of October 7 and 8, 1989 in Berlin. About 150 reports had been gathered by the time this material was made available to the public a couple of weeks later. They were published by the West German Protestant News Service on November 3, 1989 in *epd Dokumentation 47/89*. The page numbers given correspond to that edition. Following are some excerpts.

Eyewitness report of the events on October 7

A group of about 100 people went from Alexanderplatz up Prenzlauer Allee, onto Dimitroff Street and then into a side street. The people went quietly, without shouting any slogans, walking on the sidewalk in accordance with Street Traffic Ordinances. One of the 'pack leaders' had sharply warned the group before starting out about remaining non-violent in every case, even if violence came from the police. Whoever couldn't guarantee that was asked to leave the group. After the group had turned into Duncker street, it was blocked off at both ends by police lines. There were no demands to break up the demonstration. On the contrary, people who wanted to leave were driven back. In spite of being encircled, people remained calm. Some sat down, some yelled "We are peaceful citizens".

A water cannon truck drove up from the back and hosed down everyone in the encirclement. Whistles and boos from the windows of the surrounding tenements were answered with a stream of water from the cannon. After that, everyone was loaded up on trucks and taken away. A bitter irony: the next day a wet GDR flag was lying on the ground, apparently torn down by the stream of water.

(signature)   p. 16

Experience Report

Intersection of Stargarder St./Pappelallee about 11-12 pm, 8/9 October.

After the demonstrators had been driven to the east side of the intersection, about 100 people gathered on the west side and began to put candles on the street and to sing (at the last 'Dona Nobis Pacem'). An officer with a bullhorn demanded that they clear the street. Almost literally:

Officer: Citizens, your behavior is illegal! Remove yourselves in the direction of Schönhauser Allee.

Demo: Is singing illegal?

Officer: Remove yourselves in the direction of Schönhauser Allee!
Otherwise the street will be cleared by the People's police!
Demo: What do you mean by 'cleared'?
Officer: You'll find out! ... Operational squad: clear 'em out!"
That was followed by a very brutal attack along the whole width of the
street (Stargarder) by police and Stasi with riot sticks, starting at a
sprint, on the people behind the candles. People were arbitrarily
arrested out of the midst of those fleeing in panic, a bus full altogether.
Residents reported very nasty handling even of women and girls.

(Name is known to the editors) p. 46

Eyewitness Report

On Sunday, October 8, 89, I unintentionally became the target of a
terrible event on Stargarder Street. Beforehand I, together with my boy
friend, had gone to visit my brother on Greifenhagener Street. On the
way back, all the entrances to Schönhauser Allee were already sealed off
by police lines. After we had spent some time in the Gethsemane
Church, we wanted to go to the streetcar stop in Pappel Allee about
11:30 pm. But in front of Pappel Allee Stargarder Street was also
completely covered with a massive, shoulder-to-shoulder line of
uniformed people, including riot police, all of whom had rubber riot
sticks. About 15 meters in front of the police line a group of about 50
young people with candles in their hands were standing on the street.
In front of them they had stuck a row of candles onto the pavement. I
observed that people just passing by, who came out of the apartment
buildings or restaurants, were also not allowed to exit, but those who,
just as clueless passersby, wanted into the encirclement were allowed to
pass. I can truthfully witness to the fact that none of the young people,
either with words or actions, provoked the police. The candle flames
actually offered a peaceful picture. Some started suddenly to sing and
more and more people joined in singing the peace song, 'Where have all
the flowers gone?'. Other young people came from the direction of the
church in order to join the singing. As the three-part canon 'Dona
Nobis Pacem' was sung, we joined in. In the meantime, the police line
had been reinforced and a bus (empty) was parked behind it. I got scared
all of a sudden and turned with my boy friend back to the church. I
wanted to get myself out of danger, since I was five months pregnant.
The loudspeaker just then announced "Attention, citizens, leave the
street in the direction of Schönhauser Allee, otherwise the street will be
cleared". The word 'cleared' seemed at the same time to be an order for
those in uniform to storm the street. The instruction couldn't have
possibly been obeyed as quick as the police caught up to us. I was

horrified to see that from the direction we were running, a whole horde of plain-clothes security forces were running towards us, also armed with riot sticks. We ran in panic to the left side, in order to find shelter in an apartment building entryway. Three plain-clothes people and a policeman were coming at us. Before they could do anything, I screamed as loud as I could "Don't hit me, I'm pregnant!". I ducked with my stomach to the wall, my boy friend protected me from behind, but all four of them beat us brutally. My boy friend yelled, "She's pregnant!", over and over. The policeman ran off but one of the plain-clothes people tried to aim for my stomach. With both of our arms we protected my stomach from the hits. I got a pretty good shot on the right breast and several of them on the right thigh (later I had big, dark bruises at those places). They were aiming for my boy friend's sex organs and knee caps. Then three of them tore him away from me. He kept yelling, "She's pregnant", but was quieted by a choke hold and was dragged down the street. Two other plain-clothes guys grabbed my arms and led me to the bus. I was able to pull my pregnant identification card from my pocket, not even looking at it, they yelled at me ,"Shut up" and, "anybody could say that". Everywhere screams and cries for help. They pushed me on the bus, which was almost full. I saw my boy friend again. Again I shouted several times, "let me out, I'm pregnant" (while crying). Finally a plain-clothes man came up to me and wanted to see proof. When he saw my pregnancy ID card, he took me off the bus as discretely as possible. I noticed the hateful looks of the other security people. Then the bus took off. I ran to the Gethsemane church in panicky fear.

(Name is known to the editors)   p. 70

Experience Report

On Sunday, October 10, '89, I was with friends in the youth center, "E. Knaack", on Greifswalder St. About 11:30 pm we decided to go to the restaurant, "Zum Anker", to get something to eat. About midnight we were at the corner of Stargarder St. and Duncker St. We were 7 people, having a good time, the street was absolutely quiet. We weren't doing anything wrong. All of a sudden a squad car and a cop truck stopped in front of us. Six policemen jumped out of the truck and formed a line in front of us. They were equipped with riot sticks. They demanded that we get on the truck. We asked "Why?" and were answered with "Shut up!" and a few whacks with the riot sticks. We were thus driven onto the truck. ... After the truck was full, we drove to the police station on Immanuelkirch St. We were driven out of the truck with the riot sticks and had to go single-file through a gauntlet of

People's Policemen, who also beat on us with their riot sticks. That's how we got to the courtyard of the station. There we had to stand next to each other in a spread-eagle position leaning against the wall. We were not allowed to move, turn our heads, otherwise whacks came immediately from the police who were standing right behind us. ... One policeman said: "You want to know what democracy is?". That was followed by a whack and a scream. A guy next to me begged to be allowed to sit because he had a heart condition. This was after an hour of standing in that position. That was followed by a whack and a little later the remark, "you can kneel, we're humane". ... After another hour four of my friends and some other people's names were called. They were led out of the courtyard. We had to continue standing. We girls were allowed to take our arms down. That was followed by comments like, "in the USA you wouldn't have been treated any differently, we'll wait until you've shit your pants, then we'll be ready to talk to you." I stood there and trembled from fear and the cold. Later we were loaded back onto a truck and waited another couple of hours in front of the station. I could tell from their conversations that they didn't know where to take us. ... About 7 o'clock two women came and conducted a body search on me in the men's bathroom. I had to take off my shoes, turn in my shoelaces, turn my socks inside out, take my jeans off, turn in my belt, pull up my pullover and they patted me down. ... About 7:30 I was taken to be questioned. That was the first time I was handled friendly. After having been there 8 hours I was told what the charges were: 'provocative activities direct against the state'. The lady couldn't even tell me what had happened the night before. After questioning was finished at 8, I was taken to the gym in the basement. ... About noon my name was called, I was given my personal belongings again, was told "unfortunately in the current situation it sometimes happens that innocent people are brought in for questioning" and then released. ... The subdural hematomas will go away, what remains is hate for and fear of green uniforms and an experience that shook me deeply and that I will never forget.

(Name is known to the editors)   p. 42-43

<u>Tape recording about being taken in for questioning from October 7, 1989 until released on October 9, 1989</u>

... After a while I asked if I could go to the bathroom. That was allowed. I went into the stall, and after I'd taken down my pants and sat down, the captain came charging in, started swinging at me and yelled that I was not permitted to close the door. After the second whack, his riot stick slipped out of his hand and rolled down by my feet. After a couple seconds of mutual shock and surprise, I slid around on the seat so he could get his riot stick again. He picked it up and hit me a couple more times, on the shoulder and neck.

I yelled. Not so much because of the pain, it wasn't that bad at the time, but rather out of fear and wanting to make the hitter unsure of himself. As I already mentioned, not all the police involved had used the same procedures, so I thought there might be differences of opinion between them. The captain left me alone. I finished going to the bathroom, pulled my pants up and went back to the hallway. ...

I also signed the protocol (of his being questioned - MJ). After that I asked the guy from the District Attorney's office where I could file charges against the captain mentioned above and his two actions of administering beatings. He didn't answer that question. He emphasized that we here in the GDR have the most humane police in all Europe. ...

After everyone had gotten their sentences, those who had only fines were given their personal effects and told to get ready to be released.

In this situation the captain was coming towards me, and since I didn't know if he had found out about my attempt to file charges against him, I decided to do something unusual. I went up to him and asked if I could ask him something. He agreed and so I asked him if he would be willing to meet with me in about a week, after we had calmed down, in order to talk. I would listen to him for a half-hour and then he would have to reciprocate. The only condition was: no sticks for hitting. After some hesitation, he said that nowadays, coming to an understanding would be impossible with people like us. Another prisoner asked why not and he explained to us that it just wasn't possible. This short conversation was very quiet, with no yelling. ...

(Names are known to the editors)   p. 63-69

The publishing house of the Protestant Churches in the GDR reconstructed a number of the meditations and church services and published them in a book called *Dona Nobis Pacem: Fürbitten und Friedensgebete Herbst '89 in Leipzig* (Dona Nobis Pacem: Intercession and Peace Prayers in the Fall of '89 in Leipzig). A few short excerpts follow.

Peace Prayer Service, September 25, 1991
St. Nikolai Church, Leipzig
Beatitudes

Blessed are the meek, for they shall inherit the earth.

Wretched are those who depend on violence, for they shall inherit ruins.

Wretched are those who do violence, for they shall ruin themselves and the country.

Wretched are those who try to enforce their authority with violence, for the country will disinherit them.

Blessed are the meek, for they shall inherit the earth.

Blessed are those who have the courage to softly step up to violence, for they shall inherit a piece of inhabitable earth.

Blessed are those who refuse to do violence, the country is waiting for them.

Blessed are those who are consciously non-violent, they can be trusted with the country.

Blessed are the softly courageous, they shall inherit the country.

Suggestions for Non-violence

Keep yourself under control and help your neighbor to do the same.

Look for conversation, with your neighbor and those on the other side.

Remain polite and correct, no swearing. Whistling and booing does not count as an invitation to dialog.

Singing together helps to get rid of your own fear and demonstrate your non-violence. Therefore, you won't have to turn your song sheets back in tonight.

If there's an attempt to arrest individual people, sit down and link elbows.

If arrested, shout your name to those who remain behind.

When in the truck, shout the number of those arrested to those who remain behind.

Don't sign anything.

During questioning, don't give any information that isn't on your ID card.

Prayer of Intercession

Lord, we pray for (names of those arrested and in prison on Sept. 25, 1989).

Lord, we pray for St. Devaty, P. Cibulka, I. Vojtkova and F. Starek, who have been sentenced to jail in CSSR for their peace and human rights activities.

We pray for S. Kulow, who had been in prison without trial since June. We pray for J.-U. Drescher, K. Kuhlman and for all those who have been unjustly imprisoned.

We pray for all victims of violence; we think of those, for example, who are struggling for their rights in southern Africa and the victims of the IRA bombings of the last weeks.

We pray for the draftees in the riot police, who are outside here every Monday against their will.   p. 30-32

Address by Bishop Hempel, October 9, 1989
St. Thomas Church, Leipzig

Dear Brothers and Sisters,

Once again in Leipzig. I would like to be in all four inner-city churches and that's hard to do in 45 minutes. So I'm going to say what I want to say right up front. But first, something personal. You would do me a big favor today, just in case such a thing should happen, if you wouldn't applaud. I'm not used to that kind of thing and want to keep a cool head at all costs. That is very important for me.

I have two things to say.

The first. There have been, as you well know, many talks between representatives of the state and representatives of the church. At those talks I have often said, and I say it publicly today, that it is my conviction that at the current time in our country there must be talks between representatives of the state and the young people who, for example, go out on the street to demonstrate their pain and bitterness. There must be talks, and the talks with us church people are no longer enough. At these talks the young people, you, must be heard out and solutions must be searched for; right now, at this time, for me that means especially talks about the release of those in prison, in-so-far as their guilt in injuring others has not been proven. For example, that means that the state refrains from a categorical, demeaning name for the demonstrators. You are all citizens and people, not rowdies. I would also like to mention that recently city hall made an offer to talk with young people. How that could best be done and be most helpful for those most affected, I still don't know. That was the first thing. The second is: I can easily imagine that not all of you are Christians. But I can't stop thinking that I'm trying to be one. That's why the second thing I have to say is, that God is watching over what happens in the GDR. And that he has a lot to say about how things develop. For the sake of my belief about this, if you agree with it or not, and against my own feeling, I ask you to keep a cool head, a clear head and to be absolutely non-violent. Violence destroys everything that is dear to us, and the most precious of all things is life. I mean physical life. So that no blood will be shed, I ask you to remain non-violent. That was the second thing.

A final note: Early today, Bishop Reineld, the catholic bishop of the diocese of Meissen-Dresden, who came to visit me, ask me to greet you in his name and to say that he thought just like I do. I have now done that. I wish for you all that you pull through in good shape. Amen.   p. 51-52

Appeal of six Leipzig citizens
October 9, 1989, St. Thomas Church

The Leipzig citizens Professor Masur, Rev. Dr. Peter Zimmermann, the caberatist Bernd-Lutz Lange and the Secretaries of the SED District Leadership Dr. Kurt Meyer, Jochen Pommert and Dr. Roland Wötzel come before all Leipzigers with the following appeal:

"Our common concern and responsibility brought us together today. We are dismayed by the developments in our city and are seeking a solution.

We all need a free exchange of opinions about the future path of Socialism in our country.

Therefore, today the above named promise all citizens that they will use all their power and authority in order that this dialog will not only take place in the district of Leipzig but also with the national government.

We implore you to remain reasonable, so that a peaceful dialog will be possible."   p.52

Meditation of the Prayer Service for Peace
Hans-Jürgen Sievers, pastor of the Reformed Church, October 9

When I was a child, I talked like a child, I thought like a child, I reasoned like a child. When I became a man, I put childish ways behind me. I Cor 13:11

Dear congregation, we have started down a path. We are on the path to becoming grown up. For years, for decades we were like children. Now we are becoming adults. It will be a long path, it will be a long process. For some it will go too slowly. We will warn them to be patient. But just as there is no way an adolescent or an adult can become a child again, there will be no turning back on the path we have started down.

In our church today we can read a banner with a saying from Martin Luther King. This black American pastor, he was assassinated in 1968, showed the people of our age that non-violence coming from Christian faith can bring about substantive changes.

As a black man, he had to witness how people like him in his area, the South of the United States, were treated like children and second-class people. In the city where he was a pastor, in Montgomery, the situation on public transportation was especially humiliating. Blacks had to sit at the back of the buses. If a white didn't have a seat, a black person had to stand up for him. One day an old woman was arrested because she refused to give up her seat for a young man. This type of thing happened every couple of days and all the people thought nothing of it. But on this day their patience ran out. It was as if a string had snapped. There were meetings. Churches had to serve as meeting places, because there was no other place to meet. The young 26 year old pastor Martin Luther King was elected leader of the movement. He had developed a teaching of non-violence based on the Bible, based on Christian faith.

The people in Montgomery decided, back then in 1954, not to ride the buses until segregation was ended and all the people were treated as adults. No one suspected what that would all entail. For more than a whole year the black people walked, in a city almost as big as Leipzig. Every morning and every night.

During this time there was no shortage of dirty tricks. Trouble makers were snuck into the movement, who were to throw stones, who were to answer violence with violence, so that there would be an excuse for even more violence.

We know that in our city there are also persistent rumors that rocks were supposedly thrown or store windows were supposedly smashed, in order to explain the need for intervention. Let us look carefully at the people who pick up stones!

Back then in Montgomery they were usually quickly able to expose these people. At that time, from that movement, there were people taken in for questioning, fined, and arrested, just like here, but the multitude of people wasn't intimidated, instead they walked and walked and walked, with great patience, a whole year. And during this time they grew. From being children they gradually came to be adults.

They became people. There were the usual problems that go along with having more freedom. Not all used this freedom appropriately; not all applied the use of their new freedom correctly. These mistakes however could be overcome.

The people there walked and walked, in the cold and in the rain. When resolution of the problem came at the end of 1955, the Supreme Court declared segregation illegal, there was one more big meeting. As here, the people met in several churches because no one church was big enough to hold them all. At that time one of the speakers read the following Bible verse: When I was a child, I talked like a child, I thought like a child, I reasoned like a child. When I became a man, I put childish ways behind me. An eye witness reported that a great shout of joy rang out. Those listening had suddenly realized that from now on they were adults, they had become real people.

Now, dear congregation, we have started down a path. We have taken the first step of a long journey. There will be many people for whom this doesn't go fast enough. Impatience is the privilege of youth, we must, however, encourage each other to have great patience. Only if we have enough persistence, only if we encourage each other again and again to be non-violent, will we reach our goal of being treated like adults in the future.

All of us, dear congregation, know what its like to be treated like a kid. We have all had those kinds of experiences when we applied for a permit to build a garage or for permission to attend a college-prep high school, not to mention what happens when we ask for permission to travel. Haven't we all had to deal with being turned down? That's when they say, 'It isn't required to give the reasons for denying permission'. One doesn't need to give reasons to a 6 or 7 year child, a child can't understand everything yet anyway. We know what it's like to be treated like a child.

A child in the first or second grade isn't able to write complete sentences. They need a pattern, they need dictation. Every year four weeks before the first of May the government shows us what they think of us. The slogans for the First of May holiday are delivered to us all neat and tidy, so that in copying them we don't make any mistakes. Small children aren't capable of writing for themselves.[1]

A third example, bad parents scare their children with the bogey man. They threaten, 'if you don't behave, the bogey man will come and get you'. Just as one threatens children, they have threatened us for

---

[1] See page 42 for an explanation.

years, for decades. 'Watch out, there is the security man, he hears and sees everything'. We were scared like children and peeked around shyly. Now we say out loud: 'We are not afraid. We are adults. We are not children who can be threatened.' We all know how hard it will be to be to grow up. But we have started down the path of putting away the things of the child. It will be a long path, it will be a difficult path. There will be no shortage of riot sticks that will pound down on our heads or trip our feet, but there is no way back on this path. We have begun to put away childish things. We will walk and walk and walk, and we won't allow ourselves to be treated like children again.

When our church service is over, some will go home very quickly. I want to thank all of those who have overcome their fear and came out tonight. Only if we continually show through our presence that we come together in great number and pray for change, will we be able to create change.

For the others who will remain in the city center, I want to thank you for showing your desire for change, your desire to be treated as a human being. I would like to ask once more for the strictest non-violence. If we have a good goal, the path to our goal must be a good path and the means we use must be good. p. 47-50

Statutes of the Student's Organization of the Theology Department of the Humboldt University

§ 1   The Student Body Assembly (SBA) is the assembly of all students of the theology department of the Humboldt University. It represents the student's interests and convenes at the beginning of every semester and can be called into special session by the Governing Council or by petition of at least one third of all the students.
Dates and agenda of all assemblies must be made public at least one week in advance. The Governing Council is responsible for the preparation and chairing of the assemblies.
Votes will be decided by simple majority of those present. Changes in the statues require 2/3 majority.

...

§ 4   These statutes were adopted on October 16, 1989. They were revised on October 30, 1989, April 4, 1990 and May 29, 1990.

After the storming of Stasi headquarters in January, 1990, opposition groups were able to look at the files that had been collected on them. The discussion that ensued and the way in which the public was allowed access to those files deserves a book of its own. Suffice it here to say that by fall 1990, selected documents from the archives of the Central Evaluation and Information Group (CEIG) of the Ministry of State Security (MoSS) had been published. The book was called "But I love you all", based on a quote of the Minister of State Security, the commander of the Stasi. He couldn't understand how the people could turn on his organization. Following is a look at how the Stasi reported the Humboldt University students' activities. 'Socially correct forces' refers to students working to further the interests of the SED.

MoSS, CEIG   Berlin, Oct. 16, 1989
Information for the eyes of Hager, Krenz, Schabowski, Mittig, MoSS circulation only.

On October 12, 1989, there was a meeting at the Humboldt University, called at the initiative of students of the departments of Cultural & Artistic Sciences, which about 500 students and faculty attended, including numerous socially correct forces sent by the local SED leadership.

...

During the meeting the following demands were presented and discussed:
• Creation of a student parliament at the University as a federation of the student assemblies of the departments independent of the FDJ; cancellation of classes for 2-5 days to allow time for creating a statute and platform for this federation.
• Abolition of Marxist-Leninist classes.
• Abolition of History of the SED classes, or a halt to giving grades in this class until it is placed on an academic footing.
• Creation of conditions for allowing uncensored bulletin boards to encourage free discussion.
• Analysis of the events of October 7 & 8 through the installation of a commission and punishment of those responsible, all under the supervision of the United Nations.
• Abolition of the policy of 'socialist democracy'.

...

During the discussion, the socially correct forces were completely ineffective.

...

The First Secretary of the FDJ District Council, who, despite repeated efforts, was not able to speak during the meeting, announced that the discussion would be continued on October 17, at 5 pm.

pages 223-224

The mood at the demonstration in Berlin on November 4 was quite different from that of a month before. The following experience report was take from "Die Revolution der Kerzen", ONCKEN VERLAG Wuppertal und Kassel, © 1990 p. 221-222. The editor, Jörg Swoboda, taught at the Baptist seminary in Buckow and is Martin's father.

An Experience Report about November 4, 1989
Martin Swoboda, 12 years old

On Friday, November 3, 1989, my mother asked me in the morning if I would like to go along to the demonstration tomorrow. Since I wanted to demonstrate, I asked my teacher if I could be excused from school the next day. She said I could be.

The next morning I left Buckow at 8 o'clock with my mother. When we changed trains at the station 'Ostkreuz' to the S-bahn in the direction of Alexanderplatz, the train was already pretty full. At the next couple of stations, there were so many people who wanted to get on, they didn't all fit and some had to keep waiting. There were already a lot of people at Alex' when we got there, and more where pouring in from every direction. It was strange to stand in the middle of so many people who were planning to do the same thing I was.

Almost half of the demostrators had banners along. There were a lot of creative sayings like "Democracy KRENZenlos" (Without borders and without Egon Krenz - a nice play on words in German), "Freedom to surf the Baltic Sea", "Sick people belong in bed, not in the government", "Long Live the November Revolution 1989" etc.

... we saw a newlywed couple in wedding clothes that walked along with the demonstration for a little ways. There were also a lot of police on the side of the street. A few people gave them flowers.

... It was a neat experience, one that I for sure will never forget.

St. Thomas Church, Leipzig
October 16, 1989
<u>Intercessory Prayer</u>
based on hand-written notes from the Prayer Request Bulletin Board

I ask that you pray for me, because I would like my Grandma to win her fight against cancer, because I would like everyone consciously to do something to perserve our environment and thus our lives, because I would like every kind of war to end and that racism would stop, because I would like our government to trust us more. (signed) Sandra

Paster: Therefore we call to God:
Congregation sings: Kyrie eleison!

... I ask you to pray for me, because we love life and want to live. I'm from Ruhla.

I ask you to pray for me that our government, our GDR, finally learns to admit to all problems and learns to govern, but without using violence. (signed) Horst

We want to pray for everyone who has to serve in the People's Army, for the People's police and the Security forces, we want to pray that no violence will be used, no one beaten or abused, we want to pray for those under arrest and their families, that justice may be done and they are set free.

Paster: Therefore we call to God:
Congregation sings: Kyrie eleison!

I ask that you pray for me, because I'm afraid that we are all destroying the earth and life will soon not be possible.

Don't forget to pray for South Africa, that apartheid may end, because all people are equal before God. And don't forget to pray for the people in Armenia and Azerbaijan.

We want to pray for the people in Poland and Hungary, in Czechoslavakia and Romania.

We want to pray that the fight against hunger will be won and that we don't only think about a better life for ourselves.

Paster: Therefore we call to God:
Congregation sings: Kyrie eleison!

Dona Nobis Pacem: Fürbitten und Friedensgebete Herbst '89 in Leipzig (Dona Nobis Pacem: Intercession and Peace Prayers in the Fall of '89 in Leipzig), 71-72

Sermon held in Augustian Church in Eufurt on October 29, 1989

by Heino Fälcke

> Again, you have heard that it was said to the
> people long ago, 'Do not break your oath, but
> keep the oaths you have made to the Lord.' But
> I tell you, Do not swear at all: either by
> heaven, for it is God's throne, or by the earth,
> for it is God's footstool, or by Jerusalem, for
> it is the city of the Great King. And do not
> swear by your head, for you cannont make even
> one hair white or black. Simply let your 'Yes'
> be 'Yes' and your 'No', 'No', anything beyond
> this comes from the evil one.
>
> Matthew 5:33-37

When Words Aren't True

Our words have to be true. This section of the Sermon on the Mount tells us that. I didn't pick it out for today. It's given in the sermon plan. But it is as if God had picked it out. That is what He wants to say about the current situation in our country. Your words must be truthful.

The crisis in our country is a crisis of trust. Trust was broken by words that were not true. They didn't match up to reality as we experienced it. On October 7 we saw right next to each other on TV the pictures of self-praise of the Party on the 40th anniversary and on West TV the pictures of departing people, mostly young, a ghostly paradox. We had an election that didn't offer us a real 'Yes' or a clear 'No' and wasn't even truthful in its numbers. We had a political system that tempted citizens to talk out of both sides of their mouths and used force, so that the mouth said 'Yes' and the heart said 'No' and we allowed ourselves to be led astray by this temptation.

Are our words true? Haven't we allowed ourselves to be lured into untruthful talk, into the well-worn half-truths, into the art of saying words that were neither completely untrue nor completely true, but certainly advantageous for us to say? We were all accomplices in the destruction of words in our society.

... We should look for the words that are not only true, but invite others to join in, words that will encourage us to seek the truth and can join in the chorus of truth. That would be a true revolution.

A great hope, perhaps too great? Let us ask God to send us people, who can find such words for our country; let us ask God that he gives us such words in our surroundings, words that are true, words that reflect our true selves, words that let others join in with us.

Ebert, Haberer and Kraft, eds., *Räumt die Steine hinweg: DDR Herbst 1989 - Geistliche Reden im politischen Aufbruch*, 29-34

We were mute for too long

Almuth Berger, pastor of St. Bartholomew Church in East Berlin
Meditation during the prayer service on November 13 in the
Gethsemane Church in East Berlin

It happens every now and then; at times like these, it happens all the time. Stories that people told each other 2,000 years ago come alive in my own experiences, the experiences of people from back then become my own.

It is an age old experience that something wonderful happens, that conditions that make one ill and people who are ill, are changed and can be made whole. This is recorded in the Bible time after time. That we should find ourselves in the middle of such a miracle, the miracle of having that which made us ill for so long, suddenly change, that we are healed; I can still hardly believe it.

Mark, who was the first to collect and write down the stories about Jesus and his friends, tells the following story. To me it sounds like my own story, like a story for all of us.

Then Jesus left the vicinity of Tyre and went through Sidon, down to the Sea of Galilee and into the region of the Decapolis. There some people brought him a man who was deaf and could hardly talk, and they begged him to place his hand on the man.

After he took him aside, away from the crowd, Jesus put his fingers into the man's ears. Then he spit and touched the man's tongue. He looked up to heaven and with a deep sigh said to him "Ephphatha!" (which means, Be opened!). At this, the man's ears were opened, his tongue was loosened and he began to speak plainly.

Jesus commanded them not to tell anyone. But the more he did so, the more they kept talking about it. People were overwhelmed with amazement. "He had done everything well", they said. "He even makes the deaf hear and the mute speak."

Mark 7:31-37

We were speechless for a long time and our tongues were tied. We were silent at parents' meetings in our schools and at work, in the parliament and in the streets. At most we would talk with a hand covering our mouth or only at home or maybe in church buildings. We taught our children to keep quiet, to keep things hidden. For many years we continually postponed talking, so long that some almost forget how and that others, many others, left, because they couldn't keep quiet any longer.

We couldn't talk to each other because of the walls between us, the visible ones built of stone and invisible ones built of stones of fear and mistrust. Some people were talking, but they had nothing to say to us, so we didn't want to listen to them anymore, not in the newspaper or on TV or anywhere else. There were others who listened in on us or interrogated us, but they never just listened and how many cries for help did we fail to hear? Many talked about each other or past each other, but not with each other. We were deaf and mute, and we didn't believe in miracles.

But the miracle happened: Hundreds of thousands took to the streets, in Leipzig and Dresden and Berlin, in Plauen or Magdeburg or Eisenach. They were not longer mute, they talked and yelled and made sure they were heard. "We are the people!" We had finally found a language for our wishes and worries, for our hopes and concerns. We'll have to make sure that in the future we will continue to be heard, that we don't forget how to speak and that we teach talking to our children.

It is wonderful to see how people are now able to talk and are free, how they blossom, the journalists for example, how something can be healed that was broken for a long time. It is wonderful to experience how after 28 years people in both parts of Germany can talk with each other and visit each other. The joy of this miracle of new meeting and new speaking has even made many speechless. ...

Sometimes I am afraid that with our considerable and understandable enthusiasm over our new found ability to talk, we'll forget that the miracle of healing a deaf mute includes opening his ears, so that he can really hear.

I think, we need very good ears so as not to miss some very quiet voices these days: voices of people who have been left behind, all alone and find the general euphoria to be especially painful, voices from doctors, nurses and orderlies and other health workers, from department and grocery store clerks, from all those for whom the absence of all those others makes their lives too hectic and themselves too tired to yell for help until they're heard. Voices from those, for example in South Africa or in Romania or in so many other countries, even a few people here in our own country, who are to be muted by prison walls, voices from people who are weak with hunger and the worry of what they'll eat tomorrow, voices from people who speak a different language and have a different skin color and are loudly told by others here that they should leave.

Thank God, we have experienced the miracle of people who were deaf and mute becoming people who can use their mouths and ears. May God grant us that we can now hear when others suffer and that we open our mouths on behalf of the mute.

from *Räumt die Steine hinweg*, 71-75.

We are victims and perpetrators

Martin Petzoldt, theology professor at Karl Marx University, Leipzig
Meditation during the prayer service on November 27 in the Thomas Church in Leipzig

It is mine to avenge, I will repay, says God. Deut. 32:35

... Last Monday during the demonstration at Karl Marx square, a voice was heard yelling "Hand grenades in the hands of the people!" It was a single voice, yelling several times, no one rebuking, no one agreeing.

Another one said "String 'em up!" A lynching mood. ...

There is no doubt that we, the people, have to a large extent been victims. Victims of a small group that wanted to force their version of socialism on us. I wonder, though, if we are only victims, or if, in different forms and to different degrees, we have been forced, seduced, blackmailed into becoming perpetrators. The very fact of living here, of choosing to remain here, casts us in the role of perpetrators. We are both, victims and perpetrators!

The difference between us and those who governed us is that they were not victims. They were exempt through their special privileges, living in their special suburb, Wandlitz[1]. Being both a victim and a perpetrator makes the task of settling up appear a little different, however. Who can throw the first stone so that it does not end up hitting oneself in the end? Such reflection does not negate the need to deal with our recent past.

Paul took our verse and recast it in non-violent terms. "It is mine to avenge, I will repay, says the Lord. Do not be overcome

---

[1] Wandlitz was a settlement on the outskirts of Berlin that was home to the highest ranking GDR government officials. Tight security and shops well stocked with Western goods served to isolate the rulers from the plight of the ruled.

by evil, but overcome evil with good." Romans 12: 19, 21. Let us continue in this mold.

from *Räumt die Steine hinweg*, 96-97.

Jürgen Fuchs studied psychology in the GDR. He spent almost a year in jail before being deported to West Germany in 1977. His book *... Und wann kommt der Hammer?* deals with psychological aspects of Stasi activities. This poem, found on page 6, was written shortly after his arrival in West Berlin.

NOW I'M OUT, NOW
I can tell it
Like it was

But that
Can't be told

And if it could
Then I would have to tell
The part I keep to myself

For example
That on Dec. 17, 1976 I sat in my cell
With my back to the door
And cried
Because that morning I turned down their offer
To work with them

And you know
What it means to work with them

Dictionary for the political Operative
Secret, Ministry of State Security

Enemy:

Persons who purposely develop, in groups or individually, political ideological views and postures divergent from Socialism and whose practical actions directly create events or conditions that damage or endanger the socialist state and society, in general or on specific issues, in hopes of making their views and postures reality.

Enemy Image, Chekist[1]:

Totality of knowledge and conceptions about the nature and laws of Imperialism, its subversive plans and goals directed against Socialism, about the modes of subversive activities and lines of attack, the enemy centers, organizations and forces, the defense of the enemy, the means and methods of enemy activities as well as the depended judgements, feelings and convictions for the struggle against the enemy.

The Chekist Enemy Image is a specific type of the scientific enemy image of the working class, which in turn is based on Marxist-Leninist analysis of class struggle and the class powers that are antagonistic to the working class and Socialism.

It contains the elements of the working class enemy image and is further refined by the experiences and knowledge gained in the conspirational struggle against subversive forces.

As a imminent part of the ideology and moral value system, the scientific, real and actual Enemy Image is one of the important characteristics of the Chekist personality.

The comprehensive, individual and flexible communication of and training in this Enemy Image grows in importance during the process of the political ideological education of operative and informal co-workers.

Concrete knowledge about the enemy is the basis for the deep feelings of hatred, disgust, disaffection and merciless towards the enemy, which are extremely important requirements for a successful conclusion of the struggle against the enemy.

The more precise and penetrating the required knowledge about the enemy with its emotional components can be brought

---

[1] *Cheka* is the nickname for one of the Soviet forerunners of the KGB, the agency on with the Stasi was modeled.

into the class consciousness training of the security forces and informal co-workers, the higher the ability to quickly recognize, uncover and prevent enemy attacks and the higher the willingness and motivation actively to battle the enemy. One-sided, absolute, watered down or distorted versions of this enemy image could lead to incorrect conclusions and actions in the political operative work and should not be allowed.

Taken from Kukutz and Havemann, *Geschützte Quelle*, 36, 44, 46.

Monika Haeger infiltrated one of the most important opposition groups as an IM for the Stasi. She confessed to the group in May, 1989, shortly before the peaceful revolution. Afterwards she answered questions that two members of the group had. Their conversation were published as *Geschützte Quelle: Gespräche mit Monika H. alias Karin Lenz* (Protected Sources: Conversations with Monika H alias Karin Lenz). The questions were asked by Irena Kukutz and Katja Havemann. The answers are Monika Haeger speaking. The following excerpt is from pages 33-37.

When did you start working for the Stasi?

In 1981.

How did they approach you?

I had a friend who told me one day that she and a bunch of other people wanted to storm the border crossing at Bornholmer street. Women and children first, so that the border troops wouldn't shoot and everybody else would just follow. In my naivete, I took that seriously and didn't know what else to do but tell it to the husband of a different friend of mine and to ask what I should do about it. 'Yah', he said, 'I'll take care of it'. A little bit latter I told it to my boss. She was like a substitute mother for me and as the party boss of our local organization she watched out for me. A day later I had the Stasi coming at me from two different angles.

Was there any truth to this planned storming of the Bornholmer Street crossing?

To this day I don't know. They were going to print leaflets. That's what really hacked me off. As a good comrade I had to tell somebody. I thought that was terrible, against our country , you know. Then the Stasi asked me if I would let them know again if I ever heard anything like that. I said, 'Of, course, I'm a comrade, a party member'. And then later they invited me to one of those apartment meeting places and asked if I would really work for them. Of course, I said. After that we met often.

I imagine, they told you what all would happen to you next.

No, they only wanted me to tell them what I heard. A half a year later I signed up officially. I didn't know that they were watching me that whole time. They told me that I could quit anytime I wanted to. And I believed that.

Did you have any doubts at that time that you were doing the right thing?

To be honest, no. In fact, I was surprised that the Stasi hadn't approached me sooner. Because I was really an absolutely reliable comrade. I told myself, 'you're being really brave. You could do something like Richard Sorge[2] or Zoya Kosmodemyanskaya[3]. You would be able to keep your mouth shut, infiltrate the enemy lines and then tell your comrades what the wicked enemy was doing.' Childish thinking, of course, today!

Did you have doubts later?

Did I ever!

How did that happen?

You weren't the enemies that I had imagined enemies to be. I always had to convince myself that you were doing terribly unpatriotic things. The cause was more important than the person.

---

[2] Richard Sorge was a German who spied for the Soviet Union during World War II. During this time he was stationed in Tokyo as a correspondent for a Nazi newspaper. His good contacts with German embassy staff there made him one of the Soviet Union's most valuable spies.

[3] Zoya Kosmodemyanskaya was a young school teacher who lived close to Moscow. She became active in partisan activites against the Germans in the winter of 1941. They captured and hung her in December 1941. The widespread publicity of her case made her a folk hero in the Soviet Union.

Notes

[1] Letter from Heydrich to Göring, published in the record of the Nürnberg Trials. Pätzold and Runge, *Progromnacht 1938*, 136.

[2] Peter Christian Ludz and Ursula Ludz, Sozialistische Einheitspartei Deutschlands (SED), *Handbuch der DDR*, 1185.

[3] In order to clear up any confusion on this in the GDR, one could simply look it up in the official *Kleines Politisches Wörterbuch* (Little Political Dictionary) under the entry Demokratie (Democracy).

[4] *Verfassung der Deutshen Demokratischen Republik*, 9.

[5] *Keine Gewalt* has a photo sequence on page 37 showing a young man who is carrying a picture of Gorbachev (!) being removed from the parade by the Stasi.

[6] The amount of pay ranged from a low up 300 Marks a month to a high of 90% of the mother's salary, based on such factors as the length of leave, number of children and having a supplementary insurance policy. These formula were similar to figuring one's disability pension if unable to work. Mutterschutz, 921-923, Krankengeld, 748-749, *DDR Handbuch*.

[7] Jugendweihe, *DDR Handbuch*, 692-693.

[8] *FDJ Statut*, 6-7.

[9] Some of this information comes from the "Conceptual Reflections of the Church Congregation of Marzahn-North", a document endorsed by the Church Board on June 4, 1987. The congregation was four and a half years old at that time. The story of getting building permits for churches in the new suburbs is long, complicated and told in part by Goeckel in *The Lutheran Church and the East German State*, 1-2, 226-7.

[10] Goeckel, 9. The Catholic Church has a somewhat different story in general, but in the statistics it also drops membership in this period, from 12% of the population in 1946 to 8% in 1964.

[11] For a short history, see the entry Bausoldaten, 151-152 in the *DDR Handbuch*. This is explained in greater detail in Theo Mechtenberg's essay on Die Friedensverantwortung der evangelischen Kirchen in der DDR, published in *Die evangelischen Kirchen in der DDR*, Reinhard Henkys, ed.. For an English version see the following footnote.

[12] Goeckel saw the rapprochement between church as an institution and a state as being based on their mutual weaknesses. Although the state obviously always had the power, it needed the church to channel and buffer some of the oppositional energy. The church as an institution was hollowed out by the drastic membership decline and needed state help to maintain its bloated nationwide structure. See especially 281-293.

In this brief a sketch of the history of church-state relationships, obviously much has been left out. Goeckel's book provides many details for anyone looking to fill in the gaps. For those who read German, Henkys' book, *Die evangelischen Kirchen in der DDR*, provides a good general overview. Both works do have a 'church primarily as institution' bias.

[13] Goeckel, 190-5.

14 According to the Stasi there were approximately 160 such groups. The report printed in *"Ich liebe euch doch alle..."* , 46-71, provides a good overview of the various types of groups, their activities and their leaders, although, of course, Stasi reports are never to be completely trusted.

15 The Stasi's account of these events can be found in *"Ich liebe euch doch alle..."*, 72-75.

16 Timothy Garton Ash is one of the most knowledgeable writer in English on the dynamics of the changes in Eastern Europe in general. See especially his books *The Uses of Adversity* and *The Magic Lantern*.

17 This only applied to the first visit of each calendar year.

18 *Fischer Weltalmanach: Sonderband DDR*, 135-6. According to the Stasi's own statistics, 125,429 GDR citizens applied for permission to emmigrate in the first six months of 1989. 36,484 had been granted that permission, 5,202 had left the country illegally in the same time period. *Ich liebe euch doch alle...!*, 84-88.

19 *Fischer Weltalmanach: Sonderband DDR*, 137-8.

20 Zeno and Sabine Zimmerling, eds., *Neue Chronik DDR*, Vol. 1, 9. *Neues Deutschland* article of August 7, 1989.

21 *Neue Chronik DDR*, Vol. 1, 9.

22 *Ibid.*, 11.

23 *Ibid.*, 18.

24 *Ibid.*, 19.

25 *Fischer Weltalmanach: Sonderband DDR*, 138.

26 *Neue Chronik DDR*, Vol. 1, 35. From a *Neues Deutschland* article of September 11, 1989.

27 *Ibid.*, 50, From a *Neues Deutschland* article of September 21, 1989.

28 *Ibid.*, 60. From a *Neues Deutschland* article of September 30, 1989.

29 *Ibid.*, 13-14.

30 A Stasi report that summarizes the opposition groups that are active in the GDR mentions Berlin as the center of the opposition. This might explain in part the decision to deport opposition leadership from here. *Ich liebe euch doch alle...!*, 49.

31 There was also no lack of confusion. This report is based on an article in the *tageszeitung*, as quoted in *Neue Chronik DDR*, Vol. 1, 24-5 and the account in *Dona Nobis Pacem*, 13.

32 For a more complete history of the Monday night Leipzig prayer services, see Friedrich Magirius' introduction to *Dona Nobis Pacem*, 7-14. The information presented here is based in part on this account. See also *Neue Chronik DDR*, Vol. 1, 51-53, 63, and Bohse, *Jetzt oder nie - Demokratie!*, 31-60.

33 *Neue Chronik DDR*, Vol. 1, 63. *Berliner Zeitung* of October 10, 1989.

34 Heber and Lehmann, eds., *Keine Gewalt*, 25.

35 *Neue Chronik DDR*, Vol. 1, 63-64.

36 *Fischer Weltalmanach: Sonderband DDR*, 150.

37 *Neue Chronik DDR*, Vol. 1, 67.

38 *Ibid.*, 68.

39 *Ibid.*, 72.

40 The most complete account of this weekend in Berlin can be found in Dahn and Kopka, eds., *und diese verdammte Ohnmacht*.

41 Ziemer, Christof, Pastor of the Kreuzkirche and Superintendent for Dresden-Mitte, in <u>Wachen und Beten für die Stadt: Christen- und Bürgergemeinde am Beispiel Dresden,</u> *Unser Glaube mischt sich ein*, 102-3.

42 *Neue Chronik DDR*, Vol. 1, 76. According to paragraph 215 of the GDR Lawbook, the charge of 'rowdiness' carried a sentence of up to 5 years in prison. It was usually applied to people under 25 years of age who had 'acted up' in public. *DDR Handbuch*, 1129.

43 Hanish, *et. al.* eds., *Dona Nobis Pacem*, 42.

44 *Neue Chonik DDR*, Vol. 1, 101-104.

45 *Ibid.*, quoting the *Neues Deutschland* of October 17, 1989, 27.

46 Mitte and Wolle, eds., *Ich liebe euch doch alle*, p. 243, *Neue Chronik DDR*, Vol. 2, 59.

47 *Neue Chronik DDR*, Vol. 2, 70, 74, 80, 83.

48 *Ibid.*, 81-83.

49 *Neue Chronik DDR*, Vol. 3, 11.

50 *Ibid.*, p. 9. See also *Neue Chronik DDR*, Vol. 2, p. 105, Vol. 3, 5, 8 for examples of similar thinking in other opposition groups.

51 *Neue Chronik DDR*, Vol. 3, 12-16.

52 *Neue Chronik DDR*, Vol. 2, 108. See also Wolfgang Ullmann, <u>Kirche und Runder Tisch</u> in *Unser Glaube mischt sich ein*, 80-91.

53 *Neue Chronik DDR*, Vol. 4/5, 31.

54 *Neue Chronik DDR*, Vol. 3, 64.

55 *Neue Chronik DDR*, Vol. 4/5, 52, 55, 76.

56 *Neues Deutschland*, January 16, 1991, 1.

57 *Neue Chornik DDR*, Vol. 4/5, 78-79.

58 Three opposition leaders from the unofficial commission withdrew from the joint commission because of their misgivings about working together with the official commission. A short summary of this process is in Dahn and Kopka, eds., *... und diese verdammte Ohnmacht*, 48-51, 325.

59 Wolf, *Einblicke*, 17.

60 Saß and von Suchololetz, eds., *feindlich-negativ*, 115, 124.

61 *Ibid.*, 16-17.

62 There were arguments at local party meetings of the Stasi about the wisdom of banning the Soviet magazine *Sputnik*. *Ibid.*, 125. According to Werner Fischer, one of the officials in charge of the dissolution of the Stasi, up to a thousand of the regular Stasi employees demonstrated for changes in the courtyard of the Normannen Street headquarters in June, 1989, *die tageszeitung*, Nov. 5, 1990, 28.

[63] 'r.l.', <u>Neue Spirale in der Stasi-Affäre: Randbemerkungen zur Entlarvung von Böhme und de Maiziere</u>, *Telegraph*, No. 17, December 21, 1990, 7-9. Also Saß and von Suchololetz, eds.,*feindlich-negativ*, 54. A little later there were even reports that the Stasi had helped to open the Wall, *die tageszeitung*, Nov. 5, 1989.

Another area of questions is why the Stasi weren't able to snuff out the opposition if they really wanted to. They had identified the roughly 600 persons who were active in the leadership councils of the opposition groups. About 60 of them were considered the hard core cases. Mitter and Wolle, *Ich liebe euch doch alle...*, 48. Why wasn't this small handful of people arrested and deported? Documents were found for plans to arrested 122 known opposition people in Leipzig in October, 1989. The list included most of the pastors in the city. A special 'Internment camp' was to be set up to hold these people. *Neue Chronik DDR*, Vol. 6, 41. Again the question, why weren't these plans carried out?

The role of the Stasi in all of these events raising interesting questions, but more research is needed to provide definitive answers.

[64] Kukutz and Havemann, *Geschutzte Quelle*, 44,46.

[65] Dahn and Kopka, eds., *...und diese verdammte Ohnmacht*, 240. The summary of the Investigative Commission explaining in greater detail how this mindset of the security forces was created and manipulated can be found on pages 239-244.

[66] *die tageszeitung*, <u>Die offizielle Liste der ehemaligen Stasi-Objekte</u>, Sonderausgabe A 2548 A, June 1990. Berlin-Mitte 1040, Tucholskystr. 6, page 4. Lichtenberg 1156, Storkowerstr. 215, 219, page 13.

[67] Fuchs, *...und wann kommt der Hammer?*, 47.

[68] *Neue Chronik DDR*, Vol. 4/5, 204.

[69] *Ibid.*, 159.

[70] *Ibid.*, 158.

[71] Portions of the story as told this far can be found in *Neue Chronik DDR*, Vol. 3, 62, and *Neue Chronik DDR*, Vol. 4, 29-30, 50-52, 151-153.

[72] This account of Honeckers stay with the Holmer family is taken from an interview with Uwe Holmer, Richter and Zylla, eds., *Mit Pflugscharen gegen Schwerter*, 66-76.

[73] *Neue Chronik DDR*, Vol. 4/5, 166-167.

[74] *Neue Chronik DDR*, Vol. 6, 23.

[75] *Neue Chronik DDR*, Vol. 4/5, 91, 93, 95, 126, 138-139.

[76] *Ibid.*, 168.

[77] *Ibid.*, 221.

[78] *Neues Deutschland*, March 17/18, 1990, 1.

[79] *Neues Deutschland*, March 15, 1990.

[80] *Berliner Morgenpost*, March 14, 1990.

[81] *Neue Chronik DDR*, Vol. 4/5, 246. The German Beer Drinkers Union only got 2,534 votes, although in the municipal elections held on May 6, 1990, they managed to win a seat on the city council of Rostock.

[82] *Neue Chronik DDR*, Vol. 6, 51.

83 The forming of the coalition government was a fascinating story in its own right. The prime minister, Lothar de Maiziere, was a violin player turned lawyer and a member of the CDU. A *ND* reporter had asked him back in November what his guiding principles were. "Something very old, and I hope something new, the Sermon on the Mount" was his reply. (*Neues Deutschland*, April 6, 1990, 3). That would certainly have been new as a standard for politics in both East and West. He was later accused of having been an informant for the Stasi. Although the charges were never proven beyond doubt, he was forced to step down from his later cabinet position in the united German government.

The Defense Minister was a pastor of the Protestant Church and an avowed pacifist, Rainer Eppelmann of the DA party. He insisted on renaming his department "Department of Disarmament and Defense". The Foreign Minister, Markus Meckel of the SPD, was also a Protestant Pastor. In fact, pastors and church leaders took over many government and party posts. The church setting had provided practice in public speaking, debating and administrating, making pastors virtually the only group of people not in the SED to be able to practice these skills. In addition, some pastors were eager to try their luck at those tasks with a bigger crowd than came to church on Sunday. This prompted a debate in the church about the proper role of pastors in politics.

84 *Neue Chronik DDR*, Vol. 6, 96-101, 115-117.

85 "Wir haben's ja so gewollt!"

86 *Ibid.*, 129-131. The CDU lost 6% off of their results in the March 18 election, the DSU 3%, the SPD 0.6%. The PDS lost 2%. The smallest and newest parties gained the most from these losses.

87 *Neues Deutschland,* May 19/20, 1990, 2.

88 *Neue Chronik DDR*, Vol. 7/8, 124.

89 The book was published with German, English and French captions. Bertsch and Hedler, eds., *SED: Stunning Eastern Design*.

90 More details of the Stoners' activities are available in the MCC Occasional Paper by Andre Stoner, *Entering Samaria: Peace ministry among U.S. military personnel in West Germany*, September 1990, available from Mennonite Central Committee, 21 South 12th Street, Akron, PA 17501-0500 or 134 Plaza Drive, Winnipeg, MB R3T 5K9, Canada. Suggested donation is $1 per copy.

91 *Ibid.,* 2.

92 Serwuschok and Dölle, *Der Besser Wessi*, 5.

93 *Ibid.*, 23.

94 A mutual acquaintance of Angelika's and mine unwittingly introduced her to the West German woman who Dr. Fink had mistaken for my 'wife' when I first got to the GDR. Erika Kreider and her real husband, Barry, came to visit Berlin and we got a chance to meet. I had that amazing coincidence story to take home with me. Barry and Erika are now working on planting a Mennonite Church in the area of Halle, near Leipzig, together with the Mennonites who live there.

95 *Neue Chronik DDR*, Vol. 1, 91, 93.

Bibliography

In keeping with my goal of letting East Germans speak for themselves, I have relied heavily on sources from the GDR. The Protestant Church's publishing house is the *Evangelische Verlagsanstalt*. The publishing houses *Forum Verlag* and *BasisDruck* grew out of the opposition groups.

Ash, Timothy Garton, *The Uses of Adversity: Essays on the Fate of Central Europe*, (New York: Random House, 1989).
_____, *The Magic Lantern: The Revolution of 89 Witnessed in Warsaw, Budapest, Berlin and Prague*, (New York: Random House, 1990).

Bertsch, Georg C., and Ernst Hedler, eds., *SED: Stunning Eastern Design*, (Cologne: Benedikt Taschen Verlag, 1990).

Bohse, Reinhard, *et al*, eds., *Jetzt oder nie - Demokratie! Leipziger Herbst '89* (2nd ed.; Leipzig: Forum Verlag, 1989).

Dahn, Daniela, and Fritz-Jochen Kopka, eds. *und diese verdammte Ohnmacht: Report der Untersuchungskommission zu den Ereignissen vom 7. und 8. Oktober 1989 in Berlin*, (Berlin: BasisDruck, 1991).

DDR Handbuch, (Cologne: Verlag Wissenschaft und Politik, 1985).

Ebert, Andreas, Johanna Haberer and Friedrich Kraft, eds., *Räumt die Steine hinweg: DDR Herbst 1989 - Geistliche Reden im politischen Aufbruch*, (Munich: Claudius Verlag, 1989).

FDJ Statut, (Berlin: Zentralrat der FDJ, Junge Welt Verlag, 1976).

Der Fischer Weltalmanach: Sonderband DDR, Frankfurt a. M.: Fischer Taschenbuch Verlag, 1990).

Fuchs, Jürgen, *"...und wann kommt der Hammer?"*, Psychologie, Opposition und Staatssicherheit, (Berlin: BasisDruck, 1990).

Gedächtnisprotokolle: Tage und Nächte nach dem 7. Oktober, (Frankfurt a. M.: epd Dokumentation Nr. 47/89, Evangelischer Pressedienst, November 3, 1989).

Goeckel, Robert F., *The Lutheran Church and the East German State: Political Conflict and Change under Ulbricht and Honecker*, (Ithaca: Cornell University Press, 1990).

Hanisch, Günter, *et al*, eds., *Dona Nobis Pacem: Fürbitten und Friedensgebete Herbst '89 in Leipzig*, (Berlin: Evangelische Verlagsanstalt, 1990).

Heber, Norbert, and Johannes Lehmann, eds., *Keine Gewalt! Der friedliche Weg zur Demokratie. Eine Chronik in Bildern.* (Berlin: Evangelische Verlagsanstalt, 1990).

Reinhard Henkys, ed., *Die evangelischen Kirchen in der DDR: Beiträge zu einer Bestandaufnahme*, (Munich: Kaiser Verlag, 1982).

Hildebrandt, Jörg, and Gerhard Thomas, *Unser Glaube mischt sich ein...: Evangelische Kirche in der DDR 1989, Berichte, Fragen, Verdeutlichungen*, (Berlin: Evangelische Verlagsanstalt, 1990).

Kleines Politisches Wörterbuch , (7th ed.; Berlin: Dietz Verlag, 1988).

Konzeptionelle Überlegungen der Kirchengemeinde Berlin-Marzahn/Nord - Gemeindekonzeption beschlossen in der Gemeindeleitung am 4. Juni 1987

Kukutz, Irena, and Katja Havemann, *Geschützte Quelle: Gespräche mit Monike H. alias Karin Lenz*, (Berlin: BasisDruck, 1990).

Mitter, Armin, and Stefan Wolle, eds., *Ich liebe euch doch alle!: Befehle und Lageberichte des MfS, Januar - November 1989*, (Berlin: BasisDruck, 1990).

Die offizielle Liste der ehemaligen Stasi-Objekte, *die tageszeitung*, Sonderausgabe A2548A (June 1990).

Pätzold, Kurt and Irene Runge, *Progromnacht 1938*, (Berlin: Dietz Verlag, 1988).

Richter, Manfred, and Elsbeth Zylla, eds., *Mit Pflugscharen gegen Schwerter: Erfahrungen in der Evangelischen Kirchen in der DDR 1949-1990*, (Bremen: Edition Temmen, 1991).

'r.l.', Neue Spirale in der Stasi-Affäre: Randbemerkungen zur Entlarvung von Böhme und de Maiziere, *Telegraph*, XVII, (Dec. 21, 1990), 7- 9.

Saß, Ulrich von, and Harriet von Suchololetz, *Feindlich-Negative: Zur politisch-operativen Arbeit einer Stasi-Zentrale*, (Berlin: Evangelische Verlagsanstalt, 1990).

Serwuschok, Ingolf and Christine Dölle, *Der Besser Wessi*, (Leipzig: Forum Verlag, 1991).

Stoner, Andre Gingerich, *Entering Samaria: Peace ministry among U.S. military personnel in West Germany*, MCC Occasional Paper No. 12, September 1990.

Swoboda, Jörg, Ed., *Die Revolution der Kerzen: Christen in den Umwälzungen der DDR*, (Hamburg: Oncken Verlag, 1990).

Verfassung der Deutshen Demokratischen Republik, (6th ed.; Berlin: Staatsverlag der DDR, 1984).

Wolf, Stephan, *Einblicke: Geschichte und Verflechtungen des MfS in der ehemaligen DDR*, (Berlin: Selbstverlag, 1990, sponsored as a project of the "Forshcungs- und Gedenkstätte für die Opfer des Stalinismus" and "Stiftung Antistalinistische Aktion Berlin - Normannenstraße" e.V.

Zimmerling, Zeno & Sabine, eds., *Neue Chronik DDR: 1.Folge 7.August - 18 Okotober 1989.*
_____, *2. Folge: 19. Oktober - 23. November 1989.*
_____, *3. Folge: 24. November 1989 - 22. Dezember 1989.*
_____, *4./5. Folge: 23.Dezember 1989 - 18 März 1990* (Berlin: all Tribüne Verlag, 1990).
_____, *6. Folge: 19. März 1990 - 6. Mai 1990*, (Berlin: Treptower Verlaghaus, 1990).
_____, *7./8. Folge: 7. Mai 1990 - 2. Oktober 1990*, (Berlin: Treptower Verlaghaus, 1991).

Chronology of Events

May 7, 1945   Unconditional surrender of Germany ends World War II in Europe.

June 1948   New currencies introduced in the Western Occupation Zones of Germany and the Soviet Occupation Zone.

May 24, 1949   Federal Republic of Germany (West Germany) is founded in the area of the three Western Occupation Zones.

Oct. 7, 1949   The German Democratic Republic is founded in the area of the Soviet Occupation Zone.

July 23, 1952   Dissolution of the five states in the GDR and the establishment of fifteen governmental districts.

June 17, 1953   Construction workers lead strike in East Berlin that is put down by Soviet troops.

Aug. 13, 1961   The border between East and West Berlin and East and West Germany is closed off. Construction of the Wall begins.

May 1971   Erich Honecker takes over from Walter Ulbricht as the leader of the GDR.

Jan. 1988   During the annual parade in honor of Rosa Luxembourg and Karl Liebknecht, members of the opposition unfurl unauthorized banners. Many arrests are made, some leaders are expelled.

Sept. 1988   My MCC term begins.

Nov. 19, 1988   The Soviet magazine *Sputnik* is banned in the GDR.

May 1, 1989   Traditional May 1 parade in East Berlin brings out 750,000 in 'support' of the government.

May 2, 1989   Hungary starts removing barriers from its border with Austria.

May 7, 1989   Local election in the GDR with official results of 98.85% yes votes leads to widespread accusations of election fraud.

June 4, 1989   Solidarity wins election in Poland. Tianammen Square massacre in Beijing.

June 7, 1989   A demonstration to protest the election results in Berlin is diverted to a meeting in the Sophien church. There are numerous arrests.

Sept. 11, 1989   The Hungarian government allows GDR citizens in Hungary to go to Austria.

Sept. 25, 1990   First Monday night demonstration in Leipzig.

Sept. 30, 1989   East Germans wishing to go to West Germany allowed to go there from West German embassies in Prague and Warsaw.

Oct. 4-6, 1989   Demonstrations in Dresden centered around the main train station there.

Oct. 7, 1989   The fortieth anniversary celebration of the GDR is marked by huge government organized demonstrations and numerous small, peaceful demonstrations of opposition.

Oct. 9, 1989   Intense governmental pressure fails to deter a large demonstration in Leipzig and several smaller demonstrations in other cities, which are allowed to run their course peacefully.

Oct. 18, 1989   Erich Honecker steps down to be succeeded by Egon Krenz.

Nov. 4, 1989   Roughly one million people demonstrate in East Berlin for democracy.

Nov. 9, 1989   The Wall is opened.

Dec. 24, 1989 Daily exchange requirement dropped for West Germans visiting the GDR.

Jan 15, 1990 The night Stasi headquarters were 'stormed'.

March 18, 1990 Free parliamentary elections are held.

May 6, 1990 Local elections are held.

July 1, 1990 The West German currency is introduced to the GDR.

Oct. 2, 1990 Elections are held for the five states of the GDR which are being recreated.

Oct. 3, 1990 East and West Germany are united.

Dec. 2, 1990 New national elections are held for all of Germany.

Sept. 1991 My MCC term concludes.